DATE DUE	
ILL 3-6-95	
BRODART	Cat. No. 23-221

THE BOOK OF
SILK

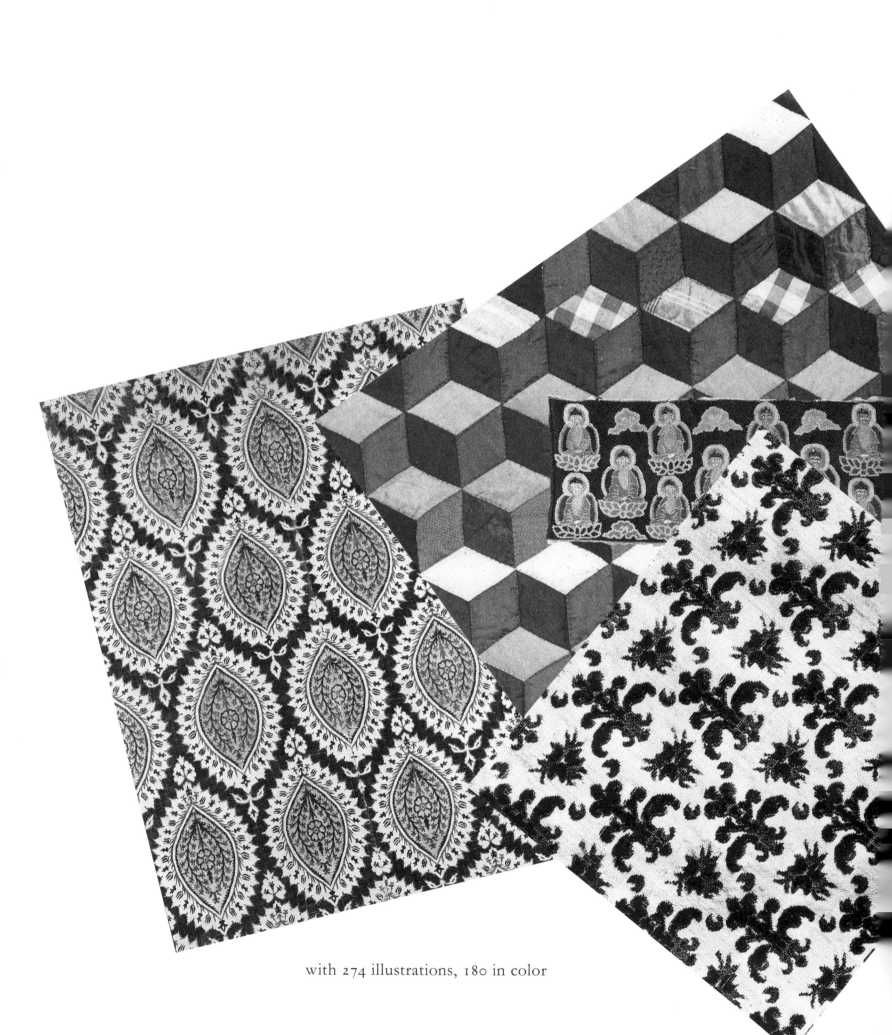

with 274 illustrations, 180 in color

PHILIPPA SCOTT

THE BOOK OF
SILK

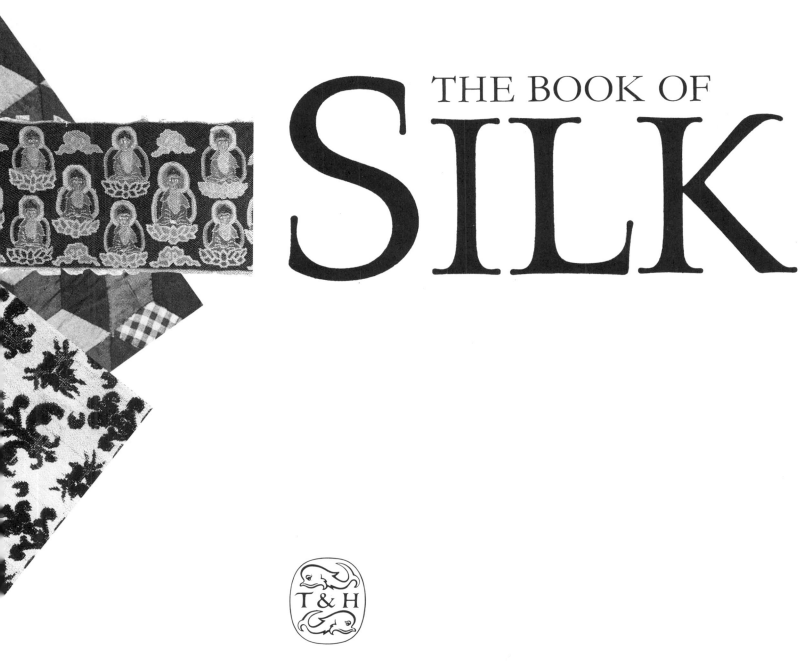

THAMES AND HUDSON

CONTENTS

Captions for illustrations on this page, the title page, and chapter-opening pages appear on p. 256.

© 1993 Thames and Hudson Ltd, London

First published in the United States of America in 1993 by Thames and Hudson Inc., 500 Fifth Avenue, New York, New York 10110

Library of Congress Catalog Card Number 93-60204

Printed and bound in Singapore

The Wonders of Silk

eidenstrassen – silk roads: the romantic term coined by Baron Ferdinand von Richthofen in the nineteenth century referred to ancient trade routes over land and sea. Along these, goods passed from east to west; silk, always an important commodity, was nevertheless one of many tradestuffs.

This book is about another – the true – silk route: a journey across the millennia whose beginning is in legend and in archaeological fragments and whose end is not in sight, the story of one of the most remarkable of all natural creations.

Silk is sumptuous, royal, heavenly; it is exotic, erotic, sensual. Most of all, it is simply sheer beauty. The qualities of silk are unrivalled by any other fibre or fabric, and any comparison to silk is flattering to the compared. 'Silken', 'soft-as-silk', 'smooth-as-silk' . . . in imagery, and metaphor, it is always desirable and esteemed. It is soft, and fluid; no other fabric drapes or falls on the body in the same way. Silk can be pleated, folded, or swirled in a bias-cut from the body's axis, to delight the most demanding and particular wearer – points vital in this century of changing fashions, when the versatility of silk has been explored and challenged in so many different ways. Think of the sculpted lines of Balenciaga's elegant robes, the subtle sinuous pleating of Fortuny and Grès, or the ripples and flutes of Vionnet's cut. Our century has seen the invention of manmade fibres, of artificial silk, but there remains nothing that has all the qualities of silk, except the real thing.

Because silk is a natural fibre, it breathes, and conducts moisture away from the body. Its isothermal properties make it cool in summer and warm in winter. Silk sheets of heavy crêpe de Chine exceed reputation and the wildest of dreams. Silk floss is the lightest and warmest wadding for quilted insulation, superior to any goose down. Silk's quality of absorbency enables it to soak up dyestuffs, making possible an infinity of shades, designs and finishes. It is even resilient and quickly recovers its former state after being deformed.

The uses and applications of silk are many and varied – tapestry, carpets, embroideries, furnishings, costume among them. Silk has been used as a ground material for painting, and many painting and printing procedures were developed as a result of experimenting and working with it.

Throughout history only the best weavers, the most skilled dyers and colourists, the most talented and gifted artists and technicians worked silk, to satisfy the demands and expectations of the most particular patrons. There is no time in silk's history when it was not sought, valued, a symbol of the best, the most royal, the most holy, an honoured gift. The Palio, Sienna's famous medieval horserace, is so-called from the Latin 'palium', a piece of silk, which today refers to the banner that is the symbolic prize to the winner. Silk has been a form of currency, worth its weight in gold, and armies, taxes and ransoms have been paid in the fabric. During the time of the Ottoman sultans, 'unwanted' princes in the Topkapi Palace were traditionally dispatched by deaf mutes, who strangled them with a silken bowstring. It is doubtful whether the victims were consoled by the fact that the bowstring had to be silk, but even this sad fact illustrates the continuing connection between silk and royalty. A happier use of silk's fineness and tensile strength is that of stringing a musical instrument. The earliest Shang pictogram for a musical instrument consists of the symbols for silk plus wood, indicating plucked silk strings stretched over wood.

Silk is rot-proof, important for sewing thread, and its fineness and strength (weight for weight it is stronger than a steel rod) have made possible the most delicate and intricate embroideries, even including the repair of the human body with fine stitches, for as pure protein the risk of irritation, or of rejection by physical tissue, is minimized. Silk has been atomized for use in cosmetic powders and make-up for this same reason, and for its absorbency. It has been tightly spun and meshed to make the strong, resilient inner tubes for bicycles competing in the Tour de France annual race: a multitude of very different uses.

All of these discoveries and inventions stem from two basic roots: firstly, the existence in China of a silk moth, whose spun filament was different from that of other silk moths, enabling it to be processed and reeled in a certain way; and secondly, the recognition of this difference, and realization of how it could be used, which led to the Chinese domestication of the silkworm, Bombyx mori. Nevertheless, the subsequent story of silk is not a linear process moving neatly through aeons and across continents in an orderly fashion. People move, borders shift, civilizations crumble and vanish, and many mysteries, many answers too, are hidden in the dust. Archaeology gives us hints of these beginnings, legends and beliefs offer further echoes, and our estimation of time is being constantly re-evaluated. The story of silk is a history of the world from a certain perspective. To tell this story, I have taken threads from many sources, and offer here a tapestry.

Elsa Schiaparelli was famous for the wit of her bold, often outrageous designs. The signature, and the perfume, of her couture house was 'Shocking Pink'. In this dramatic, full, Forties ruffled skirt, Shocking Pink and green satin highlight moiré black taffeta.

A 12th-century Moorish silk, surviving as a fragment of the Virgin's mantle from Thuir in the Pyrennees, represents the grand tradition of silk-weaving. The ancient regal emblem of double-headed eagle – like silk itself – travelled from the East to the West through the centuries. The birds' wings are patterned with textured roundels and their heads have feathered 'horns', often seen in Persian silks.

Opposite English embroidery of the 15th century. Such ecclesiastical embroidery from England was famed as 'Opus Anglicanum' during the Middle Ages. The eagle panel is part of an ecclesiastical vestment, embroidered in coloured silks and gold thread.

The Venetians were famous for the alto-e-basso velvet technique, in which an embossed effect is obtained by cutting the pile in more than one, and sometimes several heights. This fabulous 15th- or 16th-century velvet (*top*) may be Venetian, or perhaps Ottoman, for the tulip of the pattern is a native Turkish flower. A Venetian brocade velvet (*above*) has rich ornament of ogival 'cells' caught by crowns.

Right, inset The design of a five-lobed palmette containing a lotus is called a 'pomegranate velvet' even when the central pomegranate has changed beyond recognition, as here, or vanished altogether (*far right*). This 15th- or 16th-century example might be Spanish or Italian, for Spanish and Italian silks closely resembled each other at the period.

Far right Detail of Bronzino's portrait of Eleanor of Toledo (1522–26), wife of the Medici Duke Cosimo I. Brocaded velvet has been even further enriched by embroidering over the outlines of the pattern with gold and silver cord. Her dress may be Italian – perhaps a gift from her husband – or Spanish, part of her trousseau: it was her wedding dress and also to be her shroud.

Persian gold brocaded velvet of the early 17th century, in the style of the court artists of Shah Abbas. The size of the graceful figures, in a Persian three-quarters pose, suggests that this was not a dress material but intended as a wall hanging. The women's tunics are embellished with bouclé (looped) silver.

Far right Artists and craftsmen moved between the Persian and Indian courts at this period: in this second Persian velvet the women wear Indian dress, and their heads are shown in exact profile in the traditional style of Indian miniatures. Perhaps the velvet was woven in Persia as a special gift for a Mogul ruler, for these were royal silks.

A Chinese 17th-century silk tapestry weave (*kesi*), showing a crane in flight against a diaper of clouds. Clouds are said to arise from the union of Yin and Yang, symbolizing good fortune and happiness, and here auspiciously introduce the first chapter of *The Book of Silk*.

1

Origins – China and Japan

呉帝元妃西陵氏
うていのけんびせいりやうし

ilk's story begins long ago. The Chinese suggest that Fo Xi, their first Emperor, taught the Chinese people to cultivate mulberry trees and to raise silkworms, although the Lady Hsi-Ling, chief wife of the Yellow Emperor Huang-Ti, is revered as the Lady of the Silkworms, and it is she who, from observing the effect of her hot tea on a cocoon which accidentally dropped from a mulberry tree into her cup, is credited with discovering how to reel silk. The reign of the Yellow Emperor is traditionally dated to 2677–2597 BC, but we know that sericulture was already a long-established and highly developed skill by this date. As techniques in excavation processes and conservation have improved, it has been possible to save textiles which in previous times would have oxidized and decomposed rapidly when exposed to air and light. Carbon-dating methods have made possible a more accurate idea of time scale. At present, the earliest excavated silk is a group of ribbons, threads and woven fragments, all dyed red, dated to 3000 BC. These were found at Qianshanyang in Zhejiang. Other early silks were found in a bamboo basket during excavations at the site of Chien-shan-yang, at Wu-hsing in Chekiang. Carbon dating put the layer in which these pieces were found to between 2850 and 2650 BC. One of the fragments, worked in a tabby weave, was examined and found to be silk from the domesticated silkworm, Bombyx mori.

There are many indigenous varieties of wild silk moths, found in a number of different countries. The key to understanding the great mystery and magic of silk, and China's domination of its production and promotion, lies with one species: the blind, flightless moth, Bombyx mori. The original wild ancestor of this cultivated species is believed to be Bombyx mandarina Moore, a silk moth living on the white mulberry tree, and unique to China. The silkworm of this particular moth produces a thread whose filament is smoother, finer and rounder than that of other silk moths, which produce silk filaments of irregular and flattened form. The flatter threads tangle easily, and therefore break easily if unwound, whereas the rounder filament can be reeled as a long, continuous – and therefore stronger – thread. Over thousands of years, during which the Chinese practised sericulture and studied and used all their types of silk moth, Bombyx mori evolved into the specialized silk producer it is today; a moth which has lost its power to fly, only capable of mating and producing eggs for the next generation of silk producers. Therein lies the secret of silk, and China's silk production.

During the Shang dynasties, between 1766 and 1401 BC, trade opened westward – Shang means, literally, 'merchant' – and the Chinese learned bronzeworking from their Siberian and Central Asian neighbours. The most famous surviving Shang silk fragments are 'ghosts', pieces of silk whose physical structure survives imprinted on the patina of bronze ritual vessels. That sacred bronzes and jade objects were wrapped in silk suggests that silk too was held in special esteem. A bronze axe now in

Stockholm reveals silk made from three different types of cocoon, while a bronze ritual vessel in Malmö, Sweden, shows the use of several kinds of thread, including silk from wild spinners. Some of the 'ghosts', or 'pseudomorphs', as they are known, display a lozenge-patterned woven structure, indicating an already sophisticated loom technology. Traces of silk embroidery in satin stitch with vestiges of what was possibly chain stitch have been identified on the Malmö bronze vessel. As silk is the embroidery thread *par excellence* it is not surprising that embroidery should have developed early in China.

The Shang communicated with the gods through a symbolic language of pictograms, inscribed on oracle bones and tortoiseshell, and many of the pictograms relate to sericulture. We learn of offerings being made to the silkworm goddess, indicating the importance of silk. It seems there was an office of Nu Cang, Mistress of the Silkworms, and war captives were sometimes sacrificed on the altar in propitation to a pantheon of silkworm deities. Literary sources such as The Book of the Shang, and The Book of the Rites, give further information about sericulture. Reeling silk and spinning were always considered household duties for women, while weaving and embroidery were carried out in workshops as well as the home.

Shang 'twill' weave pattern, reconstructed from traces left on bronze more than three millennia ago. The warp runs vertically on the page. (after V. Sylwan)

Calligraphy and painting were always highly esteemed by the Chinese, and these arts influenced the decoration of their precious silks. Elegant curvilinear brushstrokes were echoed in embroidery techniques, and sometimes a combination of techniques enhanced the beauty of the silks. An old Chinese saying, literally 'to add designs to brocade', means to make something almost too beautiful, akin to the English expression 'to gild the lily'. That the results achieved by skilled embroiderers fulfilled aesthetic requirements so perfectly may be one reason why tapestry weaving was not developed in China until a later period, having been learned from westerly wool-and-linen cultures.

From ancient times, the Chinese evolved strict systems of rituals, and a philosophy of 'Li', which has been translated as 'the virtue of orderliness and principled refinements', or, 'the virtue of propriety'. This complex and all-encompassing philosophy has a relevance to the subject of silk. There was a hierarchy which influenced everything. At a very early date in Chinese history, rules were drawn up regulating clothes, colours, fabrics and decoration, and punishments were meted out if these were transgressed. No motif or colour was merely decorative, all had symbolic significance.

The principal forces of the universe were Yin and Yang. Yin is found in darkness, water and moon, and is feminine; Yang is contained in the sun, light and male energy. Harmony is achieved when Yin and Yang are in balance, and this is the aim of life and art. The relationship between the universe and human history is explained in terms of five phases, associated with the five elements of wood, metal, fire, water and earth. Dynasties were represented by different elements and adopted the colours

T-shaped silk painting, found draped over the inner coffin of a woman in Tomb No. 1 at Mawangdui. It is a *fei-i*, or 'flying garment' for the soul. The owners of the tombs were buried between 160 and 150 BC, during the period of the Western Han. The upper part of the design shows the snake-tailed deity Fu-Xi flanked by the sun (Yang) and the crescent moon (Yin). The moon-goddess Chang-e is seen flying up to the moon, where she is the keeper of the Elixir of Longevity. Below this division, people are wearing skirts and robes which are a true reflection of the finds in the tomb. The detail (*left*) from the lower portion shows two dragons passing through a jade *pi* disc carved with dots which suggest silkworm seeds. Beneath, a heavy curtain is parted to reveal a feast, or perhaps a sacrificial ceremony, supported by a giant astride a serpent.

Wall-hanging found at Noin-Ula, with chain stitch embroidery in coloured silks on purple wool, 1st century BC.

that matched them – green, white, red, black and yellow. Thus the Qin (221–206 BC) declared itself to be a dynasty of water and its emblematic colour was black. In this way it assumed a natural succession from the Zhou who were symbolized by fire and the colour red. Water had quenched fire. The five directions were also symbolized by colours and by their symbolic beasts. The emperor was a priest-king, the Son of Heaven, and as such he had to ensure that correct balance was maintained.

Dyeing and textiles seem to have evolved together, and there are some beautiful early examples, such as the Warring States silks excavated at Mashan, of the third and fourth century BC. A painting on silk of a lady shows an elaborate flowing robe which must surely be made of silk. Chain stitch embroideries depict Yang dragons and Yin phoenixes and scrolling-cloud motifs. A woman's tomb here contained many shrouds and silk garments, some finely embroidered as well as coloured.

Although silk had travelled west centuries earlier, the Silk Road is generally referred to as having been 'opened' in the second century BC during the time of the Romans and the reign of the Han Emperor Wu. Wu's ambassadors travelled as far west as Persia and Mesopotamia, bearing gifts including silks. A Han embassy reached Baghdad in AD 97, and important finds of Han silks have been made along the Silk Road; for instance Sir Marc Aurel Stein discovered forty-five monochrome and polychrome figured silks at Lou-Lan in the Tarim Basin, and the Soviet archaeologist P. K. Kozlov excavated some twenty patterned silks in nomadic burial mounds at Noin-Ula in Northern Mongolia. A looped-warp patterned silk was found at Noin-Ula, and a type of 'pile brocade' was found at Mawangdui in Hunan Province, dating from around 145 BC. Another site at Mawangdui yielded fifteen samples of polychrome pile warp silks, precursors of velvet, twelve of which were borders for garments. The pile was raised over a thread rather than a rod, and the thread was later removed, an example of the innovation possible with a simple loom and a skilled weaver.

Spectacular finds from richly furnished tombs have established that the inclusion of precious silk garments, as well as shrouds, with both woven and embroidered patterns, formed part of burial rituals. The famous Tomb of Lady Dai at Mawangdui (Western Han, *c.* 170 BC) contained more than one hundred examples of silks and silk garments, and displayed a variety of intricate weaves and various printing techniques. The early silks are usually fine gauzes, either plain or patterned on the warp-face with small, geometric repeating motifs, some self-coloured and some polychrome.

Designs of cloud-bands, tree-coral, spiral wave scrolls, birds, animals and mythical beasts, flow with continuous, undulating lines and soft, fluid colour transitions. These patterns were achieved by laboriously lengthening and manipulating the warp-floats by hand. The decoration of these early silks is always warp-faced; the weft is visible on the face of the fabric, and the thread has little or no twist.

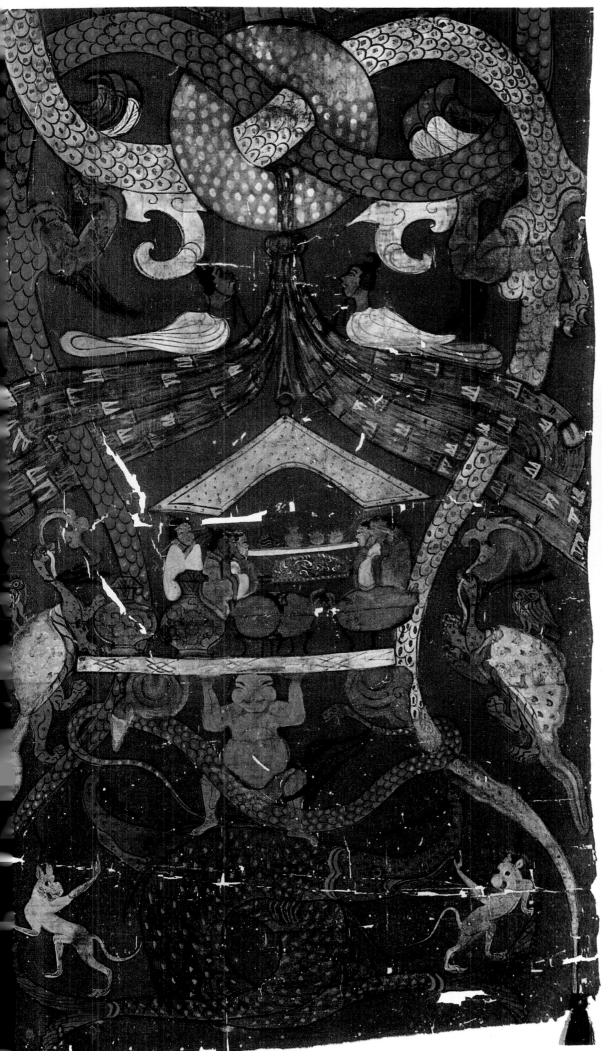

From left to right
Song dynasty tapestry panel (10–11th century AD) showing Yang blue tigers, and Yin peacocks symbolizing dignity and beauty, their bodies woven of gold-wrapped thread. This combination of creatures denotes protection.

Song dynasty votive hanging embroidered with the Guardian King of the West, depicted with the red face signifying a holy man in Chinese theatre, holding a serpent in his right hand and a jewel in his left. On either side are beribboned vases containing lotus

flowers. The figure is seated beneath an arch of ribbon-like cloud-bands. Lotus-borne characters below are embroidered in couched gold thread.

Ming dynasty (1368–1644) silk brocade dramatized by a black background and the use of flat, gilded paper for woven highlights. The bold repeating design of *Linghzi* fungi, symbolizing longevity, supports *shou* characters of long life, together with flaming pearls, swastikas, and Precious Things. The swastika, an early form of the character *fang*, is one of the oldest symbols in

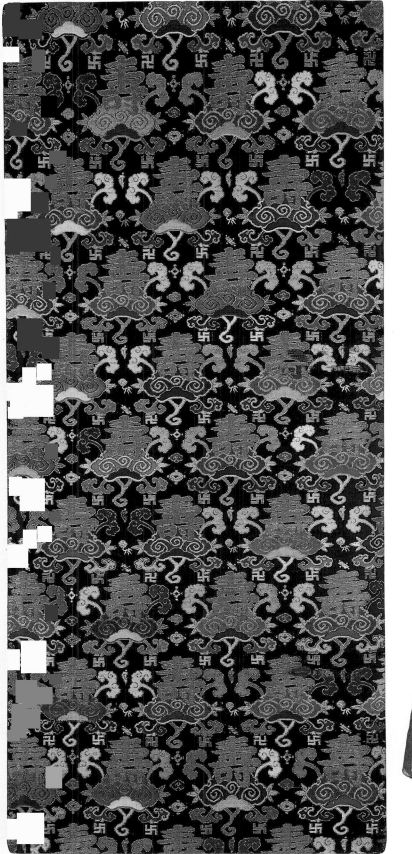

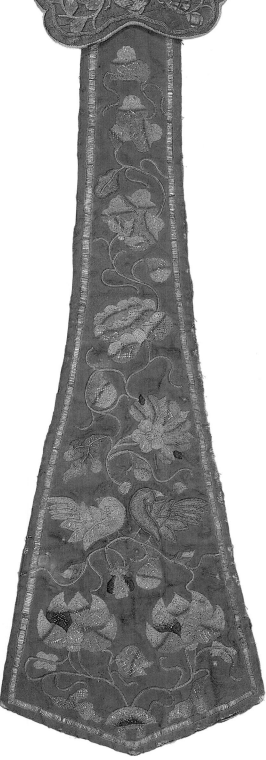

China, meaning the four regions of the world, or, since *c.* AD 700, ten thousand, symbolizing infinity.

Yuan dynasty (1260–1368) needle-loop panels. The shaped panel (*above*) is damask embroidered in needle-loop over gilded membrane. Lotus and peony flowers issue from a single stem, and two birds perch on a branch. The second panel (*right*) has each petal of the five flat blossom-heads worked in a different, intricate, pattern of stitches.

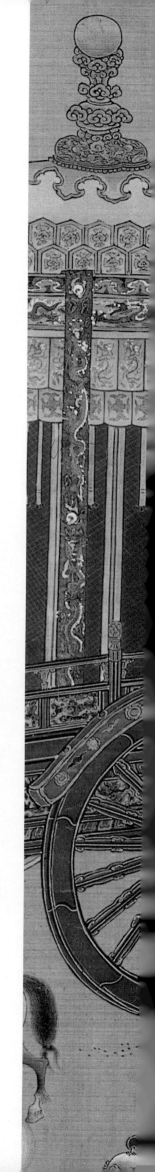

Silk-gauze festival symbol for a Ming imperial robe. Couched gold thread makes a five-clawed dragon chasing a Flaming Pearl. The lozenge-patterned background is embroidered in a twisted silk, once bright yellow. Chrysanthemum flowers, waves and rocks are embroidered in floss silk. The chrysanthemum festival took place in autumn, when these flowers were displayed before the emperor.

Ming painting on silk depicting the Emperor Tai Tsu dressed in a magnificent robe embroidered with roundels of dragons and clouds.

Opposite The Ming imperial chariot, with the enclosed, silk-curtained litter and silk banners fluttering, embroidered with auspicious designs.

Left Qing satin robe, 18th century, embroidered with phoenixes, peonies and bamboo in coloured silks and couched gold thread (detail *above*). In north-west China the phoenix represents the lover, the peony the beloved, and when these are combined in a design, the bamboo means 'modesty'.

Above Qing wedding robe, with typical betasselled floating panels and layered cloud collars. Clouds with five colours symbolize five-fold happiness. The robe is embroidered with auspicious symbols, and red – denoting beauty, wealth and life – is still the most important colour in a traditional eastern wedding.

Right The famous Manchu Dragon robe, worn for a portrait painted on silk in the 18th century.

Although patterns of Han brocades related closely to the contemporary style of painting on lacquer, and the motifs are characteristically Chinese, a medallion and square-lozenge arrangement which sometimes appears has been seen as suggestive of western influence.

The time of the Han coincided with Roman expansion, and many sources quote a Roman complaint that her citizens' demand for imported silks was so great as to be damaging to the Roman economy. Although China exported silks at this time, her home demand was high, and it seems doubtful that she would have exported silk in such quantity. It seems highly probable, however, that sericulture was established at an early period in certain areas of Central Asia, at least during the time of the Han (206 BC–AD 221), if not earlier, and that if there were grounds for the Roman complaints of excessive imports, the production-area could as well have been Sogdiana (Bactria), or even India, at that time also actively trading with Rome. China made no strenuous early efforts to maintain the monopoly of silk production, and much of the silk leaving the country was as likely to be given away as sold. For example, bolts of silk were presented as annual tributes to tribes bordering on China's provinces, in attempts to ensure peace and cooperation. Moreover Chinese emigrants took sericulture to Korea around 200 BC, and silk fabrics in Japan are recorded from about 28 BC. Many colourful stories explain the dissemination of this knowledge, telling of beautiful princesses hiding silkworm eggs in their coiffures when they were sent to marry foreign princes. A painted panel of around the seventh century AD discovered by Stein shows a richly dressed lady with a high diadem on her head, and girls kneeling by her side. One attendant figure points to the lady's diadem, where there is a basket of fruitlike objects. Stein suggests it was under this 'diadem' that the princess smuggled 'silkworm seeds' out of China, and the 'fruits' are cocoons, a story related by a Chinese pilgrim, Hsuan-tsang, in AD 600. An object at the other end of the panel is a loom. Hiroshi Wada suggests another interpretation, that the scene shows the ritual offering of silkworm eggs to the silkworm goddess, and weaving as the concluding act of the rite.

The Han dynasty was succeeded by the Three Kingdoms (AD 220–265) and the Two Jin (AD 265–420), and it seems that during this period, gold from the West began to be woven into silks for the first time.

Technical improvements continued throughout the following period of the Northern and Southern dynasties (420–589) and developments in weaving weft-patterned, instead of warp-patterned, silks allowed more complex designs and a wider cloth. Western influence became more obvious in some of these textiles, and in those of the Tang dynasty which followed (618–906). The Tang were fascinated by the exotic, the foreign, and the beautiful silks of Parthian and Sassanian Persia made a strong impression. The handsome Tang fabrics preserved in the Shoso-in and Horyuji Treasuries in Japan display the popular images, designs and symbols of

Tang brocade patterned with
'dancing phoenixes' in roundels,
7th century.

Sassanian Persia, but adapted to the Tang idiom (Pl. p. 53). One of the fabrics in the Horyuji, for example, is patterned with beaded roundels, in each of which are four bearded kings mounted on winged horses. The horses have Chinese characters branded on their haunches, and are drawn very much in the Chinese manner – more rounded steeds than those which prance on Near Eastern weavings.

A prose poem written at the end of the eighth century, entitled 'Rhapsody on the Figured Brocades offered by Men from Abroad', describes a pattern of dancing phoenixes 'with double corollas and layered leaves intermingled conformably with them so as to make a pattern'. Animals shown in a 'floral scroll' or roundel is a typically Sassanian device, and the royal gifts mentioned in the poem must have been the prototypes of well-known Tang brocades showing phoenixes in roundels.

Immense quantities of silks were demanded by rich patrons during the Tang. It is said that seven hundred weavers were devoted entirely to providing the silks demanded by Yang the Precious Consort, clearly an aptly titled lady. From time to time sumptuary decrees were issued. In 771 for instance, Tai Tsung decreed that the manufacture of certain cloths with complicated figures, including both monochrome and polychrome damasks and patterned gauzes, was considered decadent, and was to be stopped. Furthermore, the detailed work was 'harmful to the female artisans'. Woven images of dragons, phoenixes, unicorns, lions, peacocks, heavenly horses and divine herbs were prohibited, though 'the regularly current white brocade of Koro and the brocade of mixed colours, as well as the regularly current damasks and brocades of small figures and graphs and the like, may still be allowed in conformity with old precedent'. A similar edict of Wen Tsung, in 829, ordered that on the first day of the new year, all the looms and reeds used in the production of gaudy and frivolous textiles were to be burned.

The Tang apparently developed an important new weave, silk satin, and their embroidery was of two main types. Buddhist images were built up in satin or chain stitch, often combined with appliqué, while the other type of embroideries were embellished with gold or silver outlines using metal-wrapped thread secured by tiny couching stitches. Buddhist symbols derived from India include the conch shell, a canopy, an umbrella, the wheel of Dharma, the lotus, goldfish, and the endless knot. The lotus was a favourite flower until the time of the Tang, but in the late seventh to early eighth century the peony became fashionable, initially due to the notorious Lady Wu Zeitan, who commanded their cultivation at the expense of other flowers. Another favourite motif is one known as 'Tang Flowers and Grasses', a design of rounded blossoms with fine stems.

Tribute gift of foreign silks to the Tang court are documented, and these include a shipment of plain weave raw silks (a type of pongee), a gift from the Emperor of Japan to his Tang cousin. This type of plain silk was suitable for the court painters to use as a ground for colours and inks. Towards the end of the eighth century came tributes of Tibetan silks to the Tang court, and several times during the centuries the Koreans sent textiles with names like 'sunrise clouds of morning bombycine'. Sericulture, as previously mentioned, had begun in Korea around 200 BC, when waves of Chinese immigrants arrived there.

China suffered a devastating defeat by Islam at the Battle of Talas in 751, and many skilled Chinese craftsmen were taken as prisoners of war and resettled in Persia and Mesopotamia. Records list certain Tang master weavers named Yue Huan and Lu Li who were sent to Iraq, where they taught local weavers their silk-weaving techniques. Under constant attack, China began to close herself off from the West. A colony of Arab merchants had settled in Canton during the Tang or earlier, and this city had subsequently become a port for a thriving east-west trade. In 874 the annals stated that rebels 'cut down the mulberry trees throughout the region [of Canton] so that for a long time there was no silk to send to the Arabian empire . . .'.

One of the most dramatic finds of Tang silks along the Silk Road was made in 1907 by Aurel Stein. Some time around 1015, Buddhist monks, possibly alarmed by the threat of invasion by a Tibetan people, the Tanguts, sealed more than ten thousand manuscripts and silk paintings, silk banners, and textiles into a room at the Caves of the Thousand Buddhas near Dunhuang. Dunhuang was a station on the old Silk Road in north-west Gansu on the frontier of Chinese Turkestan, an area formerly under Chinese rule. The eight- and ninth-century silk banners and silk fragments and other treasures are now divided among three museums: the National Museum, New Delhi, the Victoria and Albert Museum and the British Museum in London. Another collection of silk fragments is in the Musée Guimet in Paris, and Sven Hedin presented a collection to the Stockholm Museum.

Silk scroll-painting from Dunhuang, 10th century, depicting the 7th-century pilgrim Hsuan-tsang returning to China with Buddhist sacred texts, and welcoming officials wearing robes in a variety of patterned silks.

Apart from fine damasks and embroidery, the Chinese textiles most familiar to us are the silk tapestries known as *k'ossu* or *kesi*. The technique appears to be one learned from western sources via the Uighurs who lived on the western borders of China during the early part of the Song. A Song writer, Hong Hao, commenting on the customs of some of the non-Christian barbarians of his time, mentions that the Turkic Uighurs 'use silk threads of the Five Colours to tapestry-weave robes they call *kesi*. They are very beautiful.' Recent western writers have inferred that the robes of the Uighurs, rather than the tapestry-fabric, were called *kesi*, and that these, like the later, familiar Dragon robes, were entirely silk tapestry. This is highly unlikely, as the earliest known examples of Chinese and Uighur tapestry are in the form of narrow strips, woven of silk or a mixture of silk with hemp warps. The Uighur had received in their midst many Persian and Sogdian refugees, driven out by the Abbasid persecutions and othr religious differences, and at this period the traditional Arab and Persian robes were decorated with 'tiraz' – fine silk and linen tapestry bands and borders. The technique of fine tapestry weaving travelled east in this form, sometimes on gifts of Robes of Honour. The term *kesi*, *kossu* or *k'ossu* would may derive from the Arabic *khazz* or Persian *qazz* – pronounced approximately 'khuzz' – meaning silk woven with another material such as linen or hemp.

Under the Song, whose dynasty began in 960, turbulent times continued, but progress was made in printing techniques, and some lovely examples of silks printed with gold patterns have survived. Sometimes the delicate patterns are highlighted with gold, either painted by hand or applied as a fine powder on to resin. A court edict of the period forbade the common people to dress in finely printed silks or to trade in blocks for printing such silks.

Typical Song patterns incorporate naturalistic flowers and plants, and small-scale transfer prints of animals – lions, phoenixes, or butterflies. Discreet floral patterns of hibiscus, peony or lotus were woven in fine gauzes, and geometrical designs such as checkerboard, tortoiseshell 'cells', snakeskin, bamboo stems and persimmon stalks gave subtle texture to damasks. The effect of these refined silks was enriched by weaving the pattern in a darker shade of the ground colour.

Early Song tapestries were, like the 'tiraz', woven as narrow strips, and were used for binding religious books and scrolls. The availability of silk in China would have led to a natural development of silk tapestry in its more familiar form, as whole robes and figurative hangings. Song *kesi* depicted naturalistic scenes, and favourite themes were taken from Buddhist and Taoist tales. The names of some of their famous weavers have been faithfully recorded, and some of the *kesi* masterpieces can be attributed to their creators.

By its very nature, tapestry weave lends itself best to geometric shapes. Little shuttles of different coloured thread are used to make the design in blocks. Changing colours produces a fine split in the weave which is sometimes invisibly sewn up after weaving. Sometimes *kesi* is made completely reversible by sewing the thread-ends into the fabric after weaving, and this is done for screens and fans, for example, because they are seen from both sides. By outlining motifs with silk or with gold threads, sweeping curves and highlights gave depth or emphasis, according to the weaver's intention. Sometimes *kesi* was woven in a manner similar to Japanese *tsuzure-ori*, fingernail weaving. Here the weaver's fingernails are serrated to form sawtooth edges, and used instead of a weaver's comb to beat down the weft threads. Some of the early *kesi* with gold discovered by Stein incorporated gilded paper strips, and in later *kesi*, fibre made from peacock feathers was used to give iridescent highlights.

The Great Wall failed to stem the onslaught of the Mongols, who swept in and established their Yuan dynasty (1260–1368). The Pope in Rome, menaced by powerful Arab states on his threshold, sought an alliance with the Mongols against the Crescent of Islam, and a period of trade and lively exchange of influences, known as the Pax Mongolica, ensued. Marco Polo and his family were among a number of merchants who made, or attempted, the journey to the fabled East during this time.

Yuan silks were woven for the Vatican, and for export to Moslem markets in Syria, Egypt and Spain, and further north to Scandinavian countries. Fragments of these have survived as church vestments, and as wrappings for relics. A Yuan silk excavated in Egypt shows a palmette meander design, antecedent of the favourite pomegranate design of Spain and Italy. Similarly, the west elaborated the central 'cone' of the lotus into the pine-cone motif. Sometimes the designs incorporate Islamic inscriptions, intended for the Mamluk market. Mongol war booty resulted in a more extensive use of gold than in previous centuries. Sometimes strips of paper

Song (960–1279) painting on silk, with a scene of ladies preparing silk. The lady smoothing the fabric wears a tortoiseshell 'cell' pattern upper garment.

were gilded by sprinkling powdered gold on resin or glue, or strips of thin gold foil were wrapped round a core of silk. A pale gold effect was achieved by wrapping silver foil round a yellow silk core.

Needle-loop embroideries appear to belong to the period of the Yuan alone, and the technique died out of fashion in the early Ming. The technique is similar to western European needle-made lace, and is a type of buttonhole stitch which fills in the pattern in segments of attached embroidery. The design was sometimes enriched by inserting strips of gilt hide or paper beneath the embroidery (Pl. p. 27). These rare embroideries were virtually unknown until recent years, when a number were discovered during the ransacking of Tibetan monasteries, where they had lain for centuries perfectly conserved at high, still altitudes.

Both Yuan and Ming weavers used gold thread extensively in certain *kesi* weavings, and these golden silks were considered appropriate coverings for religious scriptures. *Kesi* became popular for robes, screens, hangings, and upholstery, particularly in the form of elbow cushions, throne seats and backs.

During the Ming period (1368–1644) China started to weave figured velvets, a technique influenced by westerly sources – whether from Safavid Persia, or farther west, is not known. By the sixteenth century Chinese workshops were already weaving, embroidering and painting textiles with European influence in their designs. Bed covers and hangings made for export were usually embroidered on yellow or cream silk, often satin, with a central medallion surrounded by meandering floral designs. Painted silk, often a light taffeta, was exported to Europe for dress and furnishing fabrics.

Carpet-making was not a great Chinese tradition, but was born of the wool-weaving skills of nomadic Turkic tribes. The earliest Chinese silk carpets date from the seventeenth and eighteen centuries, and they usually have the designs and colours of eastern Turkestan, or are small shaped 'throne' mats.

During the last great dynasty of China, the Manchu Qing (1644–1911), *chinoiserie* became the height of fashion in Europe, and shawls were made of fringed, embroidered Chinese silks. The popular image of Chinese traditional dress is the Manchu Dragon robe, and these robes survive in greater numbers and variety of colours than any other Chinese garments. The dragon symbolizes imperial authority, and the whole pattern shows the universe, worn on the axis of the human body. Yellow was the dynastic colour of the Manchu, and a certain bright, clear yellow was reserved for the emperor and his chief consort. 'Mandarin squares' on robes distinguished the various ranks of civil and military officials, and were sometimes embroidered, sometimes tapestry woven.

In the Revolution of 1911, the Imperial city of Peking was looted and the palace wardrobes and coffers ransacked; some of their magnificent contents have since found their way to the West.

Ming embroidered roundel with cloud-bands. It depicts the legend of the white Hare or Rabbit who lives in the moon, and mixes with pestle and mortar the Elixir of Immortality.

An embroidered 'Mandarin square', worn on the robe to signify rank, late Ming.

Fragment of *tsujigahana*, a combination of tie-dyeing and hand-painting techniques. The pattern shows the sun and crescent moon, with a plum-blossom-head within the full orb, rendered in soft but clear lines, mixing delicacy with strength and definition. *Tsujigahana* was a product of medieval Japan, and developed between the 14th and early 17th century. In *tsujigahana*, tie-dyeing is the basis, but no single technique stands out; stencil and embroidery may be added, all contributing to the harmony of the whole.

Japan

'The garment was the person; it was the direct expression of his or her personality.' Lady Murasaki's remark in *The Tale of Genji* (Heian period, 794–1185) offers us an insight into the role of silk in Japan, where every colour, every hue, every juxtaposition, every choice of pattern, was a matter of crucial importance. Her descriptions have preserved images which would otherwise have been lost to us: for example, at the ceremony of the bathing of a newborn imperial prince, the lady-in-waiting who held up a tiger's head before the face of the child was gowned in an outer robe patterned with pine cones, the train woven with a design of seaweed and waves.

The kimono is the most important Japanese garment, worn with long, widely cut loose trousers, usually in a shade of red. In Lady Murasaki's time the kimono was a very voluminous garment, for both men and women. Its sleeves, too, were full and long, and a fashionable lady might wear as many as twenty kimonos at a time, each made of the thinnest, finest, most transparent silk, giving a rainbow appearance as the colouring of each layer overlaid and melted into those above and below. The harmonies visible at the neck, front edges and ample sleeves were all-important fashion points; criticism was severe, and Lady Murasaki commented that when a certain lady went before the Emperor, everyone noticed there was a fault in the colour combination of her dress – not serious, but one colour was 'a little too pale'. The coloured layers themselves were given descriptive names, such as 'azalea' layers, or 'pine' layers. Over these layered kimonos two or more short cloaks, preferably of imported Chinese brocade, would complete an elegant dress.

By Lady Murasaki's era, silk was a long established feature of elegant life, but just when Bombyx mori and Chinese silk technology reached Japan is uncertain – Japan's Yamamai silk moth is believed to be an indigenous species. Chinese annals record silk fabrics in Japan around 28 BC, and Japanese envoys visited the Chinese court in AD 37, 109, and 238. In AD 188, the Emperor received a gift of silkworm eggs, evidently not the first, from a Chinese ruler.

In the third century, the widowed Empress Jingu led her imperial troops into Korea, a triumphant invasion with several important results for silk. Under treaty the rulers of the three Korean kingdoms agreed to render annual tribute of silks forever, and a Korean weaver or weavers, brought to Japan, introduced pattern-weaving. The first patterned Japanese silks were self-coloured, with a simple geometric motif, similar to Chinese silks of the period, and these were known as 'aya'.

Succeeding emperors encouraged sericulture, and several times during the following centuries, Korean and Chinese weavers were brought to Japan and embassies were sent abroad, ensuring progress in technology. The Chinese found some of the Japanese patterned silks so beautiful they called them 'mystery weaves'.

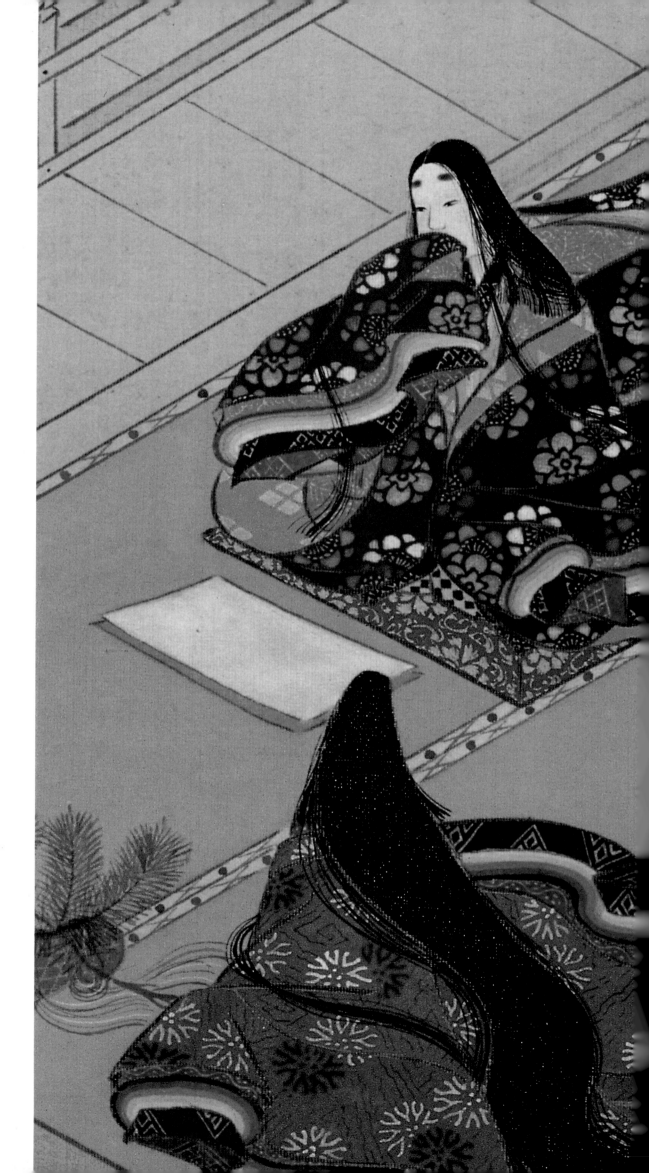

The slit-tapestry technique known as *k'ossu* or *kesi*: a swooping phoenix, against a background of clouds and peonies, late Ming.

Right, and opposite below Lady Murasaki Shikibu writing *The Tale of Genji*. Lady Murasaki was born about AD 978, when girls were not educated, but she contrived to be present while her brother was being tutored, and learned quickly. Married then widowed, she was sent to attend the young Empress Akiko. Her *Tale* contains a wealth of detail about the dress of the period. The 19th-century paintings show her wearing the many-layered kimonos then fashionable, with the top kimono patterned with blossom-heads.

Opposite above The luxurious type of brocade, woven with gilded paper, known as 'kinran'. The technique of weaving with paper-backed gold developed in China during the Song, and was first practised in Japan in the 16th century. This example dates from the 17th or 18th century.

Far right, top to bottom Fragments that once formed part of sumptuous 18th-century kimonos: a kinran with rosettes; a gauze of a bird with luxuriant plumage, turning in flight, and a more sombre type of brocade, patterned with cloud-forms and rosettes.

Silk was still reserved for the court, or used for taxation and tribute, and ordinary Japanese people dressed in homespun of hemp and ramie. In 486 Emperor Kensho asked two weavers to make silks of a more ordinary quality to be sent out to the provinces to be copied, probably the first Japanese attempt to popularize silk.

The introduction of Buddhism to Japan, sometime after 500 AD, is important in silk history, for silks are preserved in the temple treasuries, and have been carefully recorded and conserved ever since they were given, either as valued gifts themselves, or as wrappings of precious offerings. Upon the death of the eighth-century Emperor Shomu, his widow donated his art treasures and household goods, including nine robes, or *kesas*, as an offering to the Buddha, and these have been preserved for centuries in the sealed Shoso-in Treasury, among many thousands of fabrics.

The *kesa*, a priestly garment, is a large, flat rectangle made up of square patches, usually seven or nine, arranged in strips. Two corners fasten on the right shoulder, and the cloth drapes across the body, passing under the left arm. It is said that the Buddha contemplated the rice fields, with the water levées that enclosed and supported each paddy – a true whole – and told his disciple Ananda to construct a cloak with a similar format, that would be a reminder and symbolic teaching to the monks. At first the patched garment was made from rags, denoting the monks' vows of poverty and humility, but in time, the patched format became a textile in its own right, and sometimes the patches were woven in the pattern of the fabric. Shomu's *kesas* have a pattern of mottled shades of grey and brown, a colouring known as 'tree bark', and this remained a favourite until the fifteenth century. Another favourite patched pattern was called *toyama*, or 'distant mountain'. Here, silk rags of many colours were overlapped, held by fine running stitches in such a way as to give a soft rippling surface. The colours are blended to give the effect of a hazy landscape.

Gauzes woven in the Nara period (eighth century) are either plain or patterned with lozenges and floral motifs. The properties of Kyoto's River Kamo have ensured its importance as Japan's prime dyeing centre, and during the Nara, dyers of Kyoto experimented with some of the pattern techniques of imported textiles, in particular wax resist (*rokechi*) and tie and dye (*kokechi*). The finest tie-dyeing was *kanoko-zome*, from *kanoko*, a fawn, and there is a story that the Emperor Daigo commanded the dyers to reproduce the delicate random spotting on the deer in his deer park.

Kyokechik, called 'jam dying', reached Japan from China in the sixth century and was well developed at the Nara period. Folded cloth was pressed between two boards perforated with designs, and dye was squeezed through the holes. Two important printing processes were the use of gold powder or leaf with a gum or resin, and a lyrical-sounding technique in which silk was stretched over carved wooden blocks, held in place with rice paste, then rubbed and stained with flower juices.

Early 15th-century armour, elaborately laced with silk cords in a pattern known as 'jay bird's feathers'.

Embroidered robe for the Nōh theatre, 16th–17th century.

The voluminous kimono of the Heian period of Lady Murasaki lost favour to more practical dress in the Kamakura period (1185–1333), overshadowed by military dictatorship and civil war. The samurai, warriors with a fierce, proud creed of honour and loyalty, wore armour fastened by strong silk cords, and the film 'Rashomon' shows the huge hat with curtain-like silk veil worn by the samurai's wife out-of-doors. Demand for fine brocades diminished, and most fine patterned silks were imported, rather than woven in Japan. The 'mon' or family crest became an important design element. Some of the oldest 'mon' are the chrysanthemum, wisteria, and various geometric arrangements, for instance a group of six squares.

The Muromachi (Ashikaga) period (1334–1573), almost contemporary with the Ming dynasty, was a time of continual civil war and lavish patronage of the arts, and saw the emergence of two important aesthetic traditions, the Nōh theatre, and the cult of the tea ceremony, both influenced by Zen. A familiar figure in Nōh drama is the sorceress, who appears first as a maiden begging to see the secret interior of a temple. When her wish is refused, she hides in the great temple bell, and is later discovered in her true form – a great white serpent. Her maidenly appearance in the initial scene is betrayed as false by the shimmer of her under-kimono, silver triangles on white, a well-known Muromachi pattern. When the bell is lifted, this is seen to be her entire costume, like the scales of a great snake. Repeating patterns such as triangles and checkerboard were often achieved by application of gold leaf.

Tapestry weaving became a fashionable courtly pastime after some priests returned from China around 1400 and set up *kossu* looms at a temple near Kyoto. The Japanese call tapestry 'fingernail weaving', *tsuzure-ori*, because the weavers battened the weft with long serrated fingernails; it is a popular silk for sashes (*obi*), and for temple hangings and festival trappings.

A stitched tie-dye, *tsujigahana*, became a method of incredible refinement (Pl. p. 41), and surviving early kimonos indicate the great skill of the dyers. Painting, applied gold, and skilled tie-dying are combined in textiles of breath-taking beauty which today are considered national treasures.

Among the refugees who sought asylum in Japan during the Momoyama (Azuchi) period (1573–1675) were skilled Chinese 'kinran' weavers, that is, experts in brocade woven with gilded membrane or parchment (Pl. p. 43). Designs became richer and bolder, with dramatic use of gold, and one of the new textiles developed during this period of strong patronage was a weave which imitated embroidery by allowing selected threads to 'float' on the surface. Embroidery itself was very popular, and the hangings frequently show patterns where large areas of silk are covered with laid or coiled couched metal threads.

The rise of the middle class to power, wealth and educational opportunities occurred during the Edo period (1616–1868), named for marshlands reclaimed by the Shogun Tokugawa Teyasu. Japan closed its doors to the outside world, and although some trade with the Dutch continued, few textiles were exported. Edo silks were made predominantly for home consumption. Throughout the Edo period, extravagance and repression alternated, and several times the manufacture and sale of silk was forbidden.

Velvet was a mystery unsolved until one day, as a story relates, among bolts imported from China a piece of velvet was found still bearing weaving-wires over which pile was looped uncut. Skilled Japanese silk weavers understood at once.

Naturalistic themes were developed in Edo kimono design: scattered open fans, falling leaves, birds, all were portrayed more realistically than ever before, and subtle shading was achieved in embroideries by varying the fineness of threads. Tie-dye became minutely detailed, and the finest type was tied over tiny silver nails. After dyeing, great skill was required to cut the threads without damaging the fabric.

During the late seventeenth century, the first catalogues of kimono designs were produced. Dramatic, sweeping images, for example ocean waves, were popular for women's formal outer kimonos, but gradually smaller designs reappeared, and

Edo period kimonos with fashionable patterns, such as the scattered open fan design (second from right), painted on a folding screen, 17th century.

shaded dyeing became the rage. 'Twilight dyeing' produced shaded hues from pale to intense, and also from one colour to another unrelated, for example from blue to pink, and the famous kimono artist Yuzen was particularly skilled at this method. He also lent his name to a traditional method which he perfected, in which the resist paste was applied with sharpened sticks resulting in very precise outlines. Yuzen, who signed himself 'the fanmaker', published a catalogue of his kimono designs, and some bore messages, reminiscent of the screen-printed T-shirts of modern times. It became a favourite pastime, while strolling in a summer evening, to compare kimonos and guess their meaning.

The *obi*, tied round the kimono in all manner of variations, was also decorated in every way, and Japanese ladies collected these, just as westerners collect fashion accessories.

During the Tempo Reformation of the late Edo period, strict sumptuary laws were enforced, expensive costumes were seized and burned, theatres banished, actors ostracized, and all production, trade, and use of silk forbidden. The people disobeyed in secret and finally stormed the governor's residence in protest.

Japan was shocked abruptly out of her island dreaming in 1853, and forced into the world of commerce and very different aesthetic values. *Japonisme* joined *chinoiserie* and orientalism as western trends. The first serious entry of Japan into the silk export market was about 1855, when silkworm disease in the West produced a demand for eggs to replenish stock. The islands of Japan had escaped the disaster, and there was a brief boom in exporting eggs. Japan turned her attention to the possibilities of expanding her silk production for home and exports, and in 1869 Japanese weavers were sent to France to learn French weaving methods and to copy French brocades. In 1876 the Japanese government purchased the most modern equipment, and set up a model factory to instruct Japanese weavers in using power-driven Jacquard looms, and to make all types of silk.

Fortunately, there were enough far-sighted Japanese to form antiquarian societies to study, rescue and revive traditional arts and crafts, and many rich collections have been formed during the twentieth century. Despite the adoption of western clothing, traditional garments are still important, and synthetic materials have never replaced silk in status. Historical textiles are collected, exhibited, studied, and published in lavish, beautifully printed books for study by textile students, designers and collectors, and Japanese technology employs sophisticated computers to reproduce the painstaking and extraordinary weaves of earlier centuries, as well as to invent new ones.

Japan's geographical situation as an island is reflected in her art, which while always restrained is highly individual. She marks the most easterly point of the Silk Road, whose westward march carried silk, sericulture and designs across the Steppes of Central Asia.

 # 2 Central Asia and the Silk Road

he first known East-West passage is that of the northern Steppes, crossing the Altai Mountains between China and the Black Sea. More southerly routes led the caravans through the deserts and valleys of Central Asia. Caravanserai and townships sprang up along the way, and the growth of the silk trade and the knowledge of sericulture led to silk production outside the main mass of China. The Iranian Plateau is considered the farthest west of this general area, and the term Central Asia includes present-day Afghanistan and the Pamirs north of Pakistan.

The geographer Ptolemy records the tale of a first-century Macedonian trader named Maes Titianos who sent agents to reconnoitre the silk route and its principal landmarks. Their journey started from Antioch, the capital of Roman Syria, crossed the Euphrates at Hierapolis, entered the Parthian Empire, passed through Ecbatana (Hamadan), Rhagae or Ray near modern Teheran, Hecatompylos and Merv, and went on to Bactra (Balkh), a city which then belonged to the Indo-Scythians. From here their route ran on to the Pamirs. Ptolemy tells of a valley of the Pamirs, in the foothills of Komedai, where a stone tower was the place of assembly for a great bazaar. At this point merchandise was exchanged between Levantine and seric (silk-carrying) caravans. At Kashgar the route forked. The northern route led to Kucha (possibly the Issedon Scythica of Alexandrian geographers) to Kara Shahr, Lou-Lan (their Issedon Serica) and the gate of Yumen Kuan, west of Dunhuang. The course of the southern route from Kashgar passed via Yarkand, Khotan, Niya and Miran to the Lob Nor. The two roads reunited at Dunhuang, then entered China proper by way of Tsu-ch'uan and Changyah and at last reached Changan, usually regarded as Ptolemy's Sera Metropolis.

The neighbouring countries of East and West Turkestan are separated by the Tien Shan mountains. The central part of Eastern, or Chinese Turkestan as it is known today, is the almost impassable Takla Makan desert. When the snows melt, they form the River Tarim that runs eastward into the lake of Lob Nor. Kashgar, Yarkand and Khotan are the most important of the oases towns situated on the margin of this inhospitable territory. Only the heavily coated Bactrian camels are strong and hardy enough to carry burdens of merchandise along this route. It is probable that conditions during the centuries when the great caravan trains passed by the now-ruined temples and monasteries were less harsh and extreme than they are today.

In contrast to these wastes, West Turkestan is a rich country, although a great part of it too is desert: the Kara Kum (Black Sand), south of the Aral Sea, known as the Graveyard of Caravans, and Kizil Kum (Red Sand), the desert north of Kara Kum. Turkestan is watered by six great rivers, which include the Amu Daria and Syr Daria, known in ancient times as the Oxus and the Iaxartes. The Amu Daria has changed its course a number of times, leaving in the centre of the Kara Kum desert the ruins of large medieval towns as markers for earlier courses of the river. Over thousands of years a system of irrigation has been developed, and the area is famous for its silks. Great trading towns were Bokhara, in the territory formerly occupied by the silk-producing Sogdians, Tamerlane's turquoise-domed capital city of Samarkand, Tashkent and Merv, once famous for its ten great libraries and rich bazaars, and now only ruined walls in a desert.

The earliest silks so far excavated in Central Asia and known to the West are Chinese silks from frozen Scythian tombs at Pazaryck in the Altai Mountains, dating to around the fourth to fifth century BC. One of these, a piece of pale silk embroidered in chain stitch with a delicate design of flowering plants and birds, is mounted on Scythian felt to make a saddle blanket. The embroidery threads, although faded, indicate their original colours: blue, crimson, sand and brown. This embroidery probably represents the type of silk recorded in Chinese annals as a 'gift' (the Chinese term) or 'tribute' (the nomad term), in other words, a bribe to ensure peaceful relations with tribes on China's borders.

Knowledge of silk and types of embroidery was disseminated beyond China in a variety of ways. Chinese girls from noble families were sometimes sent in marriage to nomad chieftains, and sometimes later ransomed. A manuscript in New York, 'Eighteen Songs of a Nomad Flute', tells the story of a young woman taken in this way. At first she is homesick, but as the years pass, and her children are born and grow, she comes to love her nomad husband and their life in the great felt yurt, and extended tribal family. When at last her ransom is paid, she tells of her sorrow, as she returns to her homeland but leaves her 'barbarian' family and all that she has come to care for behind her. When the birds migrate each season, her memories become more poignant. The illustrations of the manuscript show rugs and fabrics, horse-trappings and tent-decorations in detail.

We do not know the antiquity of sericulture outside China. Varieties of silkworm were introduced to Central Asia during the Han, and two yellow cocoons from this period have been excavated in the Uighur Autonomous region of Chinese Central Asia. At this time, Bombyx mori was one among many types being raised for silk production.

In 323 BC Alexander the Great defeated the Persian King Darius, burnt Persepolis and marched his armies further eastward, while another Steppes people, the Parthians, moved west to settle and dominate the Iranian Plateau. Statues of Parthian kings at Hatra (in present-day Iraq) show an elegant fashion for swathed trousers and belted tunic, decorated with what appear to be appliqué gold elements. The Parthian king Mithradates (123–87 BC) encouraged trade along the Silk Road and challenged the power of Rome. It is recorded that the unfurled silk banners of the Parthians at the Battle of Carrhae amazed the Roman battalions. The earliest silk so far found in present-day Iran is from the Parthian period: a green silk cord decorating a child's felt garment, excavated at Shahr-i-Qumis (now in New York, the Metropolitan

Parthian costume of finely swathed silks, a tunic and trousers with appliqué decorations, from Palmyra, AD 150.

Museum). An important Parthian deity was the Water Goddess Anahita, and her symbol the pomegranate recurs time and again in silk patterns.

The defeat of the Parthians in AD 224 marked the beginning of the Sassanian dynasty. No longer content with acting as middlemen for the raw and woven silk travelling westward, the Sassanians set to work to establish their own silk industry. The designs developed by Sassanian weavers are highly distinctive, and their influence can be traced through the centuries to the present day. The Sassanians themselves were heirs to the decorative designs of the Assyrians and Scythians. An Assyrian carved stone cylinder seal shows Marduk wearing a robe decorated with the large-scale repeating medallions we associate with the Sassanians, and Scythian tombs unearthed in Bactria contained a number of rich garments decorated with appliqué gold elements (*bractea*) which formed an all-over repeat pattern. These types of decoration, embellished further by framing the motifs with pearls or beads, are the historical antecedents for Sassanian pearled roundel brocades.

Sassanian compound weft twill silks were woven on the drawloom, an advance in loom technology which allows patterns to be repeated automatically once they have been set on the loom, and although the question is still debated, current opinion is that the technique originated in Egypt or Syria but was developed in Persia. There are accounts of Syrian weavers taken in war and settled in Persia, and an inscription of Shapur I at Naqsh-i-Rustam mentions that he resettled his 'Roman' prisoners, who included many technicians, in his new cities of Gundeshapur and Bishapur.

The Taq-i-Bustan reliefs of Khusrau II (AD 591–628) show the Sassanian king wearing robes decorated with a mythological hybrid creature, the senmurv, isolated and in roundels. The senmurv, with mastif head, peacock tail and lion-like paws, was said to have the power to heal, and to bring rain. The design can be compared with textile fragments and a wonderful robe excavated in the Caucasus (now in St Petersburg, Hermitage Museum). Another senmurv silk is the shroud of St Remi in Rheims. These silks are now thought to have been woven in Persia or Transoxiana, between the first and ninth centuries.

Typical Sassanian motifs are the beaded roundels containing confronted animals and Trees of Life, hunting scenes, mythical beasts and birds. Animals and birds are usually depicted with pearl necklets and fluttering ribbons, while the Sassanian royal crown was often circled with pearls.

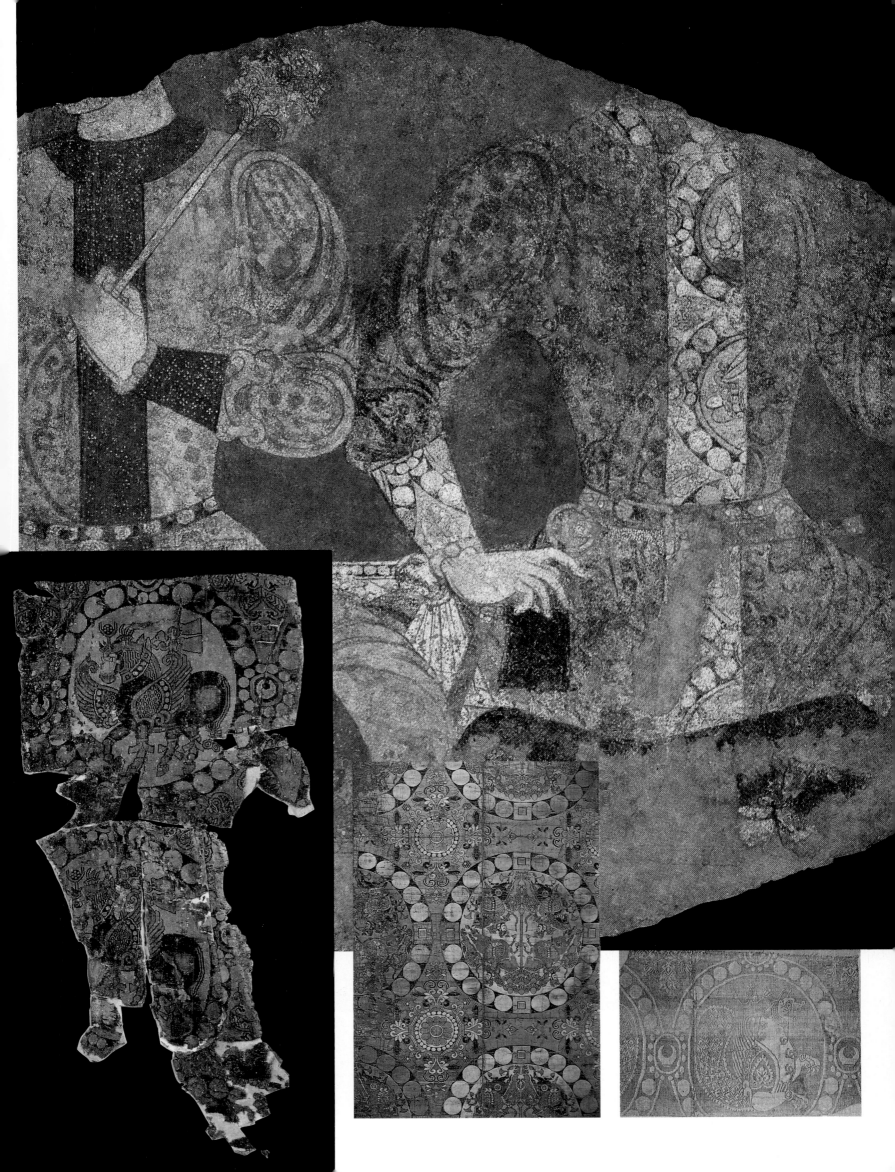

For the mounted tribesmen of Central Asia, their horses were as important as their womenfolk and weapons, and the elegant accoutrements of each were a public reflection of the man himself. A 19th-century Shakrisyab *shabrak* or saddle-cloth from the Bokhara region (ancient Sogdiana) is embroidered in fine silk cross stitch with a border of tulips.

A woman's leather boot, from Yarkand in Chinese Turkestan, embroidered with silk chain stitch, with a floss-silk frill down the centre front. Boots like this can be seen illustrated in many miniature paintings, visible below the hems of silk robes. It is very much an indoor boot; for heavy weather and riding more substantial decorated footwear was needed.

A Tekke woman's *chirpe* of yellow taffeta embroidered with a pattern of stylized flowers. Lilies, tulips and daisies are the most popular. Yellow is the colour worn by married women in Turkestan. The vestigial sleeves are purely decorative, hanging down the back like birds' wings, and the garment is usually worn draped over a headdress, in the manner of a cloak.

The crescent, another important symbol, also frequently appears in conjunction with pearls, for pearls are symbolically connected with the moon through water. Pairs of figures, addorsed or affronted, often with a central Tree of Life or flowering plant, hark back to Assyrian mythology, and addorsed figures are related to the double-headed eagle which later became the symbol of the Byzantine Empire.

Sassanian silks were copied, notably by the Chinese Tang and the Sogdians along the Silk Road, and many Sogdians silks have been excavated. A seventh-century painted frieze from a palace on the site of Afrasiyab depicts a procession of ambassadors whose caftans show repeating beaded roundels enclosing boars' heads, senmurvs, peacocks and elephants, all typical Sassanian motifs, and similar patterns were produced locally on Sogdian looms. Zandana, a Sogdian town near Bokhara, wove twill silks in a debased imitation of Sassanian designs. An inscription 'Zandanici' appears on a number of silks, suggesting a place of manufacture.

Indian missionaries carried Buddhism along the Silk Road from the third century AD. Through the intermediary of the Mongol rulers of Persia, Buddhist from 1260, the lotus, Chinese peony, dragon and cloud-band became part of Persian design, and the phoenix became the simurgh. These motifs remained in design vocabularies after the Mongol conversion to Islam.

While the Hunnish Hordes and the horsemen, the nomads and merchant caravans valued and traded silks, the skills of sericulture itself could only be practised by settled peoples living round oases. The early silks found along the silk route have been identified as Chinese, Sogdian and Persian. It is believed that some of the silks excavated at Dunhuang by Stein (see p. 35) were woven by the Uighur, a Turkic people who settled in the area. The Uighur are described by Chinese sources as wearing beautiful and colourful tapestry-woven robes, and it is probable that the skill of tapestry weaving was learned by the Chinese via this source.

Most of the wonderful silks familiar to us today as Central Asian date from the eighteenth and nineteenth centuries, and were traded in the great bazaars of Bokhara, Tashkent and Samarkand. (After about 1865, when railway tracks were laid across the Steppes, Western Turkestan became part of Russia.)

Silk has always been important in Central Asian dress, for both men and women. The cut of Central Asian caftans or *khelats* today differs little if at all from those painted or carved on walls, or depicted in miniatures or pottery from ancient times. The Turkestan woman's silk over-garment is the *chirpe*, a splendidly embroidered robe with long false sleeves that hang down the back like birds' wings. Colour indicates the age and marital status of the wearer, and during her life a woman might embroider three: one green, worn by young women, one yellow, worn by married women, and one white, worn by the older women, the rarest. The tradition of the 'Robe of Honour' was an important one, and an honoured guest might be presented with a great number.

Young woman's red silk robe from Yarkand, Turkestan, 19th century. Chinese influence is discernible in the embroidered motifs and 'magic mountain' border.

Fine, cross-stitch, geometrically designed small embroideries were made by an Uzbek sub-tribe, the Lakai, and another type of completely embroidered cross-stitch textile, for caftans, *shabraks* (saddle cloths) and spreads, with large bold designs, is usually attributed to Shakrisyab. Embroideries were worked in strips which were afterwards joined, and the work was usually divided among several embroiderers.

'Suzanis', so-named from the Persian word for needle, were made for dowries. In the eighteenth century a quantity of silk was produced locally, and stimulated the tradition of heavily embroidered suzanis. These are usually about the size of European single bedcovers, and the silk embroidery was worked on narrow loom-widths of linen (sometimes cotton, occasionally silk), later joined. Patterns and colours vary according to the centre of manufacture. Those of Nurata, for example, usually have a star-shaped central medallion as part of their distinctive design. The most popular stitch is a chain stitch using a tambour hook. Red is the predominant colour, and the range of shades runs through aubergine and maroon to crimson, scarlet and coral. The theme of flowers and plants predominates: full fat blossoms, sinuous vines and lotus, with motifs such as pomegranates, coffee pots or water jugs, and tiny occasional birds, which may be sprinkled or massed. Sometimes the field is directional, with a prayer niche at one end. The boldest suzanis, a type from Tashkent, are covered with large 'moons', and indeed the pattern is called 'oi-paliak', meaning moon-sky.

A rare and beautiful robe from Bokhara, of Chinese figured silk-damask embroidered in typical 'suzani' style, 19th century. White was reserved for elderly women.

Suzani embroidered with the large red moons, Tashkent, 19th century.

Similar embroideries have been observed in remote areas of East Turkestan, usually as the decorated portions of women's trousers, and this style is clearly characteristic of the Turkic peoples of Central Asia. In Western Turkestan, the embroideries, now less fine, are produced in government workshops.

Suzanis and caftans were traditionally lined with block-printed cotton or with the beautiful silk generally known as 'ikat' (Turkish *abr*, a cloud) – a material made with resist-dyed warp and/or weft – and narrower strips of this silk edged and emphasized the embroidery. Patterns are varied: they might be linear, curved, or geometric. Taffetas were often glazed with egg-white, a finish that wears off and washes out. Silk brocades were woven with gold and silver thread. The patterns often include rosettes on a checkerboard ground, reminiscent of the blossom-heads on suzanis, and even older silks.

The ikat technique of warp and/or weft dyeing was also used to make the rich silk velvets of the Uzbeks. This extraordinarily complex procedure required a team of specialist craftsman. Ikat patterned velvet was sometimes double-sided, with a positive and negative of the pattern, for use as gorgeous belts or ceremonial girths, with turn-backs to display the reverse. The ikat velvets of Bokhara are the most dramatic of the type. The silk pile is flat and shimmering, the repeat designs are dramatic, coloured golden-yellow, red, purple, green, white, blue, and the type of velvet was highly prized for special caftans.

Marco Polo remarked on the silk industry of Shemakha and Barda, in present-day Azerbaijan. Armenia, Azerbaijan and the Caucasus region have produced silk for many centuries, and still do. In the sixteenth century, three centuries after Marco Polo's visit, an English traveller and merchant, Anthony Jenkinson, paid a courtesy call on the local ruler, then in residence at Shirvan, and described him sitting in a luxurious marquee embroidered with silk and gold. Adam Olearius, in the 1630s, wrote of the quantity of 'weaving, spinning and silk and cotton embroidery' carried out at Shemakha; and a hundred years later another traveller, the Dutchman J.J. Streiss, enthusiastically described Shemakha's bazaar and its many stalls selling embroideries. A quantity of the velvet was produced here, and used throughout the Azerbaijan and neighbouring regions.

Azerbaijani embroiderers stitched with home-produced silk, and sometimes worked imported metal threads, spangles, beads and pearls into their designs. The style of embroidery is generally very geometrical, and related to both architectural elements, and the carpet designs of the Caucasus region. During the seventeenth and eighteenth centuries a group (or groups) of embroideries, generally termed 'Caucasian' or 'Azerbaijan', were made with fine cross-stitch or a darning stitch which gives a twilled effect. Darning stitch embroideries sometimes reproduce patterns from recognizable Persian silks, with figures and scenery, such as those on the Persian coat shown on page 146. The cross-stitch embroideries also sometimes show figures, but these are simply geometric renderings of dragons, birds, foxes or double-headed eagles, like those of Caucasian carpets. Another type is a diagonal floral pattern, imitative of Persian silk brocade strips, worked with silks that often have little twist. This was made for women's trouser-cuffs, but in the West was sold as 'gilet Persan' – Persian waistcoat material.

The Orthodox Church, steeped in Byzantine ritual and splendour, was always a patron for silks, and the Church and court retained their heritage of Byzantine and oriental richness until the time of Peter the Great, who determined that Russia should be closer to Europe. By the 1670s, Russian was producing some of the finest ecclesiastical needlework, derived from eastern and western styles, incorporating pearls, sequins, gold and silver lace on rich silk brocade and velvet grounds, and its church treasuries have conserved an inheritance of precious oriental silks.

The Caucasus, Armenia, and Gilan south of the Caspian formed part of the ancient Silk Road long before its 'official' opening in the second century BC during the time of the Romans and the Han. Silk had travelled to the Mediterranean and Europe from Greek trading posts on the Black Sea, and has been found in the Danube region, embroidered and woven into garments of the Hallstatt culture of the sixth century BC, and in several other early sites. But before we reach the destinations of the Silk Road around the Mediterranean there is another ancient source to consider: India.

 India's Woven Winds

ndia like China has ancient textile skills, practised in the cities of Mohenjo Daro and Harappa some four thousand years ago. The Dravidian inhabitants of these cities lived in large, well-planned communities, wove fabrics, knew how to use mordents and dye with madder, and sailed to trade with the Sumerians. Bronze needles tell us that they sewed, and sculptures show figures wearing jewellery and draped patterned cloth. India's textile history is complex and rich, silk-ruled, but climate and the customs of cremation of the dead have combined to destroy fabrics and dress. Thread of mixed wild silk and cotton, dated to the second half of the second millennium BC, has been found at archaeological sites at Nevasa and Chandoi, but apart from such fragments, the oldest surviving Indian textiles appear to be fifteenth-century Jain silk embroideries. For the rest, we must depend on Indian and other texts, paintings and sculpture.

The story of India and her silks is different from that of other countries. She has a number of indigenous silk moths, many of whose cocoons are suitable for weaving, and her famous textured silks (tussahs) are made from these native spinners. Early Indian texts termed certain textured silks woven from wild cocoons 'bark cloth', and in the region around Mirzapur in Uttar Pradesh, tussahs are still known by this name. Although most of the wild moths must break the filaments of their cocoons to escape, one tussah moth, Antheraea pernyl, leaves an opening in the cocoon that it seals with sericin, so that the filament remains intact.

As recently as the seventeenth century, Europeans believed tussahs were spun from a plant – hence the name 'herba goods' for these silks – and the eminent Dutch botanist Rumphius was surprised, when he dissected a 'fruit', to find a chrysalis inside. Customs surrounding the care and gathering of wild cocoons have become ritualized, and are likely to have been practised little changed for thousands of years. The 'silk forests' are considered sacred, and tribal people protect the caterpillars from predators such as birds, and later harvest the cocoons.

A Buddhist monk or missionary is credited with bringing the Chinese techniques of silk-reeling to India during the Gupta period (AD 400–600). Presumably he, or a previous traveller, also brought the eggs of Bombyx mori, for the technique of reeling is only applicable to that particular type of cocoon. Records of temple donations listed as thanks-offerings from silk-weavers for increased production may substantiate the story. In Assam, the Bodo tribe who originally migrated from Central Asia are said to have brought the art of silk reeling with them.

Around the first century AD, a maritime geography of East-West trade, the *Periplus Maris Erithreae*, documents Barbaricum on the Indus delta as a busy port, trading in silk yarn as well as muslin, indigo, turquoise, lapiz-lazuli and spices. Greek and Indian traders were active in bringing Chinese silks to India, a perilous voyage where many lives and cargoes were lost, and various trade routes, overland and by sea, connected India with the Near East and ultimately with the Mediterranean. During the period of Hellenistic and Roman expansion, Indian wild silks were exported with her fine cotton muslins. These silks were probably plain woven, some natural-coloured but some gloriously dyed. The Anglo-Saxon Synod of Calcyth warned priests against wearing garments coloured with vivid Indian dyes, as did the Venerable Bede in his 'Life of St Cuthbert', while St Jerome's fourth-century Latin translation of the Bible attributes to Job the observation that wisdom is beyond even the dyed colours of India.

Paintings in the Ajanta caves of the sixth to seventh centuries A D show figures dressed in resist-dyed and ikat-patterned textiles, and a contemporary text, the *Harshacharita*, is rich with descriptions of woven hangings. We read that for a royal marriage, the palace of King Harsha of Kannu was hung with fabrics 'like thousands of rainbows, linen, cotton, bark silk, spider's thread, muslin and shot silk'.

Fine, tightly woven silk was valued not only for its beauty and luxury, but also for its purity. Silk was deemed by Hindus to be a pure substance – so pure that it was not considered necessary to wash it before ceremonial use; according to the religious Mitakashara law, mere exposure was sufficient, for silk was 'washed by air'. Orthodox Vaishnavite Hindus and Jains abhor the taking of life, and certain holy centres, such as Benares, produce a silk known as *mukta* from the cocoons of moths which have completed their cycle and broken out of their cocoons. Since no killing is involved, this silk, like that of the moth Antheraea pernyl, is considered unpolluted, and suitable for the ropes of sacred processional chariots and for ritual swings used during the Krishna festival of Sawan, as well as for garments. Broken cocoons must be spun as short staple fibres, and *mukta* is an inferior fabric so far as utilitarian and aesthetic values are concerned. It also makes a fairly coarse yarn, and is one of those used to make the famous gold and silver brocades of Benares, known by the Persian term 'kincob', because it is better able to support the heavy gold patterns.

Gold thread runs through the history of Indian textiles. The Rig Veda, the Vedic scripture composed some three thousand years ago, mentions the cloth of gold worn by the gods in their resplendent chariots, and in the Sanskrit epic the *Ramayana*, Ravana the demon king wears a golden fabric. These golden silks were embroidered or else plain-woven with decorative borders, for Benares tradition credits the introduction of brocade weaving and drawloom techniques to skilled Persian brocade-weavers who came many centuries later, in the wake of the Mogul conquerors. Although we do not know how gold thread may have been made in those distant times, in recent centuries luxurious metal thread is usually interwoven with silk or cotton, and the gold thread can be of fine, flat strips, or wrapped round a silk or cotton core (known as *zari*). The thread core may be white, yellow or red, and the colour used affects the finished appearance of the metal. Gold saris were sent to a special craftsman in the bazaar to be burnished by beating.

Silk canopy from a Jain temple,
embroidered with a mandala
representing the Jain universe,
18th or early 19th century.

Jainism, one of many movements of religious reform originating in the sixth century, was always particularly strong in the state of Gujerat, where the famous Calico Museum in Ahmedabad has a rich collection of Jain silks, for example a canopy embroidered with a mystic diagram of the universe, and covers for sacred texts and temple hangings. Articles for religious use are traditionally replaced as soon as wear and tear has destroyed their perfection, and the earliest datable Indian textiles to have survived, after fragments found at Fostat in Egypt, appear to be Jain embroideries of the fifteenth century. The Jain sacred texts, Sutras, indicate that certain textiles always commanded fabulous prices, which suggests that some of them were luxurious items woven with precious gold and silver threads. The *Yasastilaka Champu* by Somadeva (AD 969) describes Punjabi soldiers wearing sashes that shine like gold.

Islam first reached India in the seventh century AD, and the long reign of Hindu states was broken at the end of the twelfth century by Moslem Turks. For two centuries, the military sultanate controlled the north and sometimes the centre of the country, exerting strict price controls and issuing sumptuary laws. Only the rich might wear silks. A Syrian traveller, Shahab-ud-din Abdul Abbas-Ahmed, who came from Egypt in the reign of Sultan Tughluq (1325–1350), reported that 'the Sultan keeps in his service five hundred manufacturers of golden tissues who weave the gold brocades worn by his wives, and given away as presents to the Amirs, and their wives'. The court atelier also wove 'makhmal', an Arabic term for velvet, among the materials used for embroidered garments and Robes of Honour.

In 1398 the Mongol conqueror Tamerlane sacked Delhi, and a period of turbulence followed until, in 1526, Babur, fifth in descent from Tamerlane, swept into India to defeat the Lodi Afghan rulers near Delhi and establish the fabulous empire of the Moguls, who brought artists and craftsworkers from the workshops of the Safavid court to work side by side with skilled Indian artists.

For Moslems, impurity must be avoided because it distracts the worshipper. Paradoxically, whereas Hindus are encouraged to use silk because it is considered a pure substance, Moslems were discouraged by 'Hadith', sayings of the Prophet, on the ground that the vanity to which it gave rise inhibited proper submission to God. Certain sultanate rulers had banned its use, but later sovereigns and learned men compromised; silk was forbidden at worship in the mosque but permissible outside. A cotton-silk mixture called *mashru* (permitted) was widely adopted. *Mashru* has silk warps and cotton wefts, and is usually a satin weave, which results in a smooth, silken right side of the fabric, and a cotton underpart that conforms to the stipulation that silk must not be worn next to the skin. The favourite design of length-wise stripes in various colours is sometimes enriched by small stripes, chevrons, ikat (resist-dye) patterns, or motifs. The material makes robes, but its most frequent use is for linings and borders of decorative hangings, and in quilting.

Once woven all over India, and known variously as *alacha, cuttanee,* or *tapseil, mashru* probably derived from the weaving traditions of the 'tiraz' factories of the caliphates. Today, Patan and Madvi in Gujerat are the only centres where it is woven. In recent years, Kutch tribal women, whose dress comprises a full skirt and short tight blouse, have adopted *mashru* with added embroidered borders in place of tie-dyed or intensively embroidered cloth.

Typically Mogul are certain types of flower and plant arrangements. Because of the close association of Persian and Indian craftsmen, the distinction between the Persian and India court textiles is not always obvious, or even apparent. Under the Mogul emperors, court painting received great patronage, and Jahangir (1605–1626) promoted studies from life inspired by his delight in the flowers of Kashmir, and possibly also by a fascination with the botanical representations in European herbals which were introduced to India at this time. Exquisite woven blooms differ in essence from those of traditional Indian representations. Gardens were woven in silks and wool as carpets, tent-hangings, embroideries and garments, and find their echoes in the architectural embellishments of the palaces, in enamelled jewellery, jade and crystal vessels, and weapons. The damask rose, the opium poppy, the iris, and the lily, are depicted with a tender touch and an elegant sense of spatial harmony. There is a delicacy in the Mogul depiction of flowers, in the drooping curve of a stem that supports a bud, and a dancing rhythm.

Pile carpet weaving was first introduced to India at this time, and some of the most breathtaking examples were woven in silk, or fine pashmina wool knotted on silk warps. In some cases these are so finely knotted that they have been mistaken for velvets.

Cut and voided silk-velvet and silver or gold embroidered velvets were made as floor-spreads and canopies, and quilted silk and cotton, embroidered in *zari*-work and silk chain stitch, provided summer carpets, hangings and screens. Royal tents and dividing screens were adorned with designs of man-high flowering plants in

Murshidabad sari, Bengal, 19th century, panelled with typical little scenes. The large panel above contains two *boteh*, the curving forms that gave rise to European 'paisley' patterns.

cusped arcaded panels, embroidered, woven, printed, or painted on velvet. A favourite technique was to apply gold powder to velvet with a gum arabic solution. The famous crimson and gold velvet tent of Jodhpur makes the most sensuous and seductive of enclosed spaces. The many tent-fragments in collections around the world point to the important role of these woven edifices.

The Persian vogue for gold, silver, and silk fringed sashes resulted in exquisite Mogul examples, known as *patkas*. Patterned with intricate stripes, chevrons, and repeating motifs, each sash-end bears bands with flowers or plants. Safavid and Mogul courts shared a taste for grand voided and brocaded silk velvets with large-scale figures, and only details of dress sometimes suggest Indian rather than Persian origin, although one known example bears the signature of a Safavid court artist who also designed silks, and who is known to have spent several years in India at the Mogul court.

The Koranic injunction to Moslems to cover all parts of the body necessitated tailoring, and the trousers and long tunic worn by Moslem women are shapes that lend themselves to all manner of decorative dyeing and embroidery techniques, and they are worn with a type of veil.

India developed the art of draping cloth, exemplified in the sari, which, although not the only form of Hindu feminine dress, may be thought to epitomize India internationally. The basic sari is a length of unsewn material. At one end there is a wide border, called a *pallav*, and the length of the sari has narrow borders which may be sewn on to or woven into the fabric. However there are many variations. Both the methods of draping the sari, of which there are more than a hundred, and the type of decoration differ from region to region.

A distinctive type of embroidered sari decoration, favoured by rich Parsi women, was carried out by a community of Chinese embroiderers at Surat in Gujerat, and is known in India as 'Chinai work'. The patterns display their Chinese origins, and the knot stitch is frequently used. Tie-dyeing and ikat techniques are well-displayed on saris, and one of the most intricate of these methods is the Gujerati double silk ikat used for *patola*, probably the most expensive of all wedding saris. *Patola* are characterized by a bold grid pattern juxtaposed with intricate geometrical and figurative motifs. Elephants, symbols of wealth, are auspicious for weddings, and frequently feature in borders.

A great deal of silk is produced and processed in southern India, and saris from the south, for example those of Kanchipuram, are of rich, heavy silk, with gold borders. During the eighteenth century beautiful painted saris were made at Tanjore in Tamil Nadu.

Bengali literature speaks of saris of the sun, the moon, and the stars, and still today, saris are woven with the phases of the moon, from the thin crescent to the full orb. Others show the sun with a radiant rim: 'taramandala' is the name given to this pattern. Chanderi saris, with fine silk warp and cotton weft, are bright but subtle, with rich gold borders patterned with coloured flowers, green parrots, all manner of delightful small motifs, and these were worn by royal and well-to-do families of north-western India. Other distinctive saris from the north-west are those of Murshidabad in Bengal, which include a type woven in the natural tussah of the area with broad red borders, and the famous Baluchari saris, developed some two hundred years ago, that use a palette of dark red, yellow, green, purple, chocolate, cream, white and blue. Their borders are patterned with compartments containing repeating pictorial themes, which range from figures smoking or conversing, holding flower-sprigs, to steam-boats, trains and aeroplanes. The various festivals are celebrated with saris of different colours: yellow for spring, black with bright colours for Kayalya Teej during the monsoon. Red is worn by brides. In recent years Indian textile historians have undertaken the daunting task of categorising and cataloguing information about saris, and have encouraged weavers to reproduce patterns that might otherwise have been lost forever.

Tie-dye is used in many ways, and one use is as a base for embroidery. A particularly fine type of tie-dye is achieved by stretching the fabric over a board on which the pattern is marked with tiny raised nails, and tying the cloth over these with fine thread to resist the dye. Unless the dyed silk is to be embroidered, it might sometimes be left unironed, so that the creases and raised points give an attractive puckered texture, which disappears after the first wash. Fine chain stitch embroidery, worked with a hooked rather than a straight needle, was done on satin for skirts (*ghagra*), tunics (*aba*), and trousers (*salvar*) by professional embroiderers of Kutch and Gujerat. Tiny pieces of mirror or mica, held in place with fine button-hole stitching, sometimes highlight the pattern. Similar embroideries on a larger scale were used on cotton skirts and canopies, and for temple trappings. Fine chain stitch in silk and metal threads embroidered objects such as little knuckle-pads worn inside a Rajput warrior's shield.

Phulkari, meaning 'flowered work', is an embroidered textile frequently seen in the West. These cloths, the embroidered veils of the Punjab, are sewn with silk on coarse cotton, usually indigo, ochre or brick-red. The predominantly geometric designs are worked in darning stitch over counted thread with untwisted silk, and the horizontal and vertical stitches allow the light to reflect in such a way as to suggest more than one shade of colour. This type of embroidery is fragile, and rubs off or wears away.

A certain type of embroidered coverlet, made during the seventeenth and eighteenth centuries for export to the West, has traditionally been termed Indo-Portuguese, and ascribed to Goa, although this attribution is currently under discussion. The ground is usually cotton, the embroidery of floss silk in yellow, indigo green, a rich carmine and paler pink shades, with gold and sometimes silver thread. Sometimes the design is very open, with large foliate scrolls surrounding a central medallion, and flower heads, but a second type is completely embroidered, so that the cotton ground cannot be seen.

Both the Portuguese and English during the sixteenth and seventeenth centuries commissioned a distinctive type of chain-stitch embroidery worked in Bengal from the natural yellow muga silk. The embroideries, usually for coverlets, depict biblical, mythological or domestic scenes, either European or Indian.

Bengal woven silks were generally known to the English of the seventeenth century as 'taffeta' or 'taffatie', a name current in Europe for fine silky fabrics. Shakespeare wrote of 'taffeta phrases, silken tearmes precise'. When introduced into India by Europeans the term became confused with Persian 'tafta', meaning 'glossy twist', already in textile usage. These Bengal silks were popular for petticoats and linings, and many were not pure silk but mixed cotton and silk, usually striped – in other words, *mashru*. During the seventeenth and eighteenth centuries, a striped material known as 'Bengal' was imported by America to be used in women's dress. An American textile, the cowboy's bandanna, derives from the Indian *bandhani*, a tie-dyed spot pattern imported as silk kerchiefs in the eighteenth century.

Portuguese, Dutch, French, British, and other European merchants all vied for the India trade, and patterns books were sent out for Indian weavers and dyers to copy. A European vogue for *chinoiserie* resulted in Indian *chinoiserie*, and culminated in Indian *chinoiserie* designs being sent from Madras to Canton to be copied in turn by Chinese embroiderers and silk-painters. French prohibitions on imported Indian textiles gave rise to the Provençal style of tiny repeating motifs based on Indian originals, and the fashion for shawls resulted in the many varieties of 'boteh' or paisley pattern adopted into the European pattern repertoire.

India is a vast repository of ancient motifs, techniques and ideas, and unique among silk-producing countries in the rich variety of her silks. She alone produces all the four commercially known varieties of silk. She ranks second, after China, among mulberry silk producers, and the largest proportion of this silk is produced in Karnataka. India is also the second largest producer of tussah silk, again after China, notably of eri silk, and the golden-yellow muga silk, obtained largely from Assam, of which she has the monopoly. Sericulture is home-based in India as in China, and the low cost of labour contributes largely to the commercial strength of both countries. In recent years Government-supported bodies have worked hard to promote the revival of hand skills in danger of dying out, and western designers have turned to India for special textile finishes and embroidery details.

Each area of India is so individually rich in textiles that a few glittering strands must suffice, threads that nonetheless weave an intricate pattern back through time, from the present to silk's mysterious early beginnings, and to its first appearance in the ancient world. India like China linked East and West through its silks.

Silk in the Ancient World, Egypt and Byzantium

ilk and spices, rare treasures, frequently travelled together, by land routes through Persia from the Central Asian passages, or by ship through the Persian Gulf to the ports at the mouths of the Tigris and Euphrates, from there to be transported by camel caravan to the souks of Syria, prime Mediterranean point for dispersal of Eastern luxuries. The northerly land routes carried Chinese silks, while Eastern vessels brought India's wild silks as well.

During the sixth century BC Greek traders settled around the Black Sea and in Asia Minor carried silk to the Mediterranean region, and such exploits as theirs gave rise to stories such as Jason and the Golden Fleece. A fifth-century BC coffin from the Kerameikos cemetery in Athens contained five different tabby silk textiles, one with traces of embroidery, and various short lengths of white silk-floss embroidery thread. Further west, Marseille, another Greek trading colony, conveniently sited at the mouth of Rhône, was probably the source for the Celtic embroiderers of the Hallstatt Iron Age, whose royal burial mounds in Hohmichele in the Württemberg-Danube area reveal that Chinese silk was used for embroidering and weaving distinctive Celtic patterns on woollen garments. Another Hallstatt barrow, discovered in 1977, was furnished with woven wall-hangings and had fine textiles on the floor. Here too, silk was used for embroidered textiles, but not for woven silk fabrics. Clearly, Chinese silk, and possibly also silk from Central Asia, was used by privileged weavers and embroiderers in Europe from at least 600 BC, many centuries before the Han-Roman trade missions of the second century BC. Strands of silk, apparently of a Chinese type, have recently been found in the hair of an Egyptian mummy, a woman, but not from a royal tomb, dating from *c*. 1000 BC. Improved investigative methods constantly push accepted thresholds further back in time.

Pliny's *Historia Naturalis* of the first century AD tells us that 'the Seres [China] are famous for the fleecy products of their forests. This pale floss, which they find growing on the leaves, they wet and then comb, furnishing thus a double task to our womenkind, in first dressing the threads, and then of weaving them into silk fabrics. So has toil to be multiplied, so have the ends of the earth to be traversed, and all that a Roman dame may exhibit her charms in transparent gauze.' There is no mention of cocoons to accompany the soaking and reeling processes, which would seem to confirm that Chinese silk reached the ancient world as yarn.

There are several wild Mediterranean silk moths of the Saturnidiie family which spin large, rather coarse cocoons whose fibres can be spun and woven into cloth similar to an Indian wild silk, and these cocoons were almost certainly the source of ancient Greece's famous 'bombyx' (literally, 'cocoon'). Pliny wrote of 'bombyx' that 'a process of unravelling and weaving a thread again was first invented in Cos by a woman named Pamphile, daughter of Plateus, who has the undoubted distinction of having devised a plan to reduce woman's clothing to nakedness' – presumably a comment on the transparency of the woven silk. The extraction of fibre from a cocoon is itself an unravelling process, and there is a popular and frequently quoted story about silk being 'unravelled' in the ancient world. The idea is based on verses written by the poet Lucan in the mid-first century A D, more than a hundred years after Cleopatra's suicide in 30 BC, describing the Queen's white breasts 'shining resplendent through Sidonian fabric, which wrought in fine texture by the skill of the Seres, the needle of the workman of the Nile has separated and has loosened' (*Candida Sidonio perlucent filo/Quod Nilotis acus percussum pectine Serum/Solvit et extenso laxavit stamina velo*). Often these lines have been understood as meaning that the silk was woven in China, dyed at Sidon (Syria), then unpicked and re-woven in Egypt. Other explanations given for the same verse are that the Egyptians 'loosened the threads by stretching the fabric', or that it was somehow picked open. Chinese silk yarn was usually unspun (although fibre might be given a twist when weaving damasks, in order to reflect light better and thus emphasize patterned weave). It is possible, though laborious, to unravel coarsely woven plain cloth made from a spun thread, such as linen or wool. The unravelled fibre must then be washed, weighted, stretched out in order to straighten the yarn – a vital part of the process – before re-weaving. However, as a technique applied to fine Chinese silks tightly woven with unspun yarn, it is likely to be unsatisfactory. The act of weaving yarn has an effect similar to 'permanent pleating' a textile, and the finer the thread and finer the weave, the tighter the crimp, effective despite silk's superior power of recovery. Present-day experiments to imitate this 'unravelling' have shown it to be impractical. A small piece of cloth, perhaps damaged or unusable in some other way, might surrender short threads that could be re-used in a decorative stripe, or for embroidery threads.

In purely practical terms, to make a woven silk more open-meshed, more net-like, by use of a needle, pin, or thorn, is as improbable a process as the complete unravelling of fine silk cloth. Even the finest needles used in this way would damage a yarn that had little or no twist. The resulting 'mesh' would in any case be restricted by the original selvedges. China's gauzes were already whisper-light, transparent enough for any fantasy, her patterned damasks soft and fine.

Undoubtedly Cleopatra would have worn silk, if silk there was to be worn, but silk in Egypt at the period was as likely to have come from India as from China. The earliest Egyptian woven silk so far known is in a woollen tunic of Ptolemaic period, excavated at Mostagedda, which has decorative stripes with a weft of white silk made, *not* from the domesticated Chinese Bombyx mori, but of a wild tussah silk from India. Dion Chrystostome (*c.* 117 BC) mentioned an important Indian colony resident in Alexandria, and translations of Homer into Indian languages, and there were other cultural links.

Spices and fabrics were undoubtedly carried in the Indian vessels that Vedic texts describe docking in Sumerian ports as early as 2400 BC, and it is tempting to surmise

Egyptian pleated gown, in silk or fine linen. This little statue of Nefertiti in the Louvre inspired Mariano Fortuny to invent his revolutionary pleated-silk dresses.

that King Solomon's fleet, manned by Phoenicians from the Syrian coast, carried gifts of silks for the Queen of Sheba from 'distant Ophir' and other far-away lands. No silks from these distant times have been discovered, but the Bible contains some interesting references, and as they are of minor importance to the text, they may have survived relatively unchanged. Best of all is the description of a virtuous woman, whose price is far above rubies: 'She maketh herself coverings of tapestry: her clothing is silk and purple' (Proverbs).

Driven into Egypt by the Hittites, the sheep-herding people of the Bible found themselves in a land of skilled weavers. Some Egyptian linen is so fine that it appears to be silk, and is only identifiable by testing. Elaborate and varied pleating techniques were perfected, which, thousands of years later, inspired the twentieth-century Venetian artist Mariano Fortuny to develop his famous silk Delphos dresses. He even used a version of the Egyptians' wooden pleating board, and registered the copyright as his own.

The Egyptians were skilled in various decorative techniques: weft loop and cut pile, appliqué, embroidery, resist-dyeing; and their tapestry-weavers used apparatus which was considerably more complicated than modern tapestry looms. The drawloom, which enabled a weaver to reproduce mechanically any number of pattern-repeats after the unit of the repeat had been set up, was a development from Egyptian tapestry methods, later perfected by the Sassanians. (Egyptian woollen transition-weaves are known, conserved in the Victoria and Albert Museum.) Drawloom silks dated between AD 300 and 500 were excavated at Antinoë in Egypt, and these have been variously attributed to Antinoë itself (Falke) and the Sassanians (Pfister). As the Sassanians, temporarily rulers in Syria, abducted many weavers and dyers to the imperial workshops in Persia in AD 360, and the Syrian textile industry was commercially and technically close to Byzantium and Roman Egypt, it is not unreasonable to imagine that loom technology and skills were transmitted eastward at this time.

Egyptian textile activities are illustrated both in papyri and wall paintings. The Ptolemaic rulers of Egypt (305–30 BC) followed the Greek custom of decking out banqueting pavilions with gold and purple hangings and figurative tapestries, and fine garments such as military cloaks were hung up for display.

After conquering Egypt, leaving his general Ptolemy as his ruling representative, Alexander continued east, married a Bactrian princess, and left Bactria to be ruled by Greeks for some centuries, with trading links down to the mouth of the Indus. The *Periplus of the Erythraean Sea*, the commericial handbook on western trade with India composed by an unknown author or authors towards the end of the first century AD, describes how Greek merchants were able to acquire silk yarn, silk cloth, and silk 'wool' which had been transported from Bactria.

It seems probable there was already an established silk industry at the oases around

the Tarim Basin, and if so, this silk could readily have been transported via Yarkand on the Silk Road to reach Greek traders at the mouth of the Indus, from where ships carried it, with goods from India including her various types of silk, to the markets of the Mediterranean and the dyers of Phoenicia.

Alexander took Tyre and Phoenicia, where the famous 'royal purple' dye was manufactured, en route to Egypt, and in the Achaemenid winter capital Susa he seized some five thousand talents worth of purple cloth that had been stored for almost two hundred years and was as fresh and vivid as when new. Many of Alexander's followers criticized his ostentatious taste in wearing all-purple robes, 'like a Persian'. Purpura mollusc was a dye obtained from the glandular secretions of certain types of sea snail, in particular the Dye murex (Murex brandaris), and the related rock shell Thais haemastomo. The Phoenicians were constantly seeking new sources of the molluscs, for the harvest was seasonal, and thousands of creatures had to be rapidly processed to produce relatively meagre quantities of dye. Silk, with its greater absorbency, needed less dye than wool or linen. The colours ranged from dark blood red, through light and dark pinks and violets to deep purples, and even an inky blue-black. The most precious Tyrian purple was double-dyed, a process that made it especially expensive. The result was a shimmering bright red, and silk dyed like this was worth its weight in gold.

Silk canopies had heralded Julius Caesar's triumphal entrances into Rome, and during the rule of the Emperor Augustus in 14 BC the Senate considered it necessary to ban Roman citizens from 'disgracing themselves with the effeminate delicacy of silk apparel'. Silk, which at the time of Aurelian was worth its weight in gold, was in the reign of Julian (AD 361–363) accessible in price to everyone; during the interim both Chinese and Indian sources record exchanges of ambassadors and trade missions to the West. During the third century, however, pressures from Germanic peoples to the north and the new Sassanian Empire of Persia in the east led to crises within the Roman Empire. The Sassanians overran Syria, sacked Antioch, the third city of the Roman world, and encouraged the creation of a separate eastern state by the Palmyran Queen Zenobia. Palmyra was sacked by the Romans in AD 273, but excavations have yielded many textiles, including silks from both China and India. Drastic price inflation prevailed all over the Empire, until in 301 Diocletian and his co-rulers issued an edict to set the maximum prices for goods and services. Nearly five hundred of the listed items in the extant text of the edict concern textiles or textile manufacture, and include references to silk and silk manufacture, for example looms for weaving pure silk damask cloth. In 408 when the Visigoths besieged Rome, their leader, Alaric, demanded (and got) from the city a ransom of four thousand tunics of silk as well as five thousand pounds of gold and other rich booty.

In 330 Constantine established a new capital and Christian city at Byzantium, renaming it Constantinople. After 394, Egypt was ruled from this, the Empire's

Quadriga silk, now at Cluny, 8th century, one of a series of silks showing four-horse chariots.

eastern capital, and except for a brief period of Persian rule in the seventh century, remained part of the Byzantine Empire until the Arab Conquest in 640.

The name Coptic, derived from the Greek *Aiguptios*, meaning Egyptian, is commonly applied to all Greco-Roman or medieval textiles found in Egypt and not of Pharaonic or Islamic origin. In recent years textile scholars have adopted the terms Late Roman and Early Byzantine, but there are no hard and fast divisions, for instance the term Late Antiquity indicates a period extending roughly from late third to the mid-seventh century AD, thus comprising both Late Roman and Early Byzantine textiles. In 323 Christianity became the state religion of Egypt, and pagan practices, among them mummification, were forbidden. From this time, the dead were buried fully clothed, and the change in burial customs combined with the dryness of Egypt's sands created ideal conditions for the preservation of textiles.

Typical Coptic tunics were decorated with embroidered or tapestry-woven stripes and medallions. Sometimes these were badges of office or rank, as in the case of the 'clavi', two vertical purple stripes running from the shoulder down the front and back, which signify senatorial or knightly rank. Such ornaments were sometimes silk appliqué on a linen tunic, sometimes appliqué tapestry, sometimes tapestry interwoven with the main body of the garment. Examples of silk appliqué were excavated at Akhmin in Egypt and are conserved in Lyon. However not every textile found in Egypt, or in Egyptian style, was made there. For example Egyptian-style costume-decorations in gold and purple silk tapestry, now in Budapest, are attributed to Syria *c.* AD 200. Textiles were imported and exported, and information about this trade exists in a number of papyri.

Some of the most famous Roman damasks are those which wrapped the body and coffin for the reburial of St Paulinus at Trier in about 395. One of these is

embroidered with the maker's mark, 'The Florentine Workshop'. As the Diocletian edict made clear, wealthy Romans could buy damask looms and silk yarn, and hire trained weavers; silk, wherever it came from, was an available luxury. Silk fragments from the Roman Empire's further outposts include a minute scrap of tabby weave found in a grave of the fourth century A D, outside Colchester in Essex. This may be imported Chinese cloth. At Holborough in Kent, silk damask had wrapped a child's body, about A D 250, and another fragment, also preserved in a lead sarcophagus, was found in Conthey in the Valais in Switzerland.

During the fifth century the gynaeceum (literally, women's quarters) in Alexandria was a silk workshop as renowned as those of Byzantium, Damascus, Antioch, Tyre or Sidon. Favourite decorative motifs included birds, flowers, figures of classical mythology and architectural elements, while oriental influences added hunting scenes and animals in combat, and figures flanking a central motif such as a tree (Pl. p. 82). A Late Antique silk from the fifth century in the collection of the Abegg Foundation, known as the Nile Silk, combines animal life and classical mythology in a charming scene (Pl. p. 81). The Nile god Nelios reclines in a chariot pulled by small boys, and a triumphal procession passes amid scenes of sea and riverside life, fishes, waterfowl and snails. The weft-faced compound twill (commonly termed samite), cherry red and white, is part of a group of silks which Falke attributed to Alexandrian looms, while Volbach offered Syria as their provenance, an illustration of the difficulties of attribution at this period.

Many texts refer to curtains with pictorial decoration, and pictures were also supplied on the floor in mosaics. Some silks can be directly related to mosaics, for example the Quadriga silk found in the shrine of St Landrada, abbess of Munsterbilzen, of the seventh century (Paris, Musée Cluny), which is similar to the

Byzantine or Late Roman silk, possibly from the looms of Alexandria, in a pattern often called 'lion wrestler' or 'Samson wrestling with the lion', 6th–7th century.

Quadriga silk from the tomb of Charlemagne, has the same stylized positioning of the wheels and axle as an earlier Roman mosaic, *c.* AD 200, at El Djem in Tunisia. Although these particular Byzantine silks are later than the mosaic, their pattern is contemporary with it, if not earlier, and they illustrate the continuity of popular designs.

Guilds controlled Byzantine silk manufacturing in both Alexandria and Constantinople, although the latter's rules were more rigorous. Imperial monopoly was secured on all types of silk, but particularly on purple and gold textiles.

In Constantinople, too, spinning, weaving, and embroidery were carried out in the gynaeceum, originally the servants' quarters of the palace; but despite its title both men and women were actively involved in the labour, and it became an institution headed by a high official dependent on the 'Count of the Sacred Largesses'. The Theodosian Code laid down regulations for the industry, imposed fines and set taxes. No chronicler has recorded where the imperial workshops of Constantinople recruited their first craftsmen, but the skilled silkweavers of the period were Egyptian, Syrian, and Persian, so they must have been brought from one or all of these countries. Heraclius (610–641) brought Persian weavers to Byzantium after his victory over Khusrau II.

The power of the ruler and of the Church were properly expressed in gold, precious stones and silk textiles. Whereas men were required to dress according to their rank, ladies might dress as lavishly as they pleased, provided they shopped at the imperial manufactories. 'The House of Lamps' in the city was so-named for its displays of silks illuminated at night to tempt 'window shoppers', but after it had been set alight during a rebellion, the exhibition was transferred to the imperial palace precincts. Justinian codified the guild system in 'The Book of the Prefect', and much later, in 912, this was followed by 'The Book of Ceremonies', which detailed clothing appropriate to different ranks. The Byzantine 'scaramangion' is described variously as a large purple cloak, and as a garment based on the Persian riding caftan, and another Byzantine garment, the 'tzitzakion', was so-called from the pet-name, 'Flower', of a Khazar princess whose robe impressed the Byzantine court when she married the Emperor Constantine V. The Khazars were a people of Turkish stock whose lands lay at the vital gateway for silk between the Black Sea and the Caspian. The Khazar kagan himself travelled in a silk-hung tent, surmounted by a gold pomegranate, and mounted on wheels in the Central Asian fashion. When another Khazar princess married, this time to the Moslem governor of Armenia, her cavalcade included ten tents mounted on wheels, 'made of the finest silk, with gold and silver plated doors, the floors covered with sable furs'.

Constantinople was jealous of its special status. The movements of foreigners were closely circumscribed; their dress had to be plain, and they were only permitted to buy cheap fabrics of narrow loom-width. Foreign merchants were forced to lodge in certain areas outside the city boundary, and the length of their stay was restricted. Some were considered unworthy even to enter the city, and their trade had to be conducted outside the walls.

The significant exception was the Syrian merchants, whose sales were guaranteed by the Emperor, who were granted freedom of movement, could stay almost as long as they pleased, and might trade in all kinds of merchandize. These unique privileges emphasize the importance of Syrian supplies. Though other types of purple dying (such as orchil, or madder mixed with indigo) could be carried out in the imperial gynaecea, the process of dyeing precious imperial purple could only be done near the source of the molluscs, along the Lebanese coast. Tyrian dyed silks, and goods from Roman Egypt too, were carried by Syrian traders.

For hundreds, possibly even thousands of years, if we consider the Assyrian example carved in stone, symbolic representations framed within repeating circular format have been used to decorate garments, and the Sassanians developed this in the characteristic beaded roundels patterning their silks. Byzantine weavers adopted this lay-out, although other repeating designs were also used. Some of the most beautiful surviving Byzantine silks are examples of those rich silks described in texts as *'cum rosis et aquilis'*, 'with rosettes and eagles', and are found as fragments in western churches. The church of St Eusebius at Auxerre has a particularly spectacular eagle samite (Pl. p. 84), said to have been laid on the body of St Germain by the Empress Galla Placida. The imperial purple ground is woven with golden yellow silk, in a repeating pattern of spread eagles holding finger rings in their beaks, interspersed with rosettes.

Justinian is credited with introducing sericulture to the Byzantine Empire. The Emperor's sumptuary laws and efforts to maintain state monopoly illustrate a state of desperation. Various attempts were made to find alternative sources of silk on order to by-pass the Persian control of silks passing through their lands, and their exorbitant taxes. In 540 the Persians invaded Syria and sacked Antioch, a further blow to Byzantine trade. Justinian turned to the Axumites, a sea-based trading nation of Chinese-Arab descent who traded with Ceylon and further east, and negotiated terms under which Axumite merchants would buy silk in Ceylon and deliver it to the Byzantine ports. The agreement failed, no silks were forthcoming, probably because the Axumites and the Persians had rather amicably divided the Eastern trade between themselves.

There are several versions of how Justinian eventually succeeded in circumventing Persian control of the supply of silk in 553/4. Procopius describes how 'certain monks arriving from the [country of] Indians, and learning that the Emperor had it much at heart that the Romans should not longer buy silk from the Persians, they promised that the Romans should not have to purchase silk from the Persians or from any other nation; for they had lived, they said, a long time in a country where there were many nations of the Indians, and which goes by the name of Serinda. And when there they had made themselves thoroughly acquainted with the way in which silk might be produced in the Roman territory.'

Theophanes, writing at the end of the sixth century, relates the story that a certain Persian 'coming away from the country of the Seres had taken with him the eggs of these worms [concealed] in a walking stick, and succeeded in bringing them safely to Byzantium'. In spring he put the eggs on the mulberry leaves where they 'developed into winged insects and performed other operations'. Perhaps the hatching was for demonstration or breeding purposes, for the silk from broken cocoons is inferior to the unbroken filament from reeled cocoons. If Justinian's monks were Persians, as some texts state, they would not have had to travel all the way to China for their silkworm eggs, but only to the Nestorian monasteries, the nearest of which was at the Persian silk centre, Nisibus. They would have been able to travel freely through Persia as pilgrims. To carry the tiny seeds protected in monks' bamboo staffs is a very practical method of transportation in the cold season: silkworm eggs need to be stored at a temperture of less than 22 degrees C/71 degrees F to prevent hatching.

Despite Justinian's interest in sericulture, the Byzantine Empire remained dependent on imported silk. Meanwhile the Central Asian Sogdians, dependent on the silk trade for their revenue, had found the Persian borders closed to them on suspicion of spying for the Turks, and sent an embassy to Khusrau to plead for permission to carry silks for sale into Persia. Khusrau dismissed their plea, and burned the Sogdian silk in front of their ambassadors. Their next mission was poisoned. The Sogdian chief Maniah approached the Turkish khan, Dizabel, to propose a joint mission to the 'Romans', and together they succeeded in forming a commercial alliance with Justinian in 568. Following a northerly route, Byzantines and Turks traded with one another for ten years, until the alliance fell apart at the khan's death.

Fine silks were produced during the eighth and ninth centuries, though the requirements of the new, vigorous Islamic dynasties provoked competition for supplies of raw material, and the golden period of Byzantine weaving came in the tenth, eleventh and twelfth centuries under the Comnenus dynasty. The tenth-century Book of Ceremonies, a compilation of trade ordinances for commerce and industry, is the major source on the Byzantine textile industry. Typical surviving silks are compound weaves with designs of animals, especially griffons, lions, elephants and eagles. A number of late tenth-century monochrome patterned silks, surviving in liturgical vestments, have patterns reminiscent of Syrian architecture, specifically that of the Palace of Samarra, indicating Syrian manufacture, and recalling the favoured status enjoyed by Syrian merchants at Constantinople.

An important Byzantine silk (now in Lyon) is recorded as a gift from King Pepin the Short to the monastery of Mozac in 761 (Pl. p. 82). The composition features a

crowned horseman hunting a lion, symmetrically repeated and with the entire figure scene enclosed in a large medallion. In Bamberg Cathedral, a rare surviving fragment from a large silk tapestry hanging, which may be of the eighth or eleventh century, represents a mounted Byzantine emperor, his horse decorated with jewelled ribbons and fine trappings, similar in style to those of the Mozac cavalier. The lion was another symbol of imperial power, and the Abbey of Siegburg conserves a silk with lions, facing forward but bodies in profile, which has a Greek inscription giving the names of two tenth-century Byzantine emperors. Pepin's famous son, Charlemagne, has left some important contributions to the history of silk. When, in 812, Byzantine ambassadors brought to Aix-la-Chapelle the recognition of his imperial title, they also brought gifts fit for an emperor, which included silks, and the Caliph Haroun al-Rashid sent Charlemagne silks from Baghdad's looms.

Silk tapestry in Bamberg Cathedral, known as the Shroud of Bishop Gunther. The entire tapestry is made of silk, and the large dimensions suggest it was designed to be hung between two columns.

Patterns of animals and medallions continued in use through the centuries. Even at the end of the eleventh century, a high-ranking Byzantine courtier would still have a full-length silk coat with a pattern so large that the length would only accommodate three medallions. And as late as the fourteenth century the Emperor Alexius V was portrayed wearing a coat with even larger animal medallions.

In 1203 the Fourth Crusade anchored its fleet in the Bosphorous and the Crusaders sacked Constantinople, almost obliterating its heritage of splendour. This was the end of the glorious woven silks of Byzantium, although gold embroidery for church vestments continued until the end of the Palaeologus dynasty. Venice became the chief repository of Byzantine art and craftsmanship. Her privileged relationship with Byzantium led to her emergence as one of the most important silk centres of the Middle Ages and the Renaissance. The roots of antiquity were transplanted; the skilled craftsmen of various races who settled and worked in Venice played an important part in the next great period of silk weaving, built on the inventions of Egypt, Syria, Byzantium, and Sassanian Persia. From tapestry to brocade was a considerable step, leading to the richest of all, the sumptuous gold brocaded silk velvets, the achievements of Italy and Spain, which are explored in a later chapter. But first, to consider the silks of a series of great empires that made their contribution to textile designs and their dissemination.

Detail of the magnificent Byzantine eagle silk known as the Mantle of Charlemagne, now in Metz Cathedral Treasury, 11–12th century. It is thought to be booty brought back from the First Crusade.

 The Tide of Islam

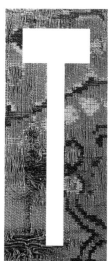**T**he Blessed may look forward to their rewards in paradise, where, robed in green garments of satin and brocaded silks, they will enjoy peace and praise Allah. Islamic lore advises the devout that he who dresses in silks in this lifetime, forfeits that luxury in the next, and for this and other reasons, silk has sometimes been forsworn; but it is usually mixed with other fibres such a cotton, so that the cotton thread touches the body but the outer surface displays its special silken opulence.

The Arab cultures were strongly textile orientated, and as they rose and spread, their principles of geometry, harmony and balance became a feature of all their arts and influenced the countries they settled, from the east to the Moorish dynasties that flourished in Spain. The Moslem victory at Nihavand (642) had brought an end to the Sassanian regime in Persia, but pre-Islamic styles persisted in textiles as in other media. The use of calligraphy pre-dates Islam; soldiers believed that holy writing could protect them in battle, and silk too was credited with protective powers. The qualities of both are beautifully combined in a yellow silk tunic decorated with Islamic calligraphy and bouquets of flowers, to be worn under chain mail (now in Brussels, Musées Royaux).

Mohammed was born about AD 570, in Mecca. In the heart of the holy city is a pre-Islamic sanctuary known as the Ka'aba, and this has always been covered with offerings of different kinds of precious textiles. Islam adopted the Ka'aba, which became the direction towards which all Moslems turn to pray. By AD 774 (AH 157) so many offerings of silks and carpets covered the walls of the shrine that it was in danger of collapsing under their accumulated weight. The Prophet covered the Ka'aba with Yemenite fabrics, and the honour of providing the annual covering, called the *kiswa*, came to imply Islamic sovereignty. Throughout the centuries each *kiswa* has been ritually cut up and distributed among the pilgrims when the time came for its yearly replacement. A pilgrim from Sicily in 1183 described the rich decoration of thirty-four lengths of green silk embroidered with calligraphy and triangular niches. Then in 1245 a great tempest rent all the coverings asunder, and since that time the *kiswa* has been black silk, with verses from the Koran embroidered or woven in gold.

The two branches of Islam are the Shi'ites and the Sunnis, but no simple, clear distinction can be made between the decorative arts of each. Both the Moguls of India and Ottomans of Turkey were Sunni, originally the more traditionalist branch, and as such might have been expected to shun the more decorative or figurative designs in favour of abstract pattern; yet both have contributed to the development and diffusion of Islamic figurative art. Prior to Islam, certain figures and images, even portraits of rulers, were emblems of sovereignty, and these were largely replaced with calligraphy, either words praising God or auspicious verses, or dedications to a ruler. In Persia the tradition of honouring by portraiture never quite disappeared, and the twentieth century has seen a revival in the form of silk rugs and mats woven with the images of Reza Shah and J.F. Kennedy.

The role of wooden furniture and paintings in European dwellings was taken by textiles in the East. The Sassanian king Khusrau I ruled from a winter palace at Ctesiphon on the Tigris. Here, in the Throne Hall, was the famous Winter Carpet, sometimes called 'The Spring of Khusrau', reputedly patterned on an actual royal garden. Joined panels of heavy silk were encrusted with jewelled gold elements, and eye-witness accounts describe its design of interlacing paths, running brooks, trees and spring flowers, their many colours depicted in precious stones. Gravel paths were imitated in pearls, and the fine details were stitched in silks. Garden imagery has always been used in carpets, and is associated with paradise (the word *pairidaeza* means 'enclosed garden'). When the Arabs captured Ctesiphon in 635 Khusrau's splendid carpet was cut into fragments as war booty. One fifth went to the Caliph Omar, one piece to the Prophet's son-in-law Ali, and the rest is said to have been divided among sixty thousand warriors.

Mohammed died in AD 632, when both Syria and the Byzantine Empire had been weakened by plagues and Sassanian attacks. Byzantium's increasingly tenuous hold over Syria was snapped by the invading Arabs, fired with the fervour of the newly converted and unified by the prospects of land and wealth. The inland cities and ports of Syria, ultimate destinations of the silk caravans, were rich reward. The first great Islamic dynasty was that of the Umayyads (661–750 in Syria, 756–1031 in Spain). From their capital at Damacus, their forces swept across to the Magreb.

In Syria as in Egypt, the Arabs took over the long-established textile traditions of Byzantium, and early Islamic silks may be expected to resemble these strongly. The Arab historian Mas'udi described the Umayyad ruler Hisham (724–43) as fond of robes and carpets, and writes that striped silk, silk banded with inscriptions and velvets were made in his day, while Idrisi praised the wonderful silks of Damascus, its precious and costly brocades resembling the finest of Byzantium, and said that every type of precious cloth was produced in the royal workshops. Damask derives its name from Damascus, and although originally a Chinese weave, it was produced and traded in various centres. Another of the famous silks of Damascus (mentioned by Migeon) was a fabric with silk pile.

Arab sources tell us that Egyptian and Mesopotamian weavers produced a variety of fabrics with both looped and cut pile, for example 'mukhmal', a valuable cloth with fine short pile, sometimes embroidered with gold thread. The same term was applied to early Indian velvets, and texts attribute the technique to Arab contacts around the tenth century. Until Italian and Spanish weavers developed ways of combining pile with other decorative weaving techniques, velvet was plain or striped, and might be embellished with embroidery and appliqué.

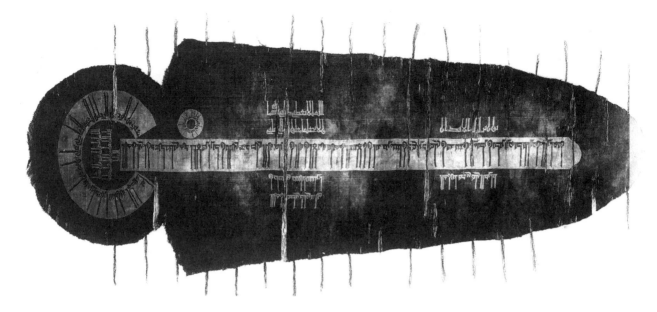

Calligraphic tomb cover of the Buyid period, 10th century: a complete loom-piece is woven to shape, with verses in kufic script referring to the face, heart, hands, and feet. The small circle would be placed over the heart.

Stripes, often including bands of calligraphy or repeating motifs, became a distinctive feature of Arab textile design, for the Prophet allowed that decorative silk strips, two to four fingers' width, were permissible, and this gave rise to embroidered calligraphic bands on otherwise plain robes. Manuscripts show turbans and garments decorated with bands of calligraphy, and the dress, banners and animal trappings of the pilgrims to Mecca shown in the manuscript of Hariri's *Maqamat* (dated Bagdhad AD 1237, AH 635, Pl. p. 103) are decorated in this way.

Embroidered bands came to be known as 'tiraz', from Arabic *tarz*, borrowed from a Persian word meaning 'embroidery', the technique first used to work their non-repeating inscriptions. Three examples attributed to Iraq in the twelfth century are worked on 'mulham', a cloth of cotton and silk mix, with the silk threads worked in crewel and split stitch, and the gold thread couched down. The gold is gilt gut wrapped round a silk core, of a type not so far found in textiles earlier than tenth-century date. The most spectacular of the three examples (now in Washington, Textile Museum) has bands of kufic letters bordering galloping winged horses, separated by trees, worked in gold and silk of blues, green and red. Later tapestry-woven strips, often of silk on cotton or linen warps, or in the most luxurious examples, using gold and silver thread, were also named 'tiraz', and eventually both the textiles and workshops where they were made were known by this name. Each minor prince boasted a tiraz factory, and gifts from prince to prince included specimens of these precious stuffs, often on Robes of Honour.

Antioch was an important weaving centre, and the best known of the silks produced there was a type of brocade patterned with fantastic animals and birds, the design highlighted by the use of gold, for example on the animals' heads. The cope of St Bernard of Clairvaux (1153) is an example of this type, woven with eagles, their heads and claws golden, while an inventory of 1315 for Canterbury Cathedral included a 'vestment of red Antioch cloth having green birds and beasts with gold heads and feet'. Antioch was devastated by the army of Baybars in 1263, so genuine silks from its looms must be prior to that date. The term 'Antioch cloth' may, however, have been used in the West to designate a type of fabric or pattern, without regard to the precise place of manufacture.

Opposite Fragment of 'tiraz', 8th-9th century. Silk tapestry bands with repeating patterns are typical of early Islamic weavings. The animal represented is probably a feline.

Aleppo's silk souks rivalled those of Damascus, and in Ibn al-Shihna's list of Aleppo taxes for 1212 we read that 'sales of a single day at Aleppo are often greater than those of a month in other cities', and that 'ten loads of silk . . . brought to Aleppo . . . are sold that very day for ready money, whereas ten loads taken to Cairo, though the largest of cities, are not sold there until the end of the month'.

Syria was replaced as centre of the caliphate by Iraq. The rival Abbasids succeeded the ruling Umayyads after a mass slaughter during a royal banquet in Damascus. One Umayyad prince escaped to make his way westward and conquer Spain, where he established an Umayyad court. The founder of the Abbasid dynasty, and creator of Bagdhad, was Mansur. In 762, four years after construction began, his capital was complete. Around his palace on the banks of the Tigris, Mansur arranged a series of 'paradises', gardens filled with flowers, trees banded with precious jewel-studded metals, their leaves gilded and silvered, ponds and waterfalls, little bridges of rare species of woods, romantic pavilions. His successor, the Caliph Haroun al-Rashid (786–809), created a court whose splendours are sung in the tales of the Thousand and One Nights, filled with treasures brought from near and far by daring merchants. The Caliph was a contemporary of Charlemagne, and embassies bearing lavish gifts, including many bolts of precious silks, passed between the two greatest courts of their period.

Early Islamic cloth-production and trade are well documented by Arab authors, although sometimes the terms used are ambiguous, and certain types of cloth have not yet been identified. Baghdad was famous in Europe for silks such as 'cramoisy' (kermes, crimson), 'siglaton' (*siqlatun*, Greek *cyclas*, a woman's gown of rounded shape), and 'baldachin' (*baudekin*), a word derived from the name Baghdad (Baudas). The term 'tabby' in English usage is said to derive from 'Attabi', and originally referred to a type of either striped or moiré cloth woven in Attabi, a district of Baghdad. One observer likens it to zebra skin.

One of the most famous accounts of the palaces of Baghdad describes the decorations for the reception of Byzantine ambassadors sent to negotiate an armistice with the Caliph Muktadir (917). Curtains and wall-hangings of gold brocades and silks embroidered with gold, and patterned with elephants, horses, camels, lions and birds, are said to number thirty-eight thousand. For a brief period the capital was transferred from Baghdad to Samarra, and wall paintings in the Jausaq Palace reproduce the patterns of Sammara's silks, still the favourite Near-Eastern design of repeating roundels enclosing birds and animals. Arab writers have left us descriptions of repeating motifs of geometric lozenges and octagonal star shapes enclosing Sassanian-inspired animal forms. One of these Abbasid silks, a Baghdad textile (Washington, Textile Museum), is worked in seven colours and gold, patterned with cocks within octagons in a stepped lozenge layout, interspersed with smaller geometric motifs.

The 'Shroud of St Josse', woven in Khurasan in eastern Persia, 10th century.

The 'Veil of St Anne', a 'Saracen' weaving probably brought back from the Crusades. The Fatimid Caliph al-Musta'li (1094-1101) is named in the inscription.

Early Arab silks are rare, for when buried in the earth, silk decomposes more readily than linen or cotton. Fortunately, some examples have survived in European churches. They were often gifts to the church, and were used for vestments, altar cloths, shrouds and wrappings for religious relics. The 'Shroud of St Josse', from this saint's reliquary at St-Josse-sur-Mer, is believed to have been brought to France after the First Crusade. A heavy silk twill, it has two rows of elephants, and Bactrian camels roped nose-to-tail, and in each corner a cock in Sassanian style. An inscription translates as 'Glory and prosperity to Qu'id Abu Mansur Bakh-takin, may God prolong his existence', naming a Turkish commander in Khurasan. (The prayer was unavailing, for the owner was executed by his Samanid ruler 'Abd al-Malik in 961.) The heritage of Sassanian Persia transmitted to the Arabs was enormous, for the Arabs conquered the Sassanian Empire entire, whereas they took possession of only outlying provinces of the Byzantine Empire.

The Fatimids (919–1171), named for the Prophet's daughter from whom the rulers claimed descent, moved eastward from the Maghreb and occupied Egypt, Syria and western Arabia. An historical romance, 'The Conquest of Bahnasa', describes the Coptic leaders, the Patriarch fine in gold-embroidered brocade, when they went to meet the Arabs in a tent upholstered in many-coloured silks, embroidered with gold and silver thread, sewn with pearls, and decorated inside and out with figures of birds and wild animals. The tent-cords were of rainbow silks, and inside the tent, a silk carpet was piled high with cushions.

The Fatimids founded Cairo as their capital, built to the north of more ancient Fostat, whose refuse has provided many textile fragments. The historian Makrizi writes that Cairo's Street of Brocade, Street of the Silk Worker, and Saifiya School combined to form an 'institution' producing brocades and other silks for the rulers. The Arabian Nights tells of the silks of Suez, among other luxuries, and of the unfolding of a piece of linen, 'and lo, in it was the figure of a gazelle worked with silk and embroidered with red gold, and facing it was the figure of another gazelle worked with silver, and having upon its neck a ring of red gold and three beads of silver'. Alexandria's silk production, and trade with India, the Maghreb and Spain, continued uninterrupted under Islam, and the troubadour romance the 'Chanson de Roland' (c. 1066–99) describes a certain person '*ki fut cuvert d'un palie alexandrine*'.

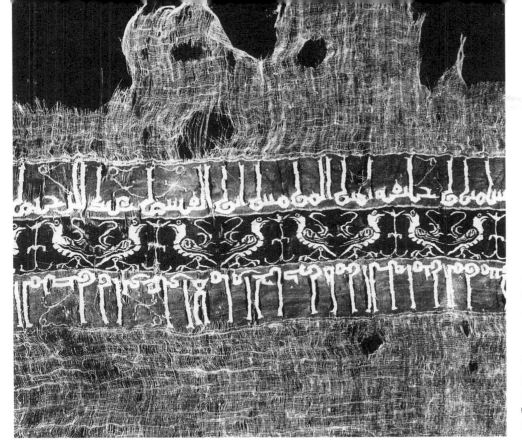

Fatimid silk-and-linen tapestry ornamented with simple kufic calligraphy and a row of birds.

Buyid period silk in the weave known as 'lampas', with raised pattern of fine bands of calligraphy and a repeating scheme of roundels containing confronted antelope or goats, with a central Tree of Life, 10th century.

The most famous Fatimid fabrics are the tiraz weaving of fine tapestry bands. Calligraphy is sometimes combined with delightful tiny animals – doves, waterfowl, desert hares and floral motifs. Such bands were usually the only decoration on a white garment. The 'Veil of St Anne', a treasure in Vaucluse, perhaps originally part of a Robe of Honour, is typically Fatimid. Three bands of silk and gold tapestry are woven with fine linen. The central band has three circles containing pairs of addorsed sphinxes. The description which originally surmounted these has been destroyed, but the calligraphy around each circle remains. The side bands show birds, animals and inscriptions, including the place of manufacture, Damietta, on the Nile Delta. Both the Lord and the Bishop of Apt, where this cloth is preserved, took part in the First Crusade, and the 'Veil' may have been plunder taken from Jerusalem in 1099. Another charming embroidery of the Fatimid period depicts a peacock, finely stitched in silver, gold and silks on linen (Abegg Stiftung). However, without provenance or inscriptions, it is virtually impossible to know exactly where such embroideries were made.

In the eleventh century a list of the costly silks of the Fatimid treasury included fifty thousand silk damasks, a quantity no less fabulous today than it seemed at the time of its compiler, Ibn Abel Aziz. A new weave appeared in the tenth or eleventh century, probably first in Buyid Persia, where what seem to be experimental stages have been found. This is a compound weave, called 'lampas' or 'diasprum', resulting from improvements in the drawloom, in which pattern-definition is achieved with a smooth ground against which the twill-woven design is slightly raised. A quilted lampas hat, probably worn with a turban, from eleventh- or twelfth-century Egypt (now in the Victoria and Albert Museum) has a yellow and blue pattern based on an eight-pointed star, with stylized birds.

In every century, a sense of great occasion has always implied the use of silk. A proposal of marriage was inscribed on white silk by a tenth-century Byzantine princess to the Caliph al-Muktaff. She described herself as 'Queen of the Franks', though this, and her claim to rule the whole western empire, was more wishful imagining than truth. Theodora's proposal was rejected, and she died unmarried, but the style of her approach made a deep and lasting impression, and Arab writers centuries later still refer to her silken letter.

'The Veil of Hisham'. Hisham II was Caliph of Cordoba, and this sheer fabric may have been part of a courtier's dress.

Moorish Spain

Although the Berbers had made a series of incursions into Spain, the first western Caliphate was established at Cordoba by 'Abd ar-Rahman, the sole surviving scion of the Umayyads, in 756. By 1031 Cordoba was economically and culturally an Islamic centre equal to Cairo and Baghdad. Silk was known, though rare, before the Arab Conquest, although the Visigoths had adopted many of the trappings of Roman civilization, and there had been a lively trade with Constantinople. Certain documents, for example the seventh-century account of the lives of the Holy Fathers of Merida, and St Isidore of Seville's Etymologies, contain references to silk.

At first the Arabs imported raw silk from the Levant, but once mulberry orchards were established, sericulture flourished in the climate of the Sierra Nevada, and baskets of cocoons were sent on muleback to Almeria and Granada. The tenth-century Almanac of Cordoba lists the season of the silkworm hatchings, and a twelfth-century book on agricultural compiled by Ibn al Awam mentions that in February 'the women of the Orient keep silk eggs in little bags in the warmth of their bosoms to incubate them'.

Early ceramics and manuscripts show figures wearing typical Eastern dress of plain cloth decorated with woven or embroidered bands, sometimes with calligraphic inscriptions. In the ninth century the Caliph 'Abd ar-Rahman II established and promoted tiraz workshops, and in 978 Andalusian tiraz was exported to Egypt, Khurasan, and the farthest corners of the Islamic world. A measure of the esteem in which Spanish textiles were held is indicated by lists of the gifts by Fatimid rulers, which include silks and carpets. To the Christian knights who had assisted him in the sacking of Santiago de Compostela, the grateful Vizir Almanzor distributed '2,285 pieces of the silken stuff called tiraz of various patterns and colours'.

Best-known among surviving Spanish tiraz is the 'Veil of Hisham' in Madrid. It bears the name of Hisham II (976–1013), with borders of kufic inscriptions and a series of octagonal medallions framing human figures, animals and birds, and is tapestry-woven in gold, coloured silks and fine linen. A distinctive group of this type of tiraz shows roundels containing human figures, usually seated, facing each other.

A regulation specifically prohibiting false inscriptions on textiles (contained in the Treatise on Hisba of al-Saqati of Malaga) suggests that they were not uncommon in eleventh- and twelfth-century Spain, and that at this period Peninsula silks were still considered provincial compared to those of Baghdad. Spelling peculiarities on a silk from Burgos, for example, suggest that it was made in Spain, not in Baghdad as the inscription claims. This particular silk (now in Boston) is part of a chasuble that was placed in the tomb of Pedro, Bishop of Osma, who was venerated as a saint after his death in 1109. The silk is patterned with roundels containing addorsed lions, on whose backs stand confronted harpies separated by a Tree of Life (Illus. p. 108).

Calligraphic banners on the pilgrim caravan to Mecca, from the manuscript of Hariri's *Maqamat*, Baghdad 1237. An 18th- or early 19th-century Turkish calligraphic banner (*inset*) illustrates the continuity of tradition.

Below left Silk banner or hanging woven with verses from the Koran, Surahs 'The Victory' and 'The Banishment' in naskhi script. The upper and lower panels include the date AH 1112 (AD 1700), and proclaim: 'For the light of the eyes

of the best of mankind, Ismail Kashani finished it out of sincerity'. The weaver's name tells us that he was a Persian from Kashan.

Below right Silk lampas tomb cover, an exquisite example of Safavid weaving. Calligraphy runs vertically and horizontally, each band separated by a border of meandering leaf, vine arabesque and quatrefoil design, punctuated with half carnation heads.

The motif has sometimes been misread as sphinxes, which appear on a number of Spanish silks, such as the textile from the coffin of St Bernard Calvo in Vich (now in Cleveland). Another silk from Vich, known as the 'tapestry of the witches', mixes all manner of elements in its design, which is dominated by double-headed monsters.

The famous peacock cope of Robert of Anjou in the basilica of St Sernin, Toulouse (with a fragment in the Victoria and Albert Museum), may have been a gift of Spanish silk to the King of Naples from his sister Blanche (Pl. p. 112). She was married to the king of Aragon, and the crown archives preserve letters showing that she frequently sent her brother gifts made in Spain.

Although Spanish dyers were skilled in their craft, and capable of reproducing rainbows should they wish to do so, Spanish silks are restrained in their combination of colours. Yellow, red, green, blue-green, sky-blue, white and purplish-black may have been chosen as the most regal colours, but equally, there may have been another significance in the restricted range. The four strings of the Andalusian lute were coloured black, white, yellow and red, representing the four Aristotlean 'humours'. A fifth string, coloured green, was introduced by Ziryab, and this represented the soul. Ziryab was the most famous and gifted singer and musician of his age, and aroused the envy of Haroun al-Rashid's Court Master of Music in Baghdad. Fearing for his life, Ziryab sought refuge at the equally famous Cordoban court of 'Abd ar-Rahman in 821. Here he was the arbiter of taste, and among the refinements he introduced was the fashion of wearing different coloured silk robes at each of the changing seasons. His songs and romances about the greatest rulers and their courts surely included the story of a certain white elephant, whose fame was recorded in the silks of Baghdad, Byzantium and Spain.

Once upon a time, an Indian ruler sent a gift of a precious white elephant to the Caliph Haroun al-Rashid. The elephant's name was Abulabbas, and the Caliph sent him, with many precious silks, as a royal gift to the Emperor Charlemagne. (Transported from Baghdad to Aachen, the elephant eventually died on a campaign against Godfried of Denmark in 810.) Although it has been suggested that the elephant-imagery in Spain springs from Central Asia, or Persia, or even Hannibal's journey through Spain, many centuries before the Arab's arrival there, might it not rather be a celebration of Abulabbas, once as famous as the great kings who owned him? The elephant silk found in Aragon (now in New York, Cooper Hewitt collection) shows an elephant within a roundel banded in guilloche and pearls, connected by small pearled circles enclosing rosettes. The ears are checkered, the trunk segmented, and stylized plants are interspersed between the roundels and above the elephants.

Another elephant silk (in the Cooper Hewitt collection, with fragments in Berlin and Florence) was found in the Monastery of Sta Maria de l'Estay in Catalonia.

Elephant silk found in the tomb of Charlemagne at Aachen (Aix-la-Chapelle), possibly woven in Baghdad.

Silk fragment found in the tomb of Pedro, Bishop of Burgos, 11th–12th century. The inscription claims that it was woven in Baghdad, although some curiosities of spelling suggest Moorish Spain.

Above right The Shroud of St Lazarus in Autun Cathedral, embroidered in Almeria, 11th century.

Alternate rows of elephants, winged horses and senmurvs are contained within pearled roundels. Though the winged horse and senmurv have Persian, Byzantine and Central Asian association, the silk has been attributed to Spain because of similarities to the group found at Vich. An elephant silk from San Isidoro in Leon has an inscription stating that it was woven for Abu Bakr in the city of Baghdad. Charlemagne himself, as Holy Roman Emperor, links Baghdad and Byzantium; and Ziryab, poet, singer and musician, took to Cordoba the tales of the glories of Haroun al-Rashid's court of the Thousand and One Nights. It is tempting to read the continuing fable of Abulabbas in a fourteenth-century Italian silk which shows a white elephant being transported in a disproportionately small four-wheeled cart.

During the medieval period, 'sendal', a light silk, was considered the most suitable fabric for banners, and the famous 'banner of St Isidore', said to have belonged to the Christian kings of Leon, is of sendal. The churches of Seville, Burgos and Toledo all preserve early banners, the mementoes of battles.

Rare examples of hispano-mauresque embroidery include the eleventh-century Shroud of St Lazarus in Autun Cathedral (fragments also in Cluny and Lyon) and the twelfth-century Chasuble of St Thomas-à-Becket, now in Fermo, Italy. The latter has a kufic inscription (now on the back, but originally part of the design) indicating that it was made in Almeria in 1166. Both these embroideries are worked in coloured silks and gold thread on a sky-blue silk. The Fermo chasuble is patterned with roundels enclosing griffins, a winged sphinx, eagles, gazelles, horsemen with hawks on their fists, and caparisoned elephants carrying ladies in howdahs. Almeria was a region elevated to a kingdom in the eleventh century, and famous for its textile production. Idrisi wrote in 1154 that Almeria 'has eight hundred textile workshops in which silks, brocades and precious mantles are produced'.

From the thirteenth century onwards, textiles with geometrical decoration predominate, especially chevrons, striped patterns formed by bands decorated with calligraphy in Moorish nakshi script, rosettes, stars, octagons and interlace. A type clearly related to the never-ending arabesques and knotted kufic patterns of stucco and tilework is known as 'Alhambra pattern'. The infinite patterns of pure geometrical shapes became embellished with plant and animal motifs, and roundels gave way to stellate and hexagonal cells.

Boabdil, last of the hispano-mauresque rulers, preferred music and verse to war, and tended to express his moods in the choice of colours in his robes. His mother's bitter words, 'Weep like a woman for what you could not defend like a man', may have echoed in his ears as, dressed in gold-embroidered black silk, he surrendered to Ferdinand and Isabella.

Upon the fall of the Nasrid dynasty in Granada many weavers fled to Morocco, where they continued to produce hispano-mauresque patterns into the sixteenth, seventeenth and eighteenth centuries. Long after the fall of Granada and the expulsion of the Moors and Jews, the historian Al Makkari (1591–1632) wrote about the still-thriving textile industry of Almeria and its beautiful silks.

The design elements of Islam merged with those of the late Gothic and the Renaissance in the style named 'Mudejar'. A distinctive Mudejar compound satin, of which there are examples in a number of collections, has confronted crowned lions within enclosed palmettes which unite at their tips to form a floral device. Another, also found in several collections, has birds and a flowering Tree of Life. It became a practice to personalize a silk by adding a coat of arms as an element in a repeating pattern which was already part of a workshop repertoire. Banded patterns also became typical of the hispano-mauresque silks.

Between Moorish and Christian kingdoms, there was a succession of wars but also a lively commercial exchange, and the main beneficiaries were the Spaniards. Spanish Christians were frequent visitors to the Moorish markets, and where Moslem and Christian weavers worked side by side, the products of Christian looms were Moorish. Almeria traded with the rest of the Peninsula, but also with the textile centres of Italy, and Italian merchants were active in the ports and markets of Spain. By the end of the thirteenth century, Malagan silks were as famous as those of Almeria, and in the fourteenth century Almeria was an important exporter of raw silk to Florence.

An important early group of silks is a type with specific heraldic devices. The Treasury of Leon has two famous stoles patterned with castles and crosses which, according to an inscription worked into the fabric, were woven by Eleonor of England and finished in 1193, and in the same collection is a textile from the coffin lid of the Abbess Berenguela patterned with the quartered shield of Castile-Leon. The chasuble of the Infante Sanche of Aragon in Toledo Cathedral Treasury has a repeating design of lions rampant, castles and eagles, each within a lozenge. Without an attribution or inscription, it is impossible to tell whether these textiles, woven in various techniques, or embroidered, were made by Moslem or Christian weavers.

The Spanish custom of using expensive silks for shrouds ensured the survival of some beautiful textiles, such as those found in the royal tombs at Las Huelgas, a Cistercian monastery near Burgos. When the casket of the Infante Don Felipe was opened in 1848, his mummy was found wrapped in a mantle of silk and gold thread, its design of rosettes banded with kufic inscriptions (Pl. p. 111). This prince had been a friend of Muhammed I of Granada (1230–1272), and in common with many Spanish Christians, he had developed a taste for Islamic robes and silks. A reaction against this 'islamicization' inspired a series of sumptuary laws, one of the earliest of which, in 1234, was imposed by James the Conqueror, in Aragon, to limit the use of silk, and permit gold and silver, as trimmings only, for cloaks and hoods. (In

Moorish silks of the 13th, 14th and 15th centuries. *Clockwise from left* Silk banded with kufic script, interlace and rosettes, one of the rich silks discovered at Las Huelgas when the royal tombs were opened; Don Felipe, of whose mantle this fragment formed part, was friendly with the Nasrid emirs at Granada, and received rich presents from them. *Top* Silk banded with open-winged eagles, a symbol of regal grandeur and opulence throughout the centuries. *Centre* Silk banded with pairs of confronted peacocks, another recurring motif. *Above right* This scheme of pairs of crowned lions sometimes incorporates a coat of arms; the design was one of a set repertoire that could be adapted to the particular client's wishes; it is a compound satin of a type attributed to Toledo. *Below right* Elegant 14th-century satin brocaded with gold thread, with addorsed hares within circlets and a repeating ogee format of palmettes and tendrils. *Below centre* Bands of plain colour, and decorative plant and tendril motifs. Decorative striped patterns such as these were shown to advantage by the simple cut of the clothes of the period.

complete contradiction, James then granted the Moor Ali and his sons the right to open a workshop manufacturing silk and gold fabrics at Jativa near Valencia.) Alfonso XI in the fourteenth century proclaimed that only he and his sons were entitled to wear silk, and even the *ricos hombres*, the wealthy, might wear gold-worked silk on their wedding day only; and furthermore, no noble should give his wife more than three silks in the first four months of marriage, and only one of these might be embroidered with gold thread. Throughout the centuries, sumptuary laws were issued from time to time, and they should be understood in relation to the necessity for the nobles to be prepared for the call to arms, which required gold. As the costly silks usually came from Moorish workshops, their purchase also constituted an indirect support of the enemy.

The Maghreb

The Maghreb comprises the countries of North Africa, which are not generally noted for silk production, although Kairawan in Tunisia was a capital city of early Islam and possessed a tiraz workshop. However, Morocco became heir to the weavers and patterns of Islamic Spain when the Catholic monarchy and the Inquisition expelled the Moors, and Moroccan looms continued to produce hispano-mauresque banded silks. Later brocades and damasks for clothes and furnishings are influenced by French fashions, sometimes with an Islamic star and crescent against a floral background. Regional embroideries retained their older, tribal character; those from Tetouan are geometrical, and stars are prominent in the strongly drawn designs; those typical of Rabat are worked in luxurious but fragile, brightly dyed, untwisted silk floss on fine silk, cotton or linen, as are those of Chechouan. Fez embroideries have sometimes been confused with certain Greek island embroideries, which at first glance they resemble in their restrained monochrome palette and precise geometric patterns. Distinctively Moroccan, the marriage band is a long stiff belt, brocaded with geometric stripes. The embroideries of neighbouring Algeria show later, Ottoman influence – Algeria was long part of the Ottoman Empire – and are worked on fine hand-loomed linen with mainly red and blue silks in repeating designs, or on satin, displaying those flowers familiar from Turkish decorative arts: the tulip, rose, carnation and hyacinth.

Sicily

The Moslems made a number of attempts to take Sicily, but were not finally in possession of the island until the late ninth to early tenth century. The Fatimid emirs established their palace tiraz workshops in Palermo. The early tiraz silks of Sicily are often impossible to distinguish from their contemporary Spanish equivalents, and in the late tenth and early eleventh century there was thriving trade between Sicily and Malaga, Almeria and Valencia.

The border of an opulent 13- or 14th- century Spanish garment, woven in compound twill with a design of bands of addorsed felines flanking a geometric Tree of Life.

Fragment of the famous peacock cope from St Sernin, Toulouse, 12th century, said to have belonged to Robert of Anjou, King of Naples. Robert's sister Blanche was the wife of the Spanish King of Aragon, and this may be her gift of Spanish silk. The likeness of the palmette-design to a silk in Salamanca also suggests a Spanish origin.

In 1071, the year of the Turkish victory over the Byzantines at Manzikert, Sicily was captured by the Norman Roger de Hauteville. In 1147, his successor, Roger II, made a military foray to the Peloponnese and as part of his victory spoils brought back a number of Byzantine weavers and Jewish craftsmen who were skilled at dyeing. These he installed in the Palermo tiraz, where they apparently worked in harmony with the Moslems. Gradually a new style emerged, incorporating Arab and Byzantine elements with those of the Romanesque, both woven and embroidered. One of the most regal silks of all time is the great coronation mantle of the Sicilian kings, known as the Mantle of Roger II (now in Vienna, Kunsthistorisches Museum, Pl. p. 154–5). Its design of animals in conflict flanking a central tree, and borders of kufic script, is classically Near Eastern, but the choice of beasts – a proud lion which has conquered, but so far spared, the camel beneath its paws – surely refers to the Norman conquest of Arab Sicily. The island itself is represented by the fruitful date palm, placed as a Tree of Life on the spine of the wearer. The mantle is red and gold silk, embroidered and appliqué, and sewn with pearls and gem-set gold elements. Under her Norman rulers Sicily continued to flourish, and the celebratory poem, 'Le Roman de Guillaume de Palerme', praises the palace and its silk hangings, gold-patterned with human figures, birds and animals.

Norman rule in Palermo was followed by that of the German Hohenstaufens in 1194. Henry VI died in Palermo before he could launch his planned invasion against Byzantium, but he was buried in funeral robes of crimson Byzantine silk, its pattern of birds and beasts worked with gold thread. Frederick I deported a group of skilled Arab craftsmen and merchants whose families had been settled in Sicily for some four hundred years, and a period of economic decline set in. In contrast, his grandson, Frederick II, was a keen patron of the arts, a progressive and enlightened despot, tolerant of Moslems and Jews, and fluent in Arabic.

Researchers have established that many of the surviving fabrics previously attributed to Sicilian workshops were in fact made in Lucca or Venice, and that Sicilian textile art was above all concerned with embroidery and tiraz. It should be remembered, however, that after the death of Manfred, and during the period of Spanish and French struggles for dominance in the island, many textile workers fled; some to Salerno, where there was a colony of Jewish weavers, some to Naples, and others to Lucca and Venice. The migration of skilled workers to these cities was part of a new phase in the history of silk, and will be described in a later chapter.

The east

While the tide of Islam swept west as far as Spain, Moslem dynasties rose and fell in the east. The Sassanian regime ended with the Moslem victory at Nihavand (642), and the Islamic prohibition against wearing silk was evaded here, as elsewhere, by mixing silk with other fibres, which in most of the patterned fabrics meant merely continuing the established use of linen interior warps. The dated and inscribed 'Shroud of St Josse' (page 100) was woven in the eastern province of Khurasan, ruled by the Samanid princes who claimed Sassanian descent, as did the Buyid dynasty in western and southern Persia where, as already mentioned, the important technique known as 'diasprum' or 'lampas' developed (p. 101). Patterns usually show a confronted pair within a unit. Eagles were popular motifs, and a dramatic silk (now in Cleveland) has six great double-headed birds in pairs, grasping lions in their talons. On their wings are cocks, and the inscription 'Pity', and their bodies support human figures. Although most of these Buyid silks are attributable to a series of tombs unearthed in the 1920s at Rayy, where Chinese silks were also found in the graves, the authenticity of several others is doubtful.

Thirteenth-century painted pottery and miniatures show figures dressed in fabrics with all-over scrolling foliation, sometimes with birds, occasionally with animals, in continuation of Buyid-Seljuq styles. A wide variety of striped fabrics are also represented, with the ogee format developed from the old Achaemenid-Sassanian roundel enclosing a single animal or pair. Other frequently represented patterns include the triple-spot or cintamani (three spots arranged in a pyramid, with two wavy lines below), chevrons, and quatrefoil lattices and honeycombs.

Under the Umayyads and Abbasids, whose rule soon became merely nominal, native and Turkish dynasties rose to power. By 1075 the Seljuq Turks from Transoxiana had spread across Persia, made Isfahan their capital, and took over the Buyid dynasty's workshops and designs. Ten years later they made themselves masters of Baghdad, proclaiming their leader Tughrul Bey 'Sultan and King of East and West' and establishing a protectorate over the Abbasid caliphate, before continuing west into Anatolia where they made Konya their capital. Not only is it difficult to distinguish between certain Buyid and Seljuq textiles, but it is difficult to know whether the few surviving Seljuq silks should be attributed to Persia or Anatolia. They are generally of two colours, and framed main motifs stand out against a background of delicate tendrils and Chinese-inspired lotus palmettes. The Seljuq emblem was the eagle, and other Seljuq favourites include pairs of birds, felines, griffins, harpies and sphinxes. The Seljuq sphinx is sometimes the Achaemenid type, male, bearded and crowned, and sometimes female as in Egyptian iconography. As well as woven silks, there exist some delicately coloured silks with resist-dyed decorations of medallions enclosing animals and birds, flowers and scrolling tendrils, and primitive nakshi script in the frames. An example of this type (now in Lyon) is said to have been found in the district of Rayy.

Before the final flowering of her textile arts under the Safavid dynasty, Persia would be unified as part of the great Mongol Empire.

Mongols, Mamluks, Ottomans

am the flail of God. If you had not committed great sins, God would not have sent a punishment like me upon you. – In Bokhara's principal mosque in 1219, there were few sheltering refugees left alive to hear these words of Ghengiz Khan. For centuries Moslems knew the Mongols as 'the Accursed of God', and the Islamic civilizations of Persia and Turkey were all but extinguished by their ferocity. It took less than fifty years for the Mongols to carve out the largest empire the world had ever seen, and at the apex of their power their territories encompassed all Russia and almost the entire land mass of Asia. Though unlettered, Ghengiz Khan recognized the power of ideas and the value of skilled craftsmen and artists, and these were spared and transported to his camp and court. Sages and philosophers were summoned, and some of these left records of their experiences. One, a Taoist named Ch'ang Ch'un, described seeing his first Moslem in the Turfan area, and a transported colony of Chinese artisans, notably silk and wool weavers. He remarked that the people in oasis cities irrigated the wasteland with canals, so that fruits could be grown, and mulberry trees cultivated for sericulture. Near Samarkand his party found a 'splendid mulberry tree whose branches could shelter a hundred men'.

After the death of Ghengiz Khan, the Mongol conquests were divided into four separate khanates – the Ilkhanate of Persia, the Golden Horde of Russia, the Ghagatai Khanate in Central Asia, and the lands of the Great Khan, the Mongolian heartland and China, where they established the Yuan dynasty. Mongol armies swept into eastern Europe, into India and the jungles of South-east Asia. Their advance was halted at last, in Syria, by the Mamluks, a dynasty of Turkish warrior-slaves, and in Japan by another emergent warrior-class, the samurai.

In 1215 the Mongols broke through the Great Wall by sheer force of numbers and at appalling cost to both sides. Ogedai Khan, son of Ghengiz, completed the conquest of north China, subjugated Korea, declared war on the Song rulers of southern China, and campaigned across north-west Persia, northern Iraq, Armenia and Azerbaijan. In 1236 eastern Europe became the focus of armies under the nominal command of Ghengiz' grandson Batu. In 1251, the title passed to Mongke, another grandson of Ghengiz, and with his brothers Kublai and Hulagu he completed the conquest of western Asia.

Kublai's education was largely the responsibility of a Confucian scholar, Yao Ji, and during years of campaigning he became increasingly Chinese in his tastes and manners, to such a degree that he felt China to be his natural home, though not until 1279 did he feel confident to proclaim himself First Emperor of the Yuan dynasty. Yuan court dress accommodated its nomadic antecedents by formalizing riding clothes, and the particular cut of robe, with slits to facilitate sitting in a saddle, remained fashionable for many years.

The Pope, concerned about the strength of Islam, sent emissaries to the Yuan emperor in the hope of forging an alliance. The period known as the Pax Mongolica lasted for a crucial century, from 1260 to 1368, and contributed much to the emergence of the great Italian silk industry, described in a later chapter. The undulating vines and palmettes of a Mongol silk excavated at Fostat in Egypt show how this pattern developed into the famous pomegranate silks of the Gothic and Renaissance period, and certain so-called artichoke or pineapple silks trace their iconography to the lotus-bud. Early European silks imitated eastern weaves and adopted their free-flowing, asymmetrical layouts which influenced first Italian silks and then, via the Italian silks, the vertical stem-patterns of Ottoman art.

The Vatican was a ready customer for silks from China, and the Yuan were active in providing these. The West had other aims too, and among the missionaries who went east in the hopes of converting the Mongols to Christianity were John of Plano Carpini and William of Rubruck. Carpini's mission, in 1245, was the first recorded European exploration of Asia. The Khan, however, assumed that the Pope was offering him homage. He was more impressed by the visiting merchant Polo family, and kept Marco in his employ for some seventeen years. William of Rubruck wrote: '[concerning the Tartars] as to their dress, you should know that silk textiles, stuffs with gold and cotton fabrics – which they use in the summer – are brought to them from Cathay and other Eastern countries, and from Persia and other Southern countries. Rich people generally have their costumes padded with silk wool, which is extremely soft and warm.'

When Kublai took the title Great Khan in 1260 he formally converted to Buddhism and became closely associated with the Tibetan 'Phags-pa Lama. Apparently the Seljuq and Yuan textiles which have come out of Tibetan monasteries in recent years reached Tibet as gifts during this period.

During the Yuan, as previously mentioned, a distinctive type of embroidery, known as needle-loop, similar to early European needle-lace, enjoyed a fashion, then mysteriously appears to have been discontinued with the end of the dynasty (Pl. p. 25). Silk velvet (or pile fabric cautiously described as the precursor of velvet) has been found in a Yuan dynasty tomb of the parents of the Prince of Wu (d. 1365). The gold in Yuan brocaded silks was not a core-wrapped thread as used in the Mediterranean regions, but fine strips of gilded membrane or parchment, a technique apparently developed during the Song dynasty, and the appearance of this type of material in a textile indicates eastern origin.

Baghdad's days of glory were over in 1258, when Ghengiz's grandson Hulagu laid waste the city. As part of the levied tribute he demanded textiles of the type described by Marco Polo as 'richly wrought with figures of beasts and birds'. The capture of Baghdad united Mesopotamia and Persia under the Ilkhanid dynasty, and Tabriz became the capital city. Chinese craftsmen were installed here, and the Ilkhanid rulers passed through a Buddhist phase before their conversion to Islam. The

Detail of the Marienkirche cope, an early 14th-century Mongol silk-and-gold lampas, or 'Tartar cloth'. The pattern includes Chinese dragons and Islamic inscriptions.

Buddhist lotus, the Chinese peony, dragon, and cloud-band became part of Persian design repertoire, while the Chinese phoenix became the Persian simurgh. In 1295 the Ilkhan Ghazan made a public conversion to Islam and decreed the destruction of churches, synagogues and Buddhist temples constructed by his predecessors. His actions were imitated later by Ozbek Khan of the Golden Horde (1312–41) and a generation later by Tamerlane (1347–63).

Few Persian textiles of the Mongolian Ilkhanid period have survived, but in these a strong Chinese influence is evident, as in the Marienkirche silk cope conserved in Berlin. The gold thread is the characteristic eastern flat gilt membrane, and a pattern of addorsed birds within dodecagons is interspersed with dragons. The birds' wings are inscribed with a benediction in circular formation: 'Glory to our master, the Sultan, al-Malik the just, the learned, Nasir al-Din'. The ruler here named was a Mamluk sultan, Nasir al-Din Muhammed (1293–1341, with interruptions). A passage from Abu'l-Fida describes camels laden with seven hundred lengths of silk bearing the sultan's name which were presented by Abu Sa'id to Nasir al-Din Muhammed in 1323, when peace was concluded between the Ilkhanids and the Mamluks. This particular silk may well have been among the cargo. Other silks bear similar inscriptions, and might be woven with addorsed birds and animals, and calligraphy, or be striped with cartouches, or bear medallions enclosing double-headed eagles and addorsed felines with script. One has bands of calligraphy forming ogival cells enclosing pomegranates, lotus blossoms, peonies and addorsed *ch'i-lins*. In accordance with Koranic prescription and Mamluk taste, Mongol silks intended for the Mamluk market are usually striped, including calligraphic bands of popular Arabic verses, for example 'Glory and Victory and Long Life', 'the Sultan, the Learned', and the characteristic Mamluk benediction, 'Glory to our Master, the Sultan'. The inscriptions were sometimes interspersed with medallions or cartouches, or written in a circular format enclosed by palmettes or medallions. Some Mongol silks with Arabic inscriptions have survived as church treasures. A striped dalmatic in Regensburg incorporates in its pattern of birds, fishes, animals and flowers, the inscription 'the work of Master Abd al-Aziz'; and a similarly patterned and inscribed silk (Victoria and Albert Museum) suggests that the weaver specialized in export silks. These Mongol silks from China and the Near East were known in Europe as 'Tartar cloths'.

Documents of this period mention 'kincob', a term adapted from a Chinese word, 'chin', designating gold-woven silk. Herat was especially famous for kinkob, and also for silver brocade. Yazd gold silks were marketed under the city name. The term 'kincob' travelled to India in the time of the Moguls with Persian brocade weavers.

The Mongols took Aleppo in 1260, then met their first defeat at the hands of the Mamluks at Ain Jalat near Nazareth. Before Hulagu could attack Damascus, he learned of the death of the Great Khan Mongke and withdrew to the Steppes for

Mamluk silk woven with lotuses and pear-shaped ornaments, bearing the inscription: 'Glory to the Lord our King' and 'al-Ashraf', a title used by several Mamluk sultans.

another 'kuriltai', election of the next Khan. It was the Mongol custom to carry their Khans back to their ancestral burial grounds in Mongolia, escorted by their clans and followers in mourning. Marco Polo described the Mongol funerary journey: the procession marched slowly and in silence, and any living being that crossed their path was killed, and 'sent to serve their master in the other world'. Twice the West was spared by the sudden death of a great Khan, when the Mongols, seemingly overnight, and, to the besieged, without apparent reason, melted back from the brink of invasion.

Few, if any, Mongol silks can be accurately attributed to a specific area of production, but the Mongols contributed greatly to the diffusion of patterns in silkweaving. A general tendency was for dark grounds – indigo blue and green, brown – with lighter-toned pattern, often enriched with, or entirely rendered in, gold thread. The shimmering effect was enhanced by a light-reflective foundation warp, warp twill or satin.

The Mamluks who stemmed the Mongol advance were descended from an élite corps of bodyguards trained in all forms of warfare and horsemanship. Initially they were drawn exclusively from Turkic tribes, and served the caliphs of Baghdad. Their sultans established an empire in Egypt and extended their rule from south-eastern Anatolia, Syria and Palestine to parts of the Sudan and Libya. The empire was consolidated under Baybars (1260–77) who had participated in the significant battle against the Mongols, and lasted until the second decade of the sixteenth century. Trade and agriculture flourished, Cairo became a prosperous city, the centre of artistic and intellectual activity, and rich textiles signified position and prosperity.

Baybars established good relations with the Byzantine emperor Michael VIII Palaeologus, and with Manfred of Sicily. He formed an alliance with Berke Khan, chief of the Golden Horde, who had converted to Islam, and an amicable rapport with the Seljuqs of Anatolia. Baybars was the first Mamluk sultan to send a ceremonial litter bearing a new *kiswa* to Mecca, and Egypt continued to supply the *kiswa* until the beginning of the twentieth century.

Luxurious patterned silks were woven in Damascus, Alexandria and Cairo, and some silk yarn was supplied by Syrian sericulture. Of the Mamluk silks that have survived, most are excavated fragments, while others were preserved in Europe as ecclesiastical vestments, but it is virtually impossible to say exactly where a particular silk was woven. The rule permitting decorative bands 'not exceeding two or four fingers' width' inspired inventiveness within restriction, and vertical or horizontal stripes were filled with inscriptions, animals and floral motifs, often accentuated by stars, rosettes and crescents. A clue to one area of production is provided by an uncut and unworn sheet of striped silk excavated at Jabal Adda (Cairo, Museum of Islamic Art), with stripes and bands filled with feline predators and prey, birds and inscriptions bestowing 'victory and long life'. One edge is stamped al-Asyut, suggesting that it was made at Asyut, a town in Upper Egypt famous for silk and linen manufacture.

During the rule of Nasir al-Din Muhammed the peace treaty was signed with Abu Sa'id, the first Ilkhanid ruler to be born a Moslem, and the Mamluk court was frequented by embassies, not only from the khans of the Golden Horde, Rasulids of Yemen, Ilkhanids of Persia, and sultans of Delhi, but also from the Pope and various Christian rulers. Documents record a substantial Mongol population in Egypt and Syria, several of whom were appointed to prestigious ranks in the Mamluk aristocracy. Gifts of Yuan silks influenced Mamluk designs, while Mongol silks produced for the Mamluk court introduce a blend of Chinese and Islamic motifs. Alliances between Mamluk sultans and Central Asian khans encouraged trading and competition with local textile industries in Syria and Egypt.

Egyptian Robes of Honour, *khila*, were exported as far as Delhi. Few Mamluk garments have survived, but one of the most important is a man's robe of heavy yellow silk, lined with linen, found in Upper Egypt in 1966 (Cairo, Museum of Islamic Art). The silk is patterned with stars enclosing eight-petalled rosettes, running animals and crosses with lobed medallions and addorsed birds.

Embroidery techniques continued, as did fine tapestry, and patterned silks. Ogival layouts in damask and brocades became popular in the late thirteenth and early fourteenth centuries, and several examples have survived, such as the silk illustrated on the previous page, and the mantle for the Virgin (originally in a church near Valencia in Spain, now in Cleveland) which bears within a pointed medallion an inscription to the Sultan al-Malik al Nassir Mohammed (1310–41), under whose reign damask designs of the Mamluk period attained their finest development. Other silks are decorated with medallions, zig-zag patterns, latticework, addorsed birds, griffins, running animals and floral motifs interspersed with calligraphy. When Mamluk weavers imitated the asymmetrical format of Yuan silks, the results are often stiffer than the originals.

Outside the narrow élite of the ruler's household unit was a body of officials known as emirs and ranked according to the number of mamluks under their command. State regulations detailed the ceremonial uniform of each rank. An Emir of a Hundred (with a hundred mamluks under his command) was invested with fur-trimmed robes of red and yellow satin embroidered with gold thread. His turban was muslin woven with silk stripes, and he wore a jewelled gold belt. Civilian notables usually wore white or black robes, and these and their turbans were decorated with tiraz borders. Streets were lined and hung with textiles during official parades, and in the imperial council each participant was identified by the silk hanging behind his place.

Although heraldic emblems had been employed by other Turkish rulers, they were generally symbols of royalty. In the Mamluk world, the blazon identified a

The splendid interior of an Ottoman military tent, embellished with appliqué and embroidery, 17th century.

specific office, and was used by the emir who held that post, and all members of his household. The word for blazon meant colour, indicating that colour was important in the identification of the signs. The emblem was always enclosed by a round, pointed, pear-shaped or oval shield, and in textiles it is usually appliqué, in silk, cotton or linen. The fleur-de-lys is one of the many symbols that appear on blazons, and although in western thought this has come to be associated with French royalty, the stylized lotus or lily is an important symbol in both the Far East and Egypt.

Italian fashions enjoyed a vogue, until al-Nasir Muhammed officially banned garments with the narrow Venetian-style sleeves he so disliked. Italian textiles were available in Egypt and Syria, but do not appear to have influenced Mamluk silks, although conversely Mamluk designs influenced those of Italy.

The distinctive Mamluk carpets appear in the fifteenth and sixteenth centuries, and the intricate geometry of their patterns is woven in the battlefield colours of sky-blue, blood-red, and holy grass-green, colour of the Prophet's banner. Only one known example is woven in silk (Vienna, Kunsthistorisches Museum, Pl. p. 125).

The Mamluks met the Ottomans in battle north of Aleppo in 1516 and were defeated. A final defeat followed in 1517 when the Ottoman sultan was formally recognized as master of Egypt and Syria. Istanbul became the seat of a new sultanate and caliphate which included the holy cities of Mecca and Medina. Although the art produced after this time continued in the Mamluk style, occasionally Turkish elements are added, and it is generally termed Ottoman.

'Ottoman' is the European term for the Osmanli, named for their ruler, Osman (1299–1326), and one among ten rival emirates who emerged to rule Turkey in the early fourteenth century. The domestic life of a nomad is lived between striking camp and re-erecting tents, with its myriad accompanying chores. The transition

Cintamani (triple-dot) design on (*above*) silk brocade and (*right*) brocaded velvet, 16th century. Compare the Tibetan Buddhist illustration (p. 130).

from sheepskin and wool to silks came with city life and settlement. In later centuries, as many miniature paintings attest, tents continued to be the favourite dwellings of sophisticated rulers. Some of the later imperial tents have survived, although none is the personal pavilion of the monarch, which took ten years to embroider and was exhibited at the Hippodrome. The meadows of Anatolia continued to flower in silk stitches, and on the Iznik ceramics of the palaces. The Ottoman camp was more than a scene of festivity or seat of war, and in the precision with which it was laid out, in streets and bazaars, cookhouses and privies, it showed the sense of order underlying Ottoman art. The first Ottoman capital was the city of Bursa, always an important centre for silk-commerce and weaving.

Fourteenth-century Turkish silks are rare, and one of these shrouds a sarcophagus in Studenica Monastery in Serbia. Striped, it bears an inscription and the name of a 'Sultan Bayazid Khan'. Bayazid I married the daughter of a Serbian prince, and this silk was probably sent as a tribute of respect on the king's death. Also tentatively attributed to the fourteenth century is a group of caftans in the Topkapi Saray. An anonymous chronicler in the fifteenth century wrote nostalgically of the days before power corrupted, when sultans walked up and down the streets of Bursa, and the earliest imperial caftans do indeed maintain a striking balance between opulence and clear proportions in the design.

'Cotton velvets of Bursa' are mentioned in fifteenth-century documents, but it is not clear whether these are a silk pile velvet with cotton foundation (the usual construction), or velvet which is entirely manufactured from cotton. Velvet technology and looms were transported from Venice to the Ottoman Empire at some early date, and there is no doubt that decorative Turkish silk velvets were woven in techniques developed by Italians. While the richest imperial velvets were brocaded with metallized threads, plain velvet has always been enhanced with appliqué and other types of embroidery. Silver- and gilt-embroidered velvet (silk or cotton pile) was used for horse-trappings, saddle-covers, boots, quivers, jackets, *salvars* (baggy Turkish trousers) and traditional wedding dresses. Even after the grand velvets and brocades were no longer made, lavish gold embroidery continued as part of regional costumes.

During the reign of Orhan (1281–1324) the Genoese had been granted trading concessions, and vied with the Florentines and Venetians. Bertrandon de la Broquière who visited Bursa in the mid-fifteenth century remarked on the continued presence of Venetians and Genoese in the market, the cosmopolitan nature of the city, its importance, and the quantities of fabrics, jewels and other costly wares in the bazaar.

The conquest of Constantinople by Mehmed II ('the Conqueror') in 1453 marked the move of the court from Bursa. Constantinople became the Ottoman capital, Istanbul. A state of war between the Ottomans and the Venetians in the period 1463

to 1475 led to closer relations with the Florentines, and during the Medici period commercial interests were fostered and developed.

Among the few Ottoman silks confidently attributed to the fifteenth century are two caftans patterned with the cintamani (triple-dot) design, believed to have belonged to Mehmed the Conqueror; a pomegranate-design crimson and gold velvet (now in Sweden, in the Treasury of Upsala Cathedral), and a number of matching fragments of cintamani-patterned gold and crimson brocaded velvet (now in various museums and private collections). Fragments of early velvets occasionally survived as bookbindings. The cintamani – a pyramidal arrangement of three dots above two wavy lines – and the tulip have become the ambassadors of Ottoman art, although foreign admiration for their native tulip may have prompted the Turks to adopt the motif. The tulip appears on datable fifteenth-century Italian silks, but does not figure in the Ottoman decorative arts until the second quarter of the sixteenth century. Turkish taste favoured the elegant, elongated form of their wild tulips rather than the rounded shape preferred by Europeans.

In order to assure their income from Bursa's lucrative silk trade the sultans built fortified hans, inside which were large scales to weigh the silk, and here the Government brokers oversaw transactions and collected payment of commissions and taxes.

A 1502 Code of Law governing trades and markets for Bursa, Edirne and Constantinople laid down guild regulations, many of which applied particularly to silk-weavers, stipulating adherence to the superior standards of twenty-five years before. The number and the weight of the warp threads, the main factors by which the quality of the fabric was determined, were both laid down, and craftsmen whose work was substandard were liable to punishment. The scope of the Bursa textile industry can be glimpsed in documents such as an inventory of 1504, which tantalisingly lists ninety-one types of fabric, each of which fulfilled a special requirement. It gives no indication of designs, so that present-day researchers are faced with difficulties in trying to match the names with such textiles as survive.

Cloth of gold or silver, where the ground is metallic and its pattern coloured silks, was deemed worthy to line a gold Qur'an binding, and for ceremonial caftans and the cushions used on thrones. The French ambassador to Constantinople presented a gown of this golden cloth to Marguerite de Valois, and it was considered to be the most precious fabric ever to be seen in France. Satin voided velvet incorporating gold and silver was made in a restrained palette, and a striking pattern found in many collections is an elegant composition of large and small fan-shaped carnations and sprays of flowers, with rich crimson silk pile, sometimes outlined with touches of chartreuse, set off against shimmering gilt. Carnation velvets became popular from the late sixteenth to the seventeenth century.

Tulip-patterned 'bohça', or wrapping cloth, embroidered with silk darning stitch on linen, 16th century.

Velvet-brocaded 'yastiks', or cushion-covers for divans, with lappet end-panels, 16th–17th century.

Silk Mamluk carpet, the world's only known example. Probably woven in Cairo around 1500, it has a design of subtle geometrical patterns derived from the ceramic-tile decorations in the courtyards of Cairo's medieval houses. In intricacy and beauty, it seems closer to some precious jewelled panel.

An edict of 1564 noted that the number of court manufactory looms had increased to 310, and that as a result of the adulteration of the silk and gold threads used, stricter controls would be exerted. Prices were fixed, and all fabrics woven with gold had to be marked with the government stamp. These regulations were maintained until the nineteenth century. A further edict of 1574 forbade the weavers in Bursa to use gold in their fabrics. Only the imperial manufactories in Istanbul would be permitted to weave gold tissue. Provided this edict was enforced, many silks with gold traditionally ascribed to Bursa must have been woven in Istanbul.

Religious friction between the Ottomans and the Persians had culminated in a 'Silk War' in 1514, when Selim I (1512–20) temporarily held the Persian capital of Tabriz, and transported artists, craftsmen, scholars and poets to Istanbul. The booty taken included ninety-one garments of Bursa silk belonging to Shah Ismail. Selim further attempted to deprive the Shah of his most vital revenue by imposing a commercial blockade. In response, the Persians developed alternative routes, and silk caravans passed through Aleppo and Iskandarun. Selim retaliated by confiscating all stocks of Persian goods whether from Arab, Ottoman or Persian merchants, and all stocks of whatever source from Persian merchants, who were transported to Rumeli and Istanbul. The resultant shortages of raw material are reflected in the silks of the time; weavers were tempted to adulterate the material, and embroiderers economized by employing stitches such as darning and couching, where all the silk was shown on the front. This is well illustrated in the predominantly red and blue embroideries of the sixteenth century.

The reign of Suleyman the Magnificent saw Ottoman military prowess at its peak. Early in his reign the Turks took Belgrade and defeated the Hungarians, and by 1529 his army was at the gates of Vienna, only retreating at the onset of a winter for which it was ill-equipped. In 1683 the Turks were finally forced back from the second siege of Vienna by Polish and German troops. Wherever they had been for any length of time, the Ottoman influence remained in customs of dress.

Although Suleyman relaxed restrictions on the silk trade, the scarcity and high price of materials eventually forced many merchants and weavers out of business. Whereas previously commerce had been in the hands of Persians and Turks, now Armenian dealers began to take over their role. Finally, the government encouraged the production of silk within the Ottoman Empire, and increased imports from the Morea (the Peloponnese), Albania and Rumeli, and from Anatolia. Sixteenth-century travellers describe the plains of Bursa as covered in mulberry orchards.

Throughout the sixteenth and seventeenth centuries, Ottoman trade and manufacture fluctuated according to the availability or shortages of silk from Persia. England had relied principally on Venetian vessels for transporting goods from the Near East, but during the time of the Ottoman-Safavid strife European merchants sought other routes, through Russian and also via the Indian Ocean.

Opposite page
Long-sleeved ceremonial caftan associated with Sultan Bayazid II (1481–1512) or possibly with one or other of Suleyman the Magnificent's sons, Şehzade Bayazid (strangled 1561) or Mustafa (d. 1553). Brilliant colours and gold thread are displayed to advantage by the design, conceived so that the fabric shows no repeat. The stylized lotus palmetes, rosettes and pomegranates are swept across the dark field by curved *saz* leaves, named after the calligrapher's reed pen.

Red and gold crescents make a striking brocade intended for a royal caftan, woven in the early 17th century.

Cane shield-cover whipped with silk thread, worked into a delicate floral pattern: a combination of weapons-of-war and decoration more suited to the soft luxury of a bedchamber.

This page
The triple-dot or 'cintamani' appears (*below*) on a long-sleeved ceremonial caftan associated with Sultana Ibrahim (1640–8), of heavy white satin with a dramatic appliqué of triple-spots or crescents, and single tiger-stripes in crimson. *Right* A quilt-cover of linen is embroidered with the cintamani; and an Ottoman miniature shows a glorious saddle-cloth decorated with the same auspicious motif.

To safeguard their trade, the Ottomans signed an agreement with England which led to the establishment of the Levant Company (later known as the Turkey Company), founded by Royal Charter of 1581. The Company built vast warehouses, notably in Smyrna (Izmir) and Aleppo, to store and trade in silk.

A peace treaty in 1613 stipulated that the Persians should send a specified amount of silk per annum, and when this was not forthcoming in 1617, the Ottomans launched another campaign. The insistence on a regular supply of Persian silk, despite increased Ottoman domestic production, gives an indication of the importance of government revenue derived from handling the silk supply. Silk remained a powerful political weapon until 1639.

Because of the frequent shortages and high cost of silk, heavier fabrics such as those for furnishings had the appearance of silk but were economically bulked out with linen and cotton. Many furnishing silks, such as *yastiks*, the rectangular divan cushion covers, were made in Istanbul in Uşkadar (Scutari), a Venetian quarter across the Bosphoros, rather than in Bursa. Most *yastiks* were woven with a great deal of cotton or linen and minimal silk. The earliest often have lappet end-panels, and their bold patterns resemble manuscript illuminations or bookbindings, with a large central medallion (Ilus. p. 123). Some have flat carnation palmettes, cleanly and elegantly spaced, and are directional, to match larger panels woven as covers for divans. The metal thread is often insubstantial, and from the seventeenth century onwards the quality deteriorated.

An unusual application of silk was for round cane shields, where the cane was wrapped with coloured silk threads and worked with a pattern, often flowers. Although strong and functional, these exquisite objects were more fitted for parade than battle. Another distinctive group of silks is known in the West as 'tomb covers'. These are woven with a satin zig-zag design, crimson and ivory or green and ivory, sometimes with alternate bands of blue and crimson, and various inscriptions are included in the pattern. They were intended to drape over the sarcophagus-shaped cenotaphs in the commemorative 'türbe' erected over the burial sites of sultans, important secular officials and holy men. Many of these (often fragmentary) silks are found in western collections: only a few, such as those in the türbe of Sultan Suleyman, are still to be found *in situ*. In the nineteenth century this type of silk was produced in the factories of Hereke, and may be identified by the golden-yellow which replaces the natural ivory in the older examples.

Designs produced for the court were often one of a kind, and displayed a wide range of dyes, whereas those made for export were limited, employing ogival or vertical stem-patterns derived from Italian prototypes, and four or five colours. Ottoman artists used the cintamani in many variations. Classical representations show crescent forms within the circles. In other versions the three dots become berry-like, the wavy lines become leaf-like, sometimes the pattern is drawn to

Tibetan apron with appliqué silks and gilt leather on silk damask, worn for ritual dances. In the fully opened Third Eye of a realized being we may find the Buddhist origin of the cintamani motif. The other element in the cintamani design, the two wavy lines, are the serene lips of the Buddha.

resemble the pelts of leopards or tigers. In Anatolia in the Ilkhanid period the cintamani and sun symbols were favourite designs for textiles associated with rulers. Peacock-feather motifs appear on some silks, and palace archives make reference to garments for the princes made from material of such patterns – often velvets with ogival or meandering layout. Chinese silks inspired lotus palmettes, meandering vines and ogival 'cells' containing arrangements of flowers, sometimes linked by Italian crowns. Chinese cloud-bands and cintamani are frequently incorporated into the overall design. Pomegranates appear, and Turkish native flowers: tulips, carnations, hyacinths. A plant motif unique to Turkish art is a stem which grows out, as it were, from a pierced leaf. It belongs to a style which has been named '*saz*', for the caligrapher's reed pen, and was created by a court artist named Sahkalu. Two examples, with large feathery leaves in brocade, are a pair of imperial caftans, one on black ground, the other on ivory, both of the sixteenth century.

Suleyman was so enthralled by the Circassian Roxelana, whom he called 'Hurrem', the laughing one, that contrary to seraglio customs he made her his legal wife. Embroidered and drawn-thread kerchiefs and headbands which must have been used by Hurrem Sultan during her life, and a brocaded and voided velvet, with gold tulips and pine cones outlined with green pile on a crimson field, were among the textiles found in her mausoleum.

The square cloths used as wrapping, named 'bohças', were as finely embroidered as their contents. Elaborate turbans once tied were left so, and turban bohças are identifiable by a central circular decoration which serves as a focus for the pattern.

Square embroideries were also made for cushion covers, usually worked on a plain silk satin. Rectangular embroideries with a directional pattern and border, though generally referred to as 'Turkish curtains', were decorative covers for quilts. The same pattern, or versions of it, were embroidered on both these and bohças; clearly a set repertoire of designs was worked by professional embroidery workshops. Narrow loom-lengths of undyed cotton or linen were usually embroidered before joining, each section probably by a different workers. The distinctive sixteenth- and early seventeenth-century embroideries, predominantely red and blue, are executed in a selection of economical stitches such as darning and couching. Little pavilions, tents and sailing ships mingle with flowers in the smaller pieces of needlework, such as kerchiefs, and gold and silver thread set off silk stitches.

Lady Mary Wortley Montagu accompanied her husband to Istanbul in 1717, and as a keen observer her letters recorded a wealth of costume detail. She described her own Turkish dress, from the rose damask brocaded with silver flowers that made her *salvar* or drawers and matched her caftan, to the *antery* or waistcoat of white and gold damask with gold fringe and pearl or diamond buttons. Oriental dress for balls and portraits became extremely fashionable in sophisticated circles in eighteenth-century Europe.

A romantic story links Turkey and France at this time, that of Aimée Dubucq de Rivery, cousin and playmate of a young girl like herself from Martinique, Josephine. Aimée was abducted by corsairs on a voyage which was to take her home from France, and sold to the Bey of Algiers who presented her to the Ottoman sultan Abdulhamid I. He named her Nakshedil, 'embroidered on the heart'. In 1789, year of the French Revolution, Abdulhamid died, and Selim III became sultan. Aimée remained at the seraglio with her son, Selim's nephew, as 'Sultan Valideh', mother of the heir apparent. For the first time, a permanent ambassador was sent from Istanbul to Paris in 1797, where Napoleon received him warmly. Everything in Paris became *à la Turque* for some weeks. Among the expertise and skills Selim imported to the Ottoman Empire from France were skilled artisans, who were brought to the Peloponnese to improve the technique of silk-reeling, and set up in textile factories in the previous Venetian colony in Uşkudar (Scutari). The textiles produced there were characterized by striped motifs, and compositions of small flowers known as 'Selimiye' after the sultan, and furnishing fabrics emulating the French style, with garlands, wreaths, ribbons and bows in multicoloured velvets. The Turks adopted French rococo with enthusiasm, and flowery European-style silks rolled off the looms for dress and furnishings. Selim was assassinated in 1807 and Aimée's son became sultan Mahmoud I in 1808. It is tempting to read the loyalty of one Martinique cousin defending another in the sudden manner in which Mahmoud turned against Napoleon, contributing to his downfall, when Napoleon, by divorce, repudiated Josephine.

Though the Ottoman court demanded woven silks and velvets, silk pile carpets were not a Turkish tradition. No silk carpets are mentioned among the numerous Turkish exhibits sent to the 1851 Great Exhibition in London, although various silks are listed as manufactured at the Imperial Government Steam Factory of Hereke. The first recorded instance appears to be a huge silk carpet woven in Hereke, which was among the many costly gifts presented to the Kaiser on his visit to Turkey in 1898.

The original Hereke factory, established in 1843 by the Armenian Dadyan brothers, was intended to produce cotton textiles. Ohnnes Dadyan, however, acquired a German silk workshop in Vienna and sent it to Hereke with the master weaver, his family and various workers. 'Bargain' machinery was brought from Lyon. Initially only ribbons, such as those for Orders and Medals, were manufactured. One inspiration for Turkish silk carpet production was probably the attention attracted by the Shah Abbas silk carpet exhibited by the Polish Count Czartoryski in the 1878 International Exhibition in Paris. Technically the first Turkish silk rugs are superb: they are woven in beautiful colours with miraculous precision, but the designs are completely derivative. Patterns taken from a Persian Safavid weaving of the sixteenth century might be juxtaposed with a border from a famous Seljuq carpet, for example. A successful design was that of niched prayer rugs, similar to the woollen ones in the Topkapi Saray. The Hereke signature was woven in Arabic script within an octagon, while others have lobed octafoils or similar designs, and today they have the word 'Hereke' woven at one end of the rug in western characters.

Silk rugs were also made in Şivas, Kayseri and Panderma, but finer than these were rugs made in Istanbul at the Kum Kapou factory. These frequently use metal thread, including multi-shaded gold, and the patterns include prayer rugs with calligraphy and Safavid-style mihrabs. They are sometimes signed by their weavers, and one famous signature is that of Zareh.

From the mid-nineteenth century Hereke produced furnishing silks including brocade *yastiks* combining Turkish features such as lappet end-panels, tulips, carnations, and European elements such as central medallions inspired by Aubusson and Savonnerie, oak-leaf wreaths, ribbons and bows. Embroidery continued to play an important role in Turkish domestic life. The most familiar example is the reversible Turkish towel which young girls were required to embroider for their dowries.

Turkish silks borrowed from neighbouring sources both technically and in their design, adding elements to create a distinctive Ottoman look. The best of these were produced in the sixteenth century, when they rivalled the Renaissance silks of Europe and those of the Safavid courts of Persia.

7 The Persian Flowering

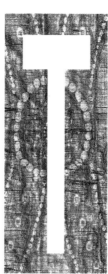he passage of silk from East to West was historically controlled by the dynasties that flourished and fell in the lands of Persia. Persian artists and craftsmen were always conscious of their inheritance, and the splendours of the Achaemenids, Parthians, Sassanians. This awareness is reflected in their silks, and the nationalistic revivals of the best of earlier designs.

By 1256 Persia was part of the Mongol Empire, stretching from China to the Mediterranean, and was at last unified. Under the Timurids, a flowering of learning, science and art graced the courts of Tabriz and Herat, and during this time Far Eastern symbols such as the cloud-band, dragon and phoenix became incorporated into Persian art. In 1404 the Spanish emissary Ruy de Clavijo visited the court of Tamerlane, and described 'the pavilions of the Great Khan, hung with silks embellished with spangles, silver plate and gilt, each spangle set with an emerald or pearl or other precious stone'.

The early years of the Safavids (1502–1736) were troubled. Tabriz, the first Safavid capital, was lost to the Ottomans in 1514, and subsequently changed hands several times. The second ruler, Shah Tahmasp (1524–1576), waged a 'holy war' against the Christians of Georgia, and a series of silks showing captors and their prisoners are believed to represent this campaign, and may have been woven as a form of propaganda (Pl. p. 137).

The earliest attributed Persian velvet is a group of fragments, plain weave foundation (now in Boston, the Cooper-Hewitt collection, and Lyon), dated to the time of Shah Tamasp by the slender figures and distinctive baton-style turbans. A mid-sixteenth-century 'carpet' of silk appliqué on leather (now in Budapest) is a type of work frequently used for tents and their trappings, and shows the young Shah Tamasp banqueting in a garden paradise, surrounded by musicians, flowers and animals. Winged beings throng the borders, and in the spandrels above the central figure the dragon and phoenix are locked in combat.

A fifteenth-century Venetian ambassador, Josafa Barbaro, visiting the Turkmen ruler Uzun Hasan of the Aq-Qoyunlu at Tabriz, wrote that the king 'caused certain silk carpets to be brought forth which were marvellous fair'. Whether these were knotted pile as is generally understood by the term 'carpet' (or the American 'rug') is not certain. We do know that Shah Tamasp presented to the Ottoman Sultan Selim II, on the latter's accession to the throne in 1566, twenty-five large rugs and other, smaller ones in silk and gold, decorated with birds, animals and flowers. Several silk carpets survive from this period, of which the most famous is a hunting carpet (now in Vienna, Museum für Angewandte Kunst). The scenes of hunting and feasting, and in the wide border the winged Blessed being waited upon by houris, closely resemble the style and draughtsmanship of Shah Tamasp's court painter Sultan Muhammad, and it has been suggested that he was responsible for the design.

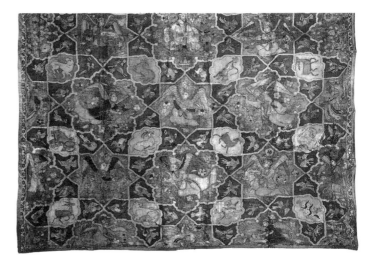

Shah Abbas's glorious reign (1587–1628) began with the loss of Georgia, Azerbaijan, Armenia, Herat and Meshed. He moved his capital from Qazvin to Isfahan, recovered the lost provinces and extended Persian frontiers to the Euphrates, the Persian Gulf and the Amu Darya. The true Safavid style blossomed during his reign, and a new repertoire of textile designs was inspired by the art of miniature painting. The inspiration for these silks came from an ideal of beauty, spirituality and mysticism expressed in poetry and heroic mythology. The lovers Layla and Majnun, Shirin and Khusrau, the exploits of heroes such as Rustem, and delicate flowers, birds, butterflies and animals, provided the motifs. Sufi mystics wrote romantic religious works centering on the rosary and the rose, and Fariduddin Attar's 'Parliament of the Birds' explained the symbol in the words of the 'passionate nightingale'. The nightingale, however, is a plain-looking bird, and in the *gul-u-bulbul* (rose and nightingale) silks, the more colourful finches are usually depicted.

Safavid colours are distinctive: a palette of peach, salmon, sugar-pink, lime green, turquoise, sky blue, often with a lavish use of gold and silver thread, either as ground-colour or for highlights, is in contrast to the reds and blues of earlier periods, which, imbued with royal significance, were beyond fashion. Unfortunately many dyes aged poorly, and their original freshness can only be discovered from threads at the back, or folded in seams which have escaped sunlight. A point of identification in Near Eastern silks is that the metal tends to wear away from the yarn, leaving the silk core intact. The result is areas of white or yellow silk where originally silver or gold was intended. (European metal thread contained a larger amount of copper in the alloy, and metal and silk tend to break at the same time.) In some Safavid velvets flat strips of metal were occasionally used, and some silks shimmer like sheets of precious metal. Mongol silks, on the other hand, used the Chinese fashion of gilt membrane or parchment.

Safavid canopy, 16th century, a silk mosaic of animals, flowers and birds, woven in fine tapestry.

Cloth of silver, 17th-century, brocaded with realistically drawn flowers and birds.

Although silks are rarely signed or dated, it is possible to assign a close date to some Safavid textiles by comparison with miniatures, although they need not have been produced in the same centres or at exactly the same time. Some of the best miniature painters made designs for textiles, and one of these, Ghiyath, worked mainly at Yazd. His signature appears in a variety of woven silks.

The stylized realism of iris, lily, tulip, hyacinth, carnation and rose, shown as singly growing plants, or in groups in the style of European *mille-fleur* tapestries, derives from miniature painting. Single motifs often have a clearly defined shape repeated across a field, sometimes in the familiar curved *boteh* known to the West as paisley (p. 74). The outline is derived from a type of oriental cypress whose tasselled tip bends over to give it this distinctive form. Birds, hares and gazelles are often included in these repeating designs, and arabesques and lattices were also popular.

Figurative velvets made during the period of Shah Abbas are distinctive. They usually have satin-weave foundations like the silk velvets made throughout the

One of a series of tapestries showing captors leading their prisoners. The slender, graceful figures and baton-style turbans date the scene to the time of Shah Tamasp (1524–76), who waged a 'holy war' against the Christians of Georgia.

Voided velvet coat depicting elegant Persian youths, presented by Tsar Alexander to Queen Christina of Sweden.

fifteenth and sixteenth centuries in Italy and Spain, and Persian weavers also used other decorative techniques invented during the period, including ciselé, or metallic bouclé (supplementary weft loops). The silk velvets produced in sixteenth-century Khurasan were said to rival those of Genoa. A gift from Shah Abbas to the Doge Marino Grimani was a Persian figurative velvet showing the Virgin with the infant Jesus, to whom an Eastern king is offering a cloak of rich material. Similarly illustrating the importance of textiles is a picturesque fashion in which velvets patterned with elegantly dressed youths were tailored into just such coats to be worn by just such youths. A coat of this type was sent as a gift to Queen Christina of Sweden.

Large-scale figured velvets were undoubtedly intended as hangings, in the manner of tapestry. Rosenborg Castle, Copenhagen, has several of these in its collection, which with brocades and silk carpets were gifts from Shah Safi's embassy to Duke Frederick of Holstein-Gottorp in 1639. Shah Abbas himself was said to be a skilled carpet weaver, and Anthony Sherley, who came to Persia as self-appointed representative of Queen Elizabeth I of England and was later sent to Europe as the Shah's own ambassador, received from the Shah lavish gifts including 'six mules, each carrying four carpets, four of silk and gold, six clear carpets, the rest very fair crewel carpets'. Crewel is of course an embroidery technique, and its use is ancient. We read of 'carpets embroidered with needles' in the description of booty taken by the Byzantine emperor Heraclius when he pillaged the palace of Khusrau II, king of the Sassanians.

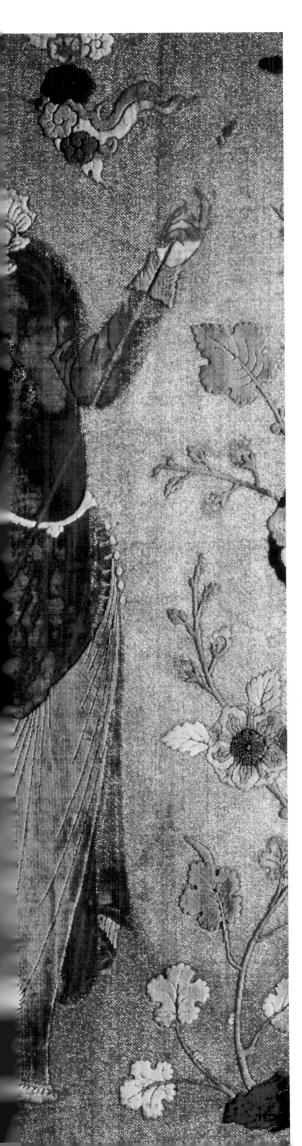

Far left 'Rose and nightingale', a favourite Safavid theme for gold and silver brocades. The nightingale, however, is a plain-looking bird, and weavers invariably replaced her image with the more colourful finch. The silk below adds a disproportionately small gazelle.

Left Safavid silk-hanging of cut and voided velvet with a gold field. Details are woven with silver bouclé (looped) thread, a technique new at the period. The style recalls the work of the court artist Riza Abbasi, while the large curved leaves resemble the popular Ottoman motif known as 'saz' leaves. The lady's dog is straining at the leash towards a smaller animal clinging to a branch.

Above An elegant 17th-century Persian coat with a diamond lozenge-shaped pattern impressed in the silver ground. Each lozenge is decorated with a marigold flower and bud, brocaded in coloured silk.

During the 16th century a number of supremely luxurious carpets were made for palace use, with the pile very finely knotted in silk instead of wool. Only three Persian medallion carpets of this kind have survived in Europe, and the example below is one of these. The carpets all depict hunters pursuing wild animals, while other animals run and prowl amid sparse floral scrolls and cloud-bands, brocaded in gold or silver thread.

Below Kurdish rugs are known more for rustic charm than fineness, but there are two notable exceptions: the close weaves of Senneh, and the rugs of Bijar, which, like the example shown here, display an attractive, confident balance of bold colour and clear design.

Bottom A so-called 'Polonaise' rug. These shimmering silk-and-metal-thread carpets were woven in the 17th and early 18th century in Isfahan and Kashan.

Below Velvet panel or floor-spread decorated with a repeating design of a turbanned youth kneeling between a tree with birds perching and a cypress, illustrating a traditional Persian romance.

Bottom A 19th-century silk Heriz rug from north-west Persia, patterned with a design known as 'minakhani': 'many flowers'.

Silk-brocade coats of the Qajar dynasty, woven with floral motifs, illustrated on a 19th-century lacquer book-cover. The Shah is shown receiving a party of European travellers.

In Persia as all over the East, whether for military campaigns, for hunting or for diplomatic missions, rulers and their retinues were equipped with elaborate tents. These 19th-century Qajar tents illustrate one particular type: a combination of fabrics and embroidery techniques, made mostly at Resht and Isfahan. Flannel and silk are cut and appliqué, and stitched into patterns with coloured silks, while pierced metal thread embroidery is worked to resemble openwork wood or stone screens, providing needful ventilation as well as ornament.

Silk is finer and stronger than wool, and has been used for the finest carpets in terms of the number of knots used, some so fine that they have been mistaken for velvet. The Carmelites, who were in Kashan in 1607, described the production of 'very fine carpets of silk and gold, brocades, velvets and other stuffs', and also 'tissues of the Arras kind', presumably the tapestry-woven rugs known as 'gelims' in Persia, 'kelims' in Turkey. These Christians probably took with them, as part of their 'missionary kit', vestments of European silks, and it has been suggested that such silks could be one source of western velvet and metal-thread techniques reaching Persian weavers at the period. However, the neighbouring Ottomans had already mastered these skills, and there were other possible sources in the traders of many nationalities who maintained open lines of East-to-West and West-to-East commerce. Some, for example the Italian Vilione family, settled in Persia for several generations.

The term 'Polonaise' became misleadingly attached to a spectacular group of silk and metal thread carpets and gelims, attributed to Kashan, after one of them, woven with a Polish coat of arms, was displayed at the Paris International Exhibition of 1878 by Prince Czartoryski. In 1601 an Armenian merchant was dispatched to Kashan to commission silk and gold rugs, tapestry-woven rugs, a tent, and other fabrics for King Sigismund III Vasa, and the detailed accounts in the Polish State Archives show extra charges for weaving blazons. Two complete gelims bearing the Vasa arms survive, but apart from these armorial examples, there is no reason to believe that all 'Polonaise'-type carpets were woven in Kashan. The so-called 'Polonaise' carpets and gelims display the typical Safavid palette, in a pattern of flowers, arabesques and palmettes. The tapestry of the gelims is dove-tailed, and figures are outlined in black, as they are for the most part in figurative velvets. Several of the gelims have motifs of animals and birds, mythical creatures such as the dragon and simurgh, or human figures, sometimes placed in cartouches with a central medallion. An example (now in the Louvre) shows the lovers Layla and Majnun in the corners, and a central horseman in combat with a spotted dragon. Rarest are the multiple medallion gelims, of which only three examples are known. One was used as a campaign cloak by the samurai Toyotomi Hideyoshi (d. 1598).

Occasionally silk was used for 'jajims', flat-woven textiles providing tent-furnishings, wrappers for bedding and clothing, saddle-bags and horse-covers. Decorated with striped geometric bands, they are illustrated in a number of miniature paintings. It is generally considered that they were woven in the Transcaucasus.

Long silk sashes, decorated with a repeating pattern, sometimes banded, with elaborate borders at the ends and fringed with silk, silver or gold, were woven by both Safavid and Mogul weavers (many of the latter Persians who went to India). As mentioned earlier, it is often difficult to distinguish Safavid from Mogul silks. Sashes

Safavid coat embroidered in silk darning stitch, Kashan, c. 1600. The design was drawn to follow the shape and dimensions of the garment before embroidery.

were woven in Poland too, inspired by those of the Persians. In 1758 Prince Michael Casimir Radziwill established a factory at Slucz and brought Armenian and Persian weavers to work here and produce scarves, sashes and cloth. These sashes are usually signed 'Slucz', and in some cases the weaver's name is also woven into the silk. Although patterned after the Persian prototypes, they are stylistically easy to identify.

Shah Abbas established Safavid control over Azerbaijan, and in keeping with his policy of promoting textile production, set up weaving workshops in the Caucasian regions of Shirvan and Karabagh. He created New Julfa, a town near Isfahan, in 1605, in an attempt to move population from an area of Armenia which was vulnerable to attack by the Ottomans. An Armenian inscription woven into the design of a 'Polonaise'-style silk carpet suggests that some of these were woven in New Julfa, as was the unique pile knotted silk cope depicting the Annunciation and the Crucifixion (see facing page).

The most common surviving Safavid period embroideries are generally termed Caucasian, Azerbaijan, or north-west Persian. The patterns of the geometrically designed panels are closely related to Caucasian carpets. Both the Ottomans and the Russians under Peter the Great invaded Azerbaijan, and although the Persian forces retaliated, they failed to recapture the whole of the original territory, and the Afghan invasion of Persia in the early eighteenth century heralded another period of conflict. Most of the surviving embroideries are examples from periods of relative stability in the late seventeenth and early eighteenth centuries. They fall into three main groups, of which the rarest, cross stitch, has equal amounts of thread on both front and back, suggesting that they were made when there was no shortage of silk. A second type is

Silk cope with a pile so fine it has been taken for velvet, although in fact it is finely knotted, a rug weave. It was woven at New Julfa in the 16th or 17th century.

surface darning, and the third, most commonly found, is surface darned on the diagonal, often with drawn-thread work.

A very distinctive pattern worked in darning stitch is a figurative type, and the male figures wear the distinctive baton turbans of Shah Tamasp period. Although the embroideries are from a later date, the designs bear close comparison to woven silks of the sixteenth and seventeenth centuries, and the previously mentioned appliqué in Budapest (p. 134). A coat made of this type of embroidery (now in Vienna, Museum für Angewandte Kunst, facing) clearly shows that the design was drawn to fit the garment before embroidery.

The last Safavid ruler, Shah Sultan Husayn (1694–1722), lived ostentatiously, and his robes were burned every seven years so that the gold in the garments could be re-used. A new floral style developed, inspired by lacquer painting, and overblown roses predominated. Another type of very distinctive Persian embroidery appears to date from this period and later. Diagonal bands of flowers are embroidered in many colours in fairly thick, lightly twisted silk threads, in imitation of Safavid finely woven narrow bands used for trimming precious brocades. These were the embroideries already mentioned as known in the West as *gilet Persan* (Persian waistcoat cloth), but in fact the decorative bands or cuffs on women's trousers, seen below the hem of the wearer's robes (p. 133).

State industries rapidly declined after the assassination of the Turkmen ruler Nadir Shah (1688–1747), and by 1750 sericulture in Mazandaran, which had flourished for fourteen hundred years, had all but vanished. Ahmed Shah founded an independent Afghan empire in the east of Persia, and the silks associated with Afghanistan today are those of the Central Asian type. Laden camel-caravans passed through Afghanistan's mountain passes to market-places in India and Pakistan. During the twentieth century, silk 'Bokharas' have been woven, but these are often Pakistani or Afghan products, and the 'silk' sometimes chemically treated cotton – *caveat emptor*. The dresses of Beluchi women, south of Afghanistan and west of Pakistan, have distinctive embroidered panels in the front, and occasionally their chocolate-dark rugs have a small motif of lime green, pink or orange silk, which shimmers like a tiny jewel, but betrays the post-1870 weaving date, as these are aniline dyes which reached the areas with the arrival of the Russian-built railways. The brilliance of the synthetic colours delighted weavers.

The famous portraits of the Qajar dynasty (1779–1925) show a wealth of costume detail, and rulers, courtiers, courtesans and acrobats wear pearl-sewn caftans, brocades and embroideries (p. 141). During the reign of Fath 'Ali Shah (1797–1834) attempts were made to restore old traditions and Safavid splendours, and Safavid silks were copied; the silkworm epidemic, pebrine, which dealt death-blows across Europe and the Near East, devastated Persian sericulture too between 1864 and 1867.

The industrial fairs of the nineteenth century heightened interest in Persian and Transcaucasian silks and other products, and brought about a revival in carpet-weaving in the later part of the nineteenth century. Silks from earlier periods of Persian history were copied, but are usually easily identified by fugitive dyes which give a muddy tone, and the spacing and proportions of the motifs lack the grace and elegance of the originals. Sericulture was re-introduced in some areas and increased in others with the introduction of healthy eggs from restocked Italy and France, while machinery and equipment was improved and developed. Silk carpets were produced in the ancient weaving centres of Kashan, Tabriz, Isfahan, Heriz, and the best of these are extremely beautiful, with fine flat pile which reflects the light in such a way that the colour appears to change according to the viewer's position. Over centuries, a distinctive type and 'look' developed in each centre, and the construction of the rugs also differs, so that the place of origin of each can be identified. Popular designs included prayer rugs, Tree of Life designs, hunting scenes, medallions and spandrels, and all-over repeating motifs. Some have scenes from Persian history or mythology, and silk carpets woven with American cartoons of the 1930s have also appeared. The most recent silk-carpet weaving centre is Qom, where looms have been in production since the 1930s. Today, silk carpets are the main, and only significant use of the material, still an important part of Persian economy and exports.

Persia's dominance in the passage and production of silk ended with the glorious silks of the Safavids, though her influence continued in the silks of the Moguls. Even before the rise of the Safavid dynasty, the great inheritance of the East had been received in the West, heralding a new era of inventiveness in designs and techniques.

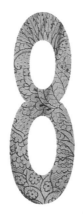

8
Silk
Weaving Comes to Europe

s knowledge of silk spread westward through the centuries, from the first domestication of Bombyx mori in ancient China, cultural development and political strength were expressed in the beauty of evolving designs and new steps in the development of weaving. The Moslem influences faded, and their place in the story of silk was taken by the merchants and weavers of Italy, who from the fourteenth to the sixteenth century controlled the silk trade and spectacularly developed silk weaving, notably velvet techniques. Although today the Italian silk production is centred in Milan and Como, historically the most important centres were Lucca, Venice, Florence and Genoa.

While there is documentary evidence for the importing and weaving of silk in Roman times, and the first silk trading centres were Amalfi, Venice and Lucca, the earliest attempts at sericulture were made in the Po Valley in the tenth century and in the area round Salerno during the first half of the eleventh century. The essentials of silk processing, and a few fundamental devices such as silk-reeling machinery, were known and used in the Byzantine and Islamic empires, and it seems that in southern Italy, most of the work of mulberry culture was carried out by Jewish, Greek and Arab immigrants who brought their expertise from the Near East.

It is likely that the art of silk weaving was introduced to Lucca, the first chief centre, by Jews from southern Italy. In the tenth century, Jewish weavers and dyers were living in Amalfi, Gaeta and Salerno, and in at least the first two cities were producing silk fabrics. There were Jews in Lucca from 1000 onward, indeed it was the most important Jewish centre north of Rome. In Sicily under Frederick II, Jews held monopolies in the dyeing industry and in the production of raw and woven silk in Palermo, Capua, Trani and Cosenza, and earlier, Roger II, the Norman king, had brought many silk technicians, including skilled Jewish dyers, to Sicily from the Byzantine lands of the Peloponnese and the Ionian islands (Pl. p. 153–5). By the time of the collapse of Frederick II's empire in 1250 Lucca's silk industry was already flourishing, but it is possible that Sicilian weavers who migrated to Lucca when the island came under Angevin rule in 1266 gave fresh impetus to the Lucchese silks, whose designs at that time combined elements from a variety of older styles: Byzantine, Sassanian, and Saracen.

Lucca, advantageously situated on the road to Pisa, Florence and Rome, had been a trade centre from Roman times. As Lucchese silk cloth was sold in substantial quantities in the medieval fairs of Champagne, her silk industry was evidently already well established by the period of their flourishing in the twelfth century. Early Lucchese designs showed strong eastern influence, with roundels and single animals of Persian and Byzantine origin, but these changed in the twelfth century to paired and stylized animals and birds, with a gradual phasing-out of enclosed framing. Lucchese weavers could make almost every kind of silk fabric known in the

Middle Ages, but a distinctive type of twelfth-century silk unmistakably attributable to Lucca is seen in narrow decorative bands woven with silk and gold in small repeating designs or motifs, often birds or animals, against a geometric or plain background, and an inscription. These were used for decorating garments and vestments, as seen in the textiles found in the tomb of Bernardo in Sta Trinità in Florence, dated to 1133. One of these strips of galon, for instance, has a repeat of waterbirds, perhaps swans, alternating with rosettes and leaf-like forms.

Inventories of the late thirteenth century list more sendals, samites, damasks, brocades, taffetas and baldachins (heavy silks brocaded with gold and silver and embellished with precious stones) from Lucca than from any other place – although many rival weaving centres, hoping to get good prices for their wares, passed them off as from Lucca. Lucchese fabrics were noted for their variety and quality, and most famous among the woven silks, because more attributable examples have survived, is her lampas or diasprum. This, another Eastern originated weave, apparently first developed in Persia (see p. 101), is a figured silk resembling damask in that the woven pattern is raised in relief from the background. It is usually monochrome, or monochrome with metal thread, but sometimes two-coloured, and favourite patterns included rows of birds or sometimes confronted pairs, especially eagles, peacocks, parrots and swans, alternating with rows of animals such as gazelles, griffons and lambs. Paired creatures frequently flanked a central palmette. Certain portions of these silks, such as the heads and feet of creatures, and roundels on birds' wings, are woven in gold.

The commercial success of Italian silks in the thirteenth century was aided by the difficulties facing the other regions producing silk fabrics at the period. Persia and Mesopotamia were suffering under Mongol invaders; Byzantium had been seized by Crusaders, and the Hohenstaufen reign in Sicily collapsed in the middle of the century. Italian cities were encouraged to tax the home production of silk, for they could still be certain to sell their silks and make large profits. In the thirteenth century medieval heraldry and Romanesque art began to influence Lucchese designs. Roundels gave way to lozenges, squares and diamonds, and animals were increasingly depicted free-standing, without a frame, a fashion developed from the preceding century. Castles often appear with fleurs-de-lys, and before the end of the century the first human figures, mounted knights reminiscent of stiffly carved medieval chessmen, are found in hunting scenes.

The rather static drawing of early Lucchese patterns gave way during the fourteenth century to a more and more fluid type of design, influenced by the Chinese silks of the Mongol Yuan dynasty, brought to the West during the period of the Pax Mongolica. Chinese flowering vines, lotus and peonies developed into the distinctive palmettes associated with the pomegranate patterned silks (Pl. p. 156). At the same time 'Gothic' motifs continued to appear, often combined with others of Eastern inspiration. Clouds and rays of sunshine gave emphasis to moated castles, feathery trees, fountains, tents, ships and water, huntresses, fluttering scarves and banners. For the first time, almost realistic human figures were depicted in woven silks, with the faces usually woven of white silk. These fall into two groups: religious subjects, and secular scenes such as hunting. To the long-familiar menagerie of eagles, lions, griffons, and so forth, new animals were added: some European, like the stag, bear, hunting dog and falcon; others, such as the dragon and *khilin*, from China, and these were less stylized, more lively, even depicted in realistic movement. Some Lucchese designs in the fourteenth century used bands of pseudo-Arabic calligraphy. However, unlike the Venetians, who always took pride in their ability to imitate oriental fabrics so skilfully that these copies were indistinguishable from the originals, the Lucchese modified oriental designs, adding elements of grace, originality and even humour.

An example of the competitiveness between city states and the way they guarded the secrets of their silk-weaving techniques is that of a Lucchese exile who brought the invention of the water-powered throwing-frame to Bologna in 1272 or 1276. He was honoured and rewarded by Bologna, while his effigy was ceremonially hanged in Lucca. The Lucca Statutes of the Arte della Seta, the silk weavers' guild, in 1308, prescribed that any man from Lucca engaging in the silk industry outside the precinct of the town should be strangled, and any woman burned.

Lucca's major contribution to the history of silk was already made by the early fourteenth century, when the Pisans sacked the city and many of her skilled textile workers were dispersed to other city states, notably Venice and Florence. Venice ensured the dependence of Lucchese refugees by means of loans which were to be repaid in Lucchese goods, thus eliminating any chance the weavers may have had of returning to their native city without incurring punishment. The Lucchese arrived destitute, and they were given looms and assigned a special quarter in the city.

The coronation mantle of Roger II of Sicily, an embroidered silk masterpiece from the royal workshops of Palermo, 1133–4. The victorious lion representing the Norman de Hauteville conquerors has subdued, but so far spared, the camel beneath its paws, which must surely represent Moslem Sicily. The fruitful date palm represents the island itself.

Below, left to right
Crimson and ivory silk lampas, *c.* 16th century, with the ancient pattern of paired beasts – in this case leopards – a Tree of Life and hunting-dogs and their prey. The silk may have been woven in Italy or Spain.

A handsome repeat of hawks with open wings within roundels, woven in 13th-century Italy. Hawking as the sport of kings and courtiers has been a theme of silks of all periods.

Crowing cockerels and roaring cockatrice, on a 13th-century silk attributed to Lucca's looms. The cockatrice, sometimes called basilisk, was a popular medieval composite beast, a mixture of serpent and winged dragon. Only three things could confound it, and one of these was a cock crowing.

155

Velvet robe patterned with lobed pomegranate palmettes, depicted in Gozzoli's fresco in the Palazzo Medici Riccardi in Florence, 1459–60. The central pomegranate shape has been opened so that it resembles a tulip or a lotus. In others of the so-called 'pomegranate silks' (*right*), the palmette appears but the pomegranate has vanished completely, or developed into a thistle, artichoke or pineapple. The red velvet (*right*), its motifs brocaded, is 16th century; the green (*far right*), 15th century, probably Venetian, is not brocaded, but its plain or voided areas have been embroidered with metal thread, the oldest method of enriching plain velvet, predating the eleborate brocaded weaves.

Intended for a table or sideboard in some palazzo, an embroidered silk cover of the 16th-17th century. The lively design includes many different types of flowers and fruits, birds, animals and insects (detail), and two-tailed sirens.

Knitted silk mitten, Italian or Sicilian, with silver and gold yarn. The back of the hands has a decoration of Chinese-cloud bands, in contrast to the geometrical pattern bands around the finger-joints and on the cuffs. Such knitted silk gloves often formed part of liturgical clothing.

An 18th-century Italian furnishing silk in the grand style, intended for curtains or upholstery

Detail of a magnificent 15th-century cope of Italian velvet cloth-of-gold, with sinuous stems surmounted by palmettes containing lotuses. Its orphreys are German embroideries, and the scale of the pattern and the richness of the cloth are both indications of extraordinary wealth.

Below Italian or Spanish cope, 15th century, of voided satin velvet. The familiar lobed palmettes no longer contain pomegranates, but instead suggest flowers on sinuous branches. The orphreys and hood are 16th-century Spanish work, embroidered in silk and silver-gilt thread.

While it is commonly believed that velvet was an Italian invention post-dating the start of the fifteenth century, and was a development of Venice, Florence and Genoa, mercantile documents show clearly that Lucca was producing a variety of sophisticated velvets before the end of the fourteenth century. Even earlier Islamic and French documents make reference to pile fabrics. It seems, however, that Italians devised the many techniques which enhanced looped-and-cut-pile cloth. The letters of the merchant Bartolomeo Balbani, for example, written in the 1390s to the Barcelona branch of Francisco Datini's company, contains glowing descriptions of velvets he was producing, and some twenty years earlier the inventory of the stock of a deceased Lucchese silk merchant lists velvets in two and three heights of pile – known as 'alto-e-basso', and particularly associated with Venice (Pl. p. 12) – and polychrome velvets in three, four or five colours of the type subsequently famous as 'velours de Gêne', or Genoese velvet (Ill. p. 167). There were cut and uncut velvets, monochrome velvet with the delicate, graceful tracery of design called 'ferronerie', and velvets brocaded with gold or silver. Listed among the dramatic polychrome velvets was one with a black ground on which red, blue and yellow flowers appear amidst a tracery of green leaves, and a crimson velvet with a floral design in a deeper shade of red mingled with yellow, black and green. Variously coloured stripes were also popular in the early velvets, though this taste faded as techniques for more complex patterning developed.

Velvet requires more yarn than any other weave, to achieve the rich lustrous pile which gives it its unique beauty, and cocoons produced in medieval Italy were never sufficient to satisfy the demands of her looms. Most of the imported raw silk came from the area around the Caspian Sea, notably Gilan and Georgia. This was transported to Genoese colonies on the Black Sea and then by sea to Genoa. During the thirteenth and fourteenth centuries silk also came from Soultanieh in Persia and Sogdiana in Turkestan. After Georgian silk, Syrian was the most popular, and the existence of Genoese and other Italian colonies in Syria during the thirteenth century explains the abundance of Syrian silk. The European part of the Byzantine Empire, known as 'Romania' in the Middle Ages, and the Iberian peninsula, were two principal regions for sericulture in Europe. Silk from Romania is frequently mentioned among Lucchese imports of the thirteenth and fourteenth centuries. Granada and Andalusia in Spain exported considerable quantities, but very little Spanish silk reached Lucca before the fifteenth century. There is no mention of the import of Sicilian silk, though some Lucchese merchants went to Sicily and even sold Lucchese silk fabrics there.

Raw silk and silk cloth travelled in long narrow canvas-wrapped and roped bales called fardels (Italian, *fardelli*, *torselli*) which often weighed about one hundred pounds, a convenient size and shape for pack animals to carry. The fardel was adopted as the emblem of the Lucchese silk merchants' guild. Although some

A charming 'boat design' such as often identifies Venetian silks specially woven for a patron, 14th-century brocade.

Opposite Designs for silks by Jacopo Bellini, 15th century.

Chinese silk reached Italy, it was generally less highly valued than that from the Caspian region or Georgia.

Never before had communication with China been as easy as in the years of the Pax Mongolica. This interlude of European access to East Asia was short; in 1368 the Chinese overthrew the Mongols and the new Ming dynasty began to close itself off from the West. Nevertheless its duration was dramatic and fruitful in terms of its exchange of ideas, influences and trade, and the most famous travellers were perhaps the Venetian Polos.

Nicolo and Maffeo Polo left Venice in 1255 and travelled for fourteen years through Asia, and then set out on a second journey in 1271 accompanied by Marco, who remained in the East until 1295. His vividly recorded experiences include lavish praise of the silks and carpets of the areas in which he travelled.

Venice had the closest ties with the East, and Venetian fabrics were among the most varied of all those made in Italy. Early silks were strongly Byzantine and Persian in their patterns, to satisfy the taste and desires of a clientèle accustomed to oriental designs.

Although the Venetians took pride in closely emulating silks from other centres, sometimes ship and boat designs identify cloth from Venice, and these have an individual charm which suggests they were privately commissioned. Venetian gold brocades were patterned with metal thread against a silk ground, and more sumptuous still was the famous 'drap d'or', or cloth-of-gold of Venice, where the background was woven in gold and the pattern in silk (Pl. p. 160). By the fifteenth century the Venetian silk industry had reached its peak of development, and artists like Jacopo Bellini designed patterns for the weavers.

In the mid-fifteenth century Venice became an important centre for velvet, and its looms produced the large, simple floral patterns which worked so well in velvet construction. Undulating panels with pomegranates or pine cones, bifurcating stems, and small blossoms lent themselves to three-dimensional pile surfaces. As techniques for combining gold and silver thread with silk pile developed, the taste for polychrome velvets gave way to monochrome ruby, violet, or blue as suitable foils for the rich metals. Subtle variations in tone were achieved by alto-e-basso pile in varying heights against satin or brocaded ground, and by brocading and looping the metal threads. So rare and valuable were these velvets that their owners would bequeath them to the Church, in common with jewels and other treasures. As specialization became even more pronouncd, velvet weavers separated from the other silk weavers to form a guild of their own, and this in turn was divided into five further branches, each with its own tests for Masters of specialized skills, and St Mark was adopted as the guild's patron saint.

At a different level, Venice protected her home market by prohibiting the importation of foreign silks and promoting the export of her own silks. This

regulation was evaded by having cheap silk fabrics woven in neighbouring towns and tailoring them into garments to be smuggled into Venice on the backs of her citizens. In turn the Senate responded by forbidding the manufacture of silks in the mainland towns of the Republic.

Venetian skill in imitating oriental factors was enhanced by various colonies of foreign merchants and tradesmen, such as Turks from the Ottoman empire, who settled and worked in their own quarter, the Fondaco dei Turchi. The Venetians had had a colony in Pera in Constantinople since Byzantine times, and in the fifteenth century, Scutari, across the water from Constantinople, was a Venetian trading centre. Textiles were woven in Scutari until the end of the Ottoman rule, and early examples display a strong Italian influence but with a certain rigidity of design, incorporating Turkish and Venetian motifs such as tulips, cintamani (triple-dots), and ogival repeats joined through crowns (Pl. p. 12). Scutari velvets, whether Venetian or Ottoman, were never as fine or sumptuous as the products of looms working under court patronage.

In Europe generally, until the beginning of the sixteenth century large-patterned silks were used for every purpose, for clothes and for furnishings. During the sixteenth century patterns became differentiated according to purpose. The so-called Spanish costume, black, gave rise to a preference for small and relatively discreet patterns, while the rise of a rich merchant class created a demand for luxurious wall-decoration and upholstery. Scattered patterns were known in Italy in the fifteenth century, though not common, and in the sixteenth century this type of design was usually a series of stylized flowers on a short twig, in asymetrical arrangements and small repeats, executed in brocade and satin-ground velvet.

Political decline led inevitably to that of the industry, and even in the sixteenth century signs of the slow shrinkage of the Venetian silk industry became apparent. Venice continued to hold her own for more than a century, but the Venetian ambassador to Paris correctly prophesied the future of silk when he remarked in 1546 that the French always preferred lighter and less durable fabrics than the Venetians, and that they soon tired of wearing costumes of the same materials.

The silk industry of Florence in the thirteenth century became famous for crimson-dyed sendal used in dresses and linings and for banners. Obtained from kermes, this crimson dye gave the softest, most sumptuous depths to velvet pile, a regal contrast to gold. In the fourteenth century the city received its share of the Lucchese weavers who fled there and settled, and became a great centre. As elsewhere in Europe, sumptuary laws were issued from time to time, which, however, were largely ignored, especially by women. The philosophy of the Florentine was quite straightforward: to be rich was honourable, to be poor disgraced. Gregorio Dati, one of Florence's international silk merchants, went so far as to say, 'A Florentine who is not a merchant, who has not travelled through the world, seeing foreign nations, and peoples, and then returned to Florence with some wealth, is a man who enjoys no esteem whatsoever.' Having acquired riches the merchant must not be chary of spending them. Giovanni Rucellai's enormous fortune was based on the famous Florentine red-purple dye, oricello, obtained from a species of Mediterranean seaweed, from which his family derived their name, and he declared that he had done himself much more honour 'by having spent money well than by having earned it'.

Information about the silk trade and silks in the fourteenth century came to light with the papers of Francesco di Marco Datini. Datini was a successful merchant and native of Prato, a city near Florence, who preserved every letter and business document he received, told the managers of all his branches to do likewise, and in his Will, provided for all these papers to be collected and preserved in his house, where they lay undisturbed for some three hundred years. They present a remarkable picture of commercial activity between Datini's branches in Avignon, Prato, Florence, Pisa, Genoa, Barcelona, Valencia, Majorca and Ibiza. His private correspondence conveys such details as the order for silks for his wife's wedding gown, which was crimson samite for three and a half florins a braccio, and white damask for two and a half florins.

Between 1463 and 1479 a state of war between the Ottomans and the Venetians allowed the Florentines to develop their own trading relationship with the Ottoman Empire. Letters written by Francesco Maringhi, who looked after the commercial interests of the great Florentine family the Medici, mentions their commerce with Bursa, the Ottoman entrepôt for raw and woven silk, and a Florentine treatise on the arts of silk weaving confirms that the city wove silks specifically for export to the Turkish market in the fifteenth century. Italian silk-weaving technology was important in enabling the Ottomans to develop their own silk production, and Italian influence is evident in many Turkish silks. Unfortunately descriptions of these silks, both in Italian documents and Ottoman, are frequently too ambiguous to enable them to be positively identified. In terms of pattern influence, it may be significant that the earliest-known woven representation of the famous Turkish tulip is an Italian, not a Turkish, silk.

Perspective, explored in the paintings of the Renaissance, was explored in silks too, and the alto-e-basso velvets, with their differing depths of pile, and combinations of textures such as velvets on satin or gold-brocaded ground, enriched with gold and silver loops, gave depth and shimmer to the silks as they reflected light.

The Bronzino portrait of Eleanor of Toledo in Florence (Pl. p. 13) shows her wearing exquisite black and white silk, the weaving highlighted with gold, enriched even further by the addition of gold and silver cord. This was her wedding dress, which was also to be her shroud. Opinions vary as to whether the silk was Florentine, and, as some suggest, commissioned by her husband Cosimo de Medici

The scene of St Augustine being consecrated Bishop, showing embroidered orpheys.

The stiff, heavily gold-brocaded silk cape of Spanish and Italian fashion: a portrait of Prince Alexander Farnese by Coello, *c*. 1560.

whom she married in 1539, or whether it was a Spanish silk brought in her dowry. A hint might be read in the discovery in St Olaf Church, Nörrkoping, of a cope of the same material, decorated with embroideries that are probably Italian.

The height of development of Florentine weaving coincided with the appearance of a motif sometimes called a pineapple (a fruit from the New World), sometimes an artichoke or thistle, and sometimes (as in the papal inventories) a pine cone. It was combined with floral motifs, pomegranates, and great serpentine curves to make dramatic velvets and brocades, frequently depicted as backdrops in paintings of the Madonna and Child, or portraits of rich patrons.

Florence was also famous for its orpheys, ecclesiastical vestment bands illustrating sacred subjects. The most commonly depicted scenes were the Annunciation, the Crucifixion, and the Nativity. Woven orpheys were a substitute for more costly embroidered versions of the fourteenth century, and they were woven several bands wide, then cut into strips. Brocatelle construction, with silk and gold weft on linen warp, made the pattern stand out. Fine tapestries were also woven in Florence, of wool, with silk and gold and silver highlights, but the city is best known for her great silks of the Quattrocento and the Renaissance, worn proudly by the elegant and noble, and so carefully depicted in paintings and frescoes (Pl. p. 156). The sixteenth-century silks are typified by ogival patterns of curvilinear branches containing pomegranate motifs, and the sixteenth and seventeenth century saw these extend into variations based on central floral motifs with symmetrically paired curved volutes and branches, and patterns composed of a vase and ogival pomegranate motif.

The fourth great silk centre, Genoa, grew to mercantile importance in the Middle Ages. The Genoese appear to have been as prominent in the trade with China as they were in Persia. However, constant warfare prevented the city reaching her potential until the fifteenth and sixteenth centuries, when the Genoese were the principal bankers of southern Europe and controlled the Spanish trade by controlling monetary and credit systems. By the late sixteenth century Genoa, like Milan, was an important lace-making centre, and some of her laces were made from silk.

Although she was not alone in producing this type of silk, Genoa was famous for, and gave her name to, polychrome velvets, 'velours de Gêne', patterned with large S-curves over voided grounds, and 'jardinière' or 'garden velvets', with large multi-coloured floral designs, popular for wall-coverings and furnishing fabrics. These furnishing velvets were often reinforced by a coarse weft (waste silk, linen or hemp) which was visible on the surface of the fabric. Alto-e-basso velvet was woven, as well as voided and plain pile, and another speciality of Genoa was 'ferronerie', a voided velvet named for its pattern, which is reminiscent of wrought-iron work. Genoa also made ciselé velvet, where selected parts of the pattern were left looped and other parts cut to achieve pile.

The famous velvet to which Genoa gave her name: 'velours de Gêne', in the type of pattern known as a 'garden velvet', 16th-17th century.

Where Venice relied for raw silk on the Levant, Genoese sources included Calabria, Spain and Sicily until the sixteenth century. Genoa's looms processed more wool than silk, but by 1531 the position was reversed and some two thousand silk weavers were listed, compared with only four hundred for wool. By the end of the sixteenth century Genoa's production exceeded that of Lucca and Venice.

It is said that the Doge of Venice, Antoniotto Adorno, declared in 1523 to the Maona of Chios, the organization which controlled the great commercial monopolies of that island, that the art of silk was more than the right eye, it was the soul of his time. This soul, above all, was coloured black. Through marriage, Naples had been ruled by the court of Aragon, and black, the official colour of the Spanish court and the Inquisition, became fashionable throughout Europe for both men and women. Apart from her velvets, Genoa was famous for her black silks, with small discreet patterns.

While the south of Spain was under Moorish domination (see pages 102–10), areas of southern France and northern Italy, and notably Sicily, Genoa and Naples, were under Spanish rule from time to time, and Spanish and Italian silks of the fourteenth to sixteenth centuries resembled each other, both displaying large-scale stately designs combining late Gothic and Renaissance elements: pomegranates, pine cone and artichoke forms, palmettes and broad undulating bands. Although Granada was named for the pomegranate, in the fourteenth century Toledo was famous for pomegranate-patterned silks. During the period of the Pax Mongolica Chinese motifs were adopted into the design repertoire of Spanish as well as Italian weavers. In the late fifteenth century a group of Italian craftsmen, including Lucchese and Genoese master weavers, emigrated to Barcelona to open a workshop there, and the influence of Lucca can be seen in the various winged creatures, including dogs – never found on Islamic silks – in certain Spanish silks of this period. A list of accredited craftsmen in Valencia in 1479 includes weavers from Venice, Florence, Lucca and Lombardy.

In contrast to the large regal patterns, a small-scale repeating spot or circle, often containing a pointed star, woven in velvet or gold brocade, was popular in Spain, notably in the fifteenth century, for doublets and breeches worn under armour or half-armour. The pattern is reminiscent of brigandine, a form of armour composed of overlapping metal or leather 'scales' covered with cloth.

As silk became more readily available to Spanish weavers, Spanish velvet was made with pure silk pile with voided satin areas, and further enriched with a variety of new techniques, especially in the use of gold. Before the discovery of the New World, the Mediterranean's source of gold was Africa, while the most famous gold thread was processed in Cyprus. When the *Madre de Dios* with her cargo was captured by the English off the Azores in 1592: 'the principall wares after the jewels . . . consisted of spices, drugges, silkes, calicos, quilts, carpets and colours . . . the silkes [being] damasks, taffatas, sarcenets, altobassos, that is, counterfeit cloth of gold, unwrought China silke, sleaved silke, white twisted silke, curled cypresse'. 'Curled cypresse' is *oro de chypre*: thin gold wrapped round silk thread; and 'altobassos', here called 'counterfeit cloth of gold', probably indicates, not velvet cut with several levels of pile, the usual meaning of the term, but fine loops of gold in up to three different sizes. In another technique of the fifteenth and sixteenth centuries, gold threads were couched in the grooves made by cut voided velvets.

Spanish sumptuary laws at the end of the sixteenth century attempted to curb both importation of cheaper foreign silks and the extravagant use of gold and silk cloth. Exempt from the decrees were the Church, war veterans, and women who were 'publicamente malas', that is, prostitutes. This last clause is likely to have been effective where other means failed, and doubtless caused many a virtuous wife a great deal of frustration.

By the early seventeenth century high taxation, cheap imports, the banishment of skilled craftsmen and merchants – Jews in 1492, *Moriscos* in 1609–1614 – and the emigration of enterprising men to the Americas had weakened the Spanish economy and contributed to the decline in silk production. By 1662 when Philip IV forbade embroidered dress, the great heyday of Spanish silks was over.

At the end of the seventeenth century Savary's famous *Dictionnaire de Commerce* summed up a change: 'Although Italy still exported large quantities of gold and silk fabrics to France, Italian persons of rank preferred to buy from France the elegant silk for their clothing.' Fashion, the sustaining force of French silks, drew silk weavers to leave Italy, and the French silk industry was founded on Italian expertise. One of the emigrés was Claude Dangon of Milan, who went to Lyon to teach technical methods and is credited with inventing, or at least introducing, an improved drawloom. French silk manufacture and fashion had begun to dominate European society, and though Spanish and Italian looms continued to produce some exquisite silks, the patterns were French in appearance, following a mode-conscious clientèle's changing moods and tastes for *chinoiserie*, rococo, bizarre and so forth. Not until the twentieth century, with haute couture, were the other nations of Europe to resume a prominent role in silk design.

9 French Style

It was to be many centuries

before silk was produced in France, and silk weaving did not become an important industry until relatively recent times, but as an imported fabric it was long known and treasured. In fifth-century Arles, the court wondered at fine silks patterned in the Sassanian style with mounted huntsmen and animals, and at his court in Toulouse, Theodoric II reserved precious purple-dyed silk couch-covers for state occasions. Imported woven silks were known as 'étoffes d'outre-mer'. *Outre-mer*, literally 'beyond the sea', denoted lands of the East, which by the time of the Crusades narrowed to specify Palestine and Syria.

Silk yarns too were imported, and treasured as embroidery threads to highlight wool and linen. The author of 'Berthes au Gran Piès' pointedly praises the embroidery skills of this legendary figure, the mother of Charlemagne, and although her devotion to the needle might be a poetic exaggeration, it was expected of all women, whatever their status, that they have textile skills. Charlemagne himself received lavish gifts of regal silks from Byzantine rulers and from Haroun al-Rashid, the Caliph of Baghdad, whose fabled court in the eighth century inspired the tales of One Thousand and One Nights. The cape in Metz Cathedral known as the Mantle of Charlemagne post-dates his period, and is in fact a twelfth-century Byzantine eagle silk, brought back from the Crusaders' sack of Constantinople (Ill. p. 92), but among the silks preserved at Aachen are some presented to him by the Caliph. Other silks, gifts to monasteries, survived as covers for religious books, or interleaving the illuminated pages of manuscripts.

Charlemagne's cousin or niece, Aye of Avignon, and her contemporary Blanchefleur, wore robes of 'porpola', a silk woven in Almeria and considered the height of elegance in France, while lengths of silk were so valuable that King Egfried paid two lengths of silk to St Benedict Biscop, the abbot of an English monastery, as the purchase price for lands. The payments were most probably robe-lengths, rather than whole bolts of richly patterned brocade, and were possibly gold-worked, of the type deemed worthy for church vestments. Imported silks have been church treasures since Merovingian times; in Chinon, an Islamic silk woven with chained leopards and an Arabic inscription of benediction (May God Bless and Protect the owner of this cloth) was used to wrap the relics and cover the tomb of St Etienne. The shroud of St Germain in Auxerre is one of the finest Byzantine eagle silks to have survived (Pl. p. 84), and other early silks to have been preserved in the same way include the shroud of St Colombe at Sens, and the chasuble of St Regnobert in Bayeux. Many oriental silks were brought back by Crusaders, and we learn that '53 saintures de soie' were brought back from Jerusalem by a certain Monsieur Gui of Marmontier. In this instance 'saintures' (belts or sashes) describes unsewn lengths.

Gregory of Tours was as passionate about the arts as he was about religion, and his writings frequently mention silken veils, 'pallia serica', which decorated the tombs

Patteur sur la tenue de Canitie sur les lices

of the pious, and altarcloths and orphreys, stressing that these were sometimes of pure silk, 'holoserica,' enriched with gold and precious stones. It was not uncommon for rich garments to be bequeathed to the Church, and these were unpicked and reshaped as altar cloths and vestments. The Abbey of St Martin at Tours was famous for its Treasury, therefore undoubtedly an attraction for the Moors, whose northward advance was halted by Charles Martel ('The Hammer') in 732 just outside the city.

The medieval age of chivalry was an age of silk. Epic poems and chansons telling of gallantry and heroic deeds were circulated by wandering troubadours; tournaments were bedecked with silk-hung tents and banners, and rich silks caparisoned the horses. Over their armour, the knights jousting wore silk 'joupons', tunics embroidered or appliqué with heraldic devices and colours, and they received a silken sleeve or veil as a 'gage', a token of her honour from the lady symbolically defended in the joust. The banners, joupons, horse-trappings, saddlery, tents, and all the fineries of battle and display were stitched by the 'brodereurs'. In later centuries the traditions of these skilled embroiderers and craftsworkers were adapted to produce specialized furnishings, saddlery, and coats of arms for ceremonial displays.

The medieval period also saw the development of trade and the rise of a rich merchant class. Silk was traded in the fairs which were held all over Europe, and the most famous of these were those of the Champagne region which commenced as early as the fifth century. The silk came in two forms: as hanks which would be dyed and used for embroidery, or woven, as decorative stripes and motifs to enliven linen or wool or as already woven stuffs. The woven silks included plain fabrics (taffetas, sendal, and so forth), and patterned (brocade, damask, etc.), and those striped silks or silk-and-cotton mixed fabrics which were always popular with Near Eastern weavers. Fairs were spread throughout the year so that merchants could attend more than one of them, and they were carefully structured. Each lasted for forty-six days,

Silk trappings for the horses and hangings for the stands add colour and splendour to a scene of jousting, from a 15th-century manuscript.

A rare, early, 14th-century French embroidery depicting 'The Return of the Hunter', worked in silk with gold and silver thread on silk velvet. The panel is one of a series of scenes of aristocratic life and pursuits.

Women collecting cocoons from a mulberry tree, and weaving silk, from a 15th-century French manuscript illumination of Boccaccio's *De Claris Mulieribus*.

divided into three trading periods, the first for cloth, the second for leather, and the last for 'other goods'. The twelfth and thirteenth centuries saw their height of posperity and influence, and at this time, commerce between France and Sicily, Italy, Constantinople and the Levant flourished.

Apart from the demands of royal courts, the Church was the most important customer for silks. Precious woven stuffs were used as wrappings for relics of saints, which were so numerous in medieval times that they were akin to tourist souvenirs, *de rigueur* for any traveller returning from the Holy Lands.

Some of the trading centres established by fairs became famous for their locally produced textiles, and workers' guilds were formed to regulate production. Roman weavers (that is, weavers from Egypt and Syria under Roman rule) and Byzantine weavers and embroiderers had worked under this system of specialized guilds for centuries – indeed, from the earliest days – and the custom was adopted by the conquering Arabs who took over Byzantine lands and weavers. The silk weavers formed guilds earlier than the embroiderers, who, although well organized with statutes dating from 1292, did not form a guild in Paris until 1471, and it has been suggested that this might be explained by an influx of weavers from Sicily (after the Norman conquest of the island from the Arabs) or from Byzantium after the First Crusade in 1096, or the Crusaders' sack of the city in 1209.

Weavers moved from one centre to another, usually propelled by political upheavals and economic pressures, and naturally continued to weave their accustomed repertoire. It is therefore often impossible to identify the exact origin of many silks, particularly when there is no weaver's mark, special local dye, or distinctive regional pattern.

Etienne Boileau's *Livre des Metiers* (Book of the Looms) published in Paris in 1258–68, records that silk weavers 'sont assez nombreux pour meritez un reglement corporatif' (were sufficiently numerous to make it worth their while to establish corporate rules), and that these silk workers included 'mestier des tissus de soie' (master weavers of patterned silks) and 'mestiers des draps de soie de Paris et de vuluyaux et de boursserie enlice' (master weavers of plain silks, velvets, and decorative trimmings). These silk workers in Paris are sometimes referred to as 'Sarazines', a term which suggests that they might indeed have been from Arab (or 'Saracen') Sicily, and tapestry weavers were known as 'faiseurs de tapis Sarazinois' (makers of Saracen carpets or tapestries), a term associating the technique with the fine silk, gold, silver and linen tapestry bands woven in oriental tiraz workshops. Indeed, a medieval romance, 'Le Chevalier au Lion' (The Knight of the Lion) describes some three hundred 'pucelles' or young girls: 'qui diverse oevres fesoient/ De fil d'or et de soie ovroient . . .' (who made various things/Working with gold thread and silk) – an image which strongly evokes some oriental palace workshop exactly like those inherited by the Norman conquerors of Sicily.

A scene at the court of Charles the Bold, Duke of Burgundy, from a 15th-century manuscript, showing a glorious silk of the period forming the baldequin in the background. Although there was already silk-weaving in the papal city of Avignon by the 14th century, production was limited, and France's great silk-weaving tradition not yet established. The baldequin illustrates the type of silk keenly sought by the northern courts, and imported by the influential merchants of Lyon and Flanders.

Opposite An illumination from a chivalric romance, the *Chronicle of Renault de Montauban*, depicting the young knight Renault and his bride Clarisse de Gascoyne in the bridal chamber. A detail of Clarisse's dress (*inset*) shows the type of rich silk a 15th-century lady would select for her best gown.

During the 18th century, Lyon in particular set the fashion, and exported far afield. Patterns that mixed fantasy with realistic motifs in witty juxtapositions developed into the complex and wonderful creations known as 'bizarre' silks (*left*). By 1728 (*far left*), fashion decreed gowns with full, soft folds, and delicate designs of scattered sprigs or floral bouquets.

The 18th-century rococo silks mix architectural and garden elements in surprising, almost dream-like combinations. *Far left* A huntsman and his hound set off from little pavilions which have an oriental air, inspired by the fashion for *chinoiserie*. *Above* An oriental tent, a triumphal archway, and a crown or headdress of ostrich plumes combine in a romantic satin brocaded with metal threads. *Left* A chasuble is brocaded with meandering, beribboned bouquets and crumbling ruins.

Guillaume de Hangest, Provost of Paris in 1303, approved regulations stipulating
that anyone doing gold thread work must sew with silk, obviously an example of
quality control; and merchants maintained control of the spinning, weaving and
embroidery of silk by a system termed 'verleger', used all over Europe. The workers
were provided with yarn and a part-wage, the balance being paid on delivery of the
finished work. Workers had thus no chance to accumulate capital and become
independent. A document of the Provost of Merchants in Paris in June 1275,
expressly 'forbade the spinsters of silk to pawn the silk the mercers give them to
work, or to sell or exchange it, under pain of banishment'.

An important use for silk was as woven ribbons and galon (trimmings) and a guild
of ribbon weavers was established in Rouen as early as 1290. There was no changing
fashion as we know it today, and clothes were recut, or given a new lease of life with
trimmings, until the fabric expired.

As international trade developed, and was increasingly conducted by correspondence as banking systems became more sophisticated, the importance of itinerant
merchants and fairs decreased. Textile production was often centred on the
monasteries, and when in 1308 the Papal seat was transferred to Avignon (at that
time just outside the kingdom of France), Pope Clement V commanded that
mulberry trees be planted around the city so that the requirements for silk could be
met locally. It is not known whether sericulture had been introduced to France
earlier than this, nor from where the seeds, plants and technology were imported;
but the Church connection and Avignon's physical proximity to Italy suggest this as
the most probable source. The city became famous for its silks, especially its velvets.
Documents record, for instance, an order for ten lengths of red satin purchased in
1399 from Avignon looms by Lyonnais city officials to make up into their robes of
office; and the 1408 inventory of the Duchess of Orleans specifies velvet hangings
woven in Avignon. In the mid-fifteenth century a special palace, 'la petite Fusterie',
was the heart of this silk commerce. During the sixteenth century, velvet weaving
was thriving there and Avignon velvets were considered to be as fine as those of
Genoa. However, the population of Avignon and the surrounding area was
decimated by plague around 1722, and the silk industry never fully recovered.

About the same time as sericulture was begun in Provence, it was introduced to
the Cevennes area, and this centre continues to produce silk the present day,
although on a relatively small scale. The wives of silk-producers no longer follow the
ancient custom of wearing, suspended between their breasts, little pouches
containing silkworm eggs in order to keep them protected and warm until they hatch
and are transferred to their feeding trays. Body heat is ideal for hatching purposes,
but nowadays incubators are used.

Today Lyon is the heart of French silk manufacture and processing, and has been
so for several centuries. However when Louis XI first attempted to establish

domestic silk manufacturing in Lyon in 1466, the merchants and bankers of the city, who made handsome profits from imported silks, resisted the conditions Louis tried to impose to ensure the success of the industry. The Lyonnais also profited from trade with the rich and proud neighbouring Burgundian dukedoms (Pl. p. 174), whose lands included Flanders and most of present-day Belgium, and so it came about that the first royal warrant for manufacture, in 1470, was for Tours, close to Bourges, where the court, in exile from Paris which was held by the English, then resided. The merchants of Tours in turn objected to the King's conditions, but this time were persuaded by the promise that profit from silk production would be for the city, and that any losses incurred would be borne by the Crown. Behind the King's project for Tours lies the colourful story of Jacques Coeur and the intrigues and power struggles of the French court.

Coeur was a native of Bourges, a self-made merchant prince who rose to the powerful position of Minister of Finance to Louis's father, Charles VII. Coeur's fortune was made through trading with the East, control of mines and the mint, and supplying the needs of the King and his court. Since both King and court borrowed great sums of money from Coeur, his monopoly of their custom was assured. His vessels sailed east and south to China, India, Damascus, Alexandria, west to Sicily, Spain, and north to Scotland, carrying silks and spices, jewels, arms and metals.

Not content with silk-importing, Coeur established a partnership in Florence to manufacture as well as trade in silks, and in November 1446 he was accepted as a fully accredited member, a 'setaiulo grosso', by the formidable silk weavers' guild, the Arte della Seta.

Not only the court of Charles VII but the King and Queen too became financially indebted to Coeur beyond hope of repayment. Plotting secured Coeur's downfall after the accession to the throne of Charles's son Louis. Coeur was tried for poisoning the King's mistress, Agnes Sorel, and sentenced; his wealth was confiscated by the Crown, and all debts were cancelled. The court lost, at the same time, its assured and constant source of luxury goods. There followed the beginnings of an independent silk production under the aegis of a king who was Coeur's enemy.

The town records of Tours list the salaries, skills and names of the first silkworkers, who included two master weavers and a skilled silk-dyer, and were all Italian. The silks of Tours resembled typical contemporary Italian patterns: the large, bold, regal repeats incorporating palmettes, artichokes, pineapples, pomegranates, in diapered or ogee format, or set in bold sinuous meanders, the silk thread richly coloured and highlighted with gold and silver, which are illustrated in paintings of the time (Pl. p. 175). The 'soieries Tourangelles', the silks of Tours, became famous, and gros de Tours, a strong heavy taffeta with a double weft and an interesting raised-surface texture, was copied by other silk-weaving centres.

A 16th-century Flemish *mille-fleurs* tapestry showing the Fates. The figures are dressed in patterned silk brocades and moiré, represented here in tapestry-weave.

The snobbery which at first attached superior qualities to imported silks was eventually overcome. The price of imported silks was prohibitive in any case, and supply was not dependable due to continual wars and political unrest in France and the silk-producing Italian states, Sicily (at this time French-held), Spain, and the Near and Far East. When the King of Portugal was welcomed into the city in 1476, the ceremonial draperies and banners were of Tours manufacture, and it was the looms of Tours which furnished the silks for the royal wedding of the Dauphin to Margaret of Austria in 1483.

By 1550, silk weaving was supporting half the population of Tours, which then had eighty thousand inhabitants. When Mary Queen of Scots entered the city on 1 October 1548, she was received on a dais decked with gold-banded crimson damask, and on the occasion of her marriage the city of Tours made a wedding gift of dozens of lengths of silks, including taffetas of her favourite colours: crimson, violet and black. However, it was not until 1602 that silkworms began to be cultivated locally in the park of the Chateau de Plessis-de-Tours, and up to that time the city was entirely dependent on the importers of Lyon for its supplies of raw silk.

Silk was desired not only for robes and garments, but for all manner of decorative purposes: for hangings and furnishings for all courtly functions and receptions, and all Church functions and ceremonies. Castle rooms and beds were hung with textiles, for decoration and for warmth. Embroidery skills were as important as weaving skills. The poems and stories of mythology, the Bible, chivalry and romance provided pictorial themes, and the language of symbols was all-important. A *mille-fleur* (literally, thousand flowers, referred to the ground design, which was covered with realistic and identifiable flowering plants) tapestry or embroidery was more than a pretty backdrop: certain recurring motifs can be recognized, and their significance be understood. The rose, the carnation or pink, the pomegranate, a fountain, unicorn, stag, lion, have both religious and secular meanings. In times

Dress-silk of Chinese figured-silk damask, imported into France where it was painted around 1780. At the top, a petal-crowned figure, possibly Flora, floats on a cloud, surrounded by the blooms of summer.

Detail of the scene at the Field of the Cloth of Gold, 1520.

when reading skills were for the privileged, the language of symbols held great power and was far reaching.

One of the great achievements of François I was the building of Fontainebleau and its costly and luxurious furnishings. François himself loved to wear rich silks and satins, while the women of the court were gorgeously clad in dresses heavy with gold. The event of the century took place in 1520, when François met Henry VIII of England at the Field of the Cloth of Gold near Calais. Even the sails on Henry's ships were of cloth of gold, and his vast tents were hung with gold and silver brocades and rich tapestries. For two weeks the kings and their courts paraded in extravagant finery, changing their garments several times a day. Realizing that the economy of his kingdom suffered from the costs of importing Spanish, Italian and Flemish fabrics, François determined to expand French home-production of silk, and to establish silk weaving in Lyon. In 1531 he reconfirmed the city's envied privilege as the only authorized 'bonded warehouse' for all silks, including gold brocades, velvets, satins and taffetas from Italy, Spain and Provence, all of which had to pass through the Lyon Customs to be stamped with their mark to show that duty had been paid.

Ideally situated on land and water crossroads, Lyon is a commercial heart whose arteries lead everywhere. Many of its bankers and merchants were Italians from the silk cities of Lucca, Genoa, Venice and Florence, and had a vested interest in protecting the lucrative import of foreign silks and yarn. However the success of Tours had diminished foreign monopoly, and in 1536 François I granted privileges and support to two Italian merchants, Etienne Turquet and Paule Nariz, to bring looms and machinery from Italy and to start manufacturing silk in Lyon. The Massacre of St Bartholomew in 1572 marked the start of religious persecutions that climaxed with the Revocation of the Edict of Nantes in 1685, and both of these events forced major exoduses of Huguenot Protestants, among them skilled weavers and silk designers. Turmoil in France contributed to the decline of the French silk industry, but before this time, Lyon had embarked on a course of competition with Tours, and the famous silks had begun to slither and rustle off Lyonnais looms.

This new industry was protected by the imposition of high duties on foreign imports. The silk-weavers were locally called 'canuts', after the special machines for cutting the pile of velvets, and the weaving quarter developed in the Croix Rousse on the bank of the Rhône, a hilly area of narrow lanes, closely built houses, hidden tunnels and passages that enabled silks to be carried from building to building protected from inclement weather. In 1540 a Silk Weavers' Association was formed, headed by Turquet and master weaver Rollet Viard, a Lyonnais by origin who had twelve velvet looms operational in Avignon. These he transferred to Lyon, and the following year built a further forty-six looms, twenty-six for velvet and the rest for taffetas.

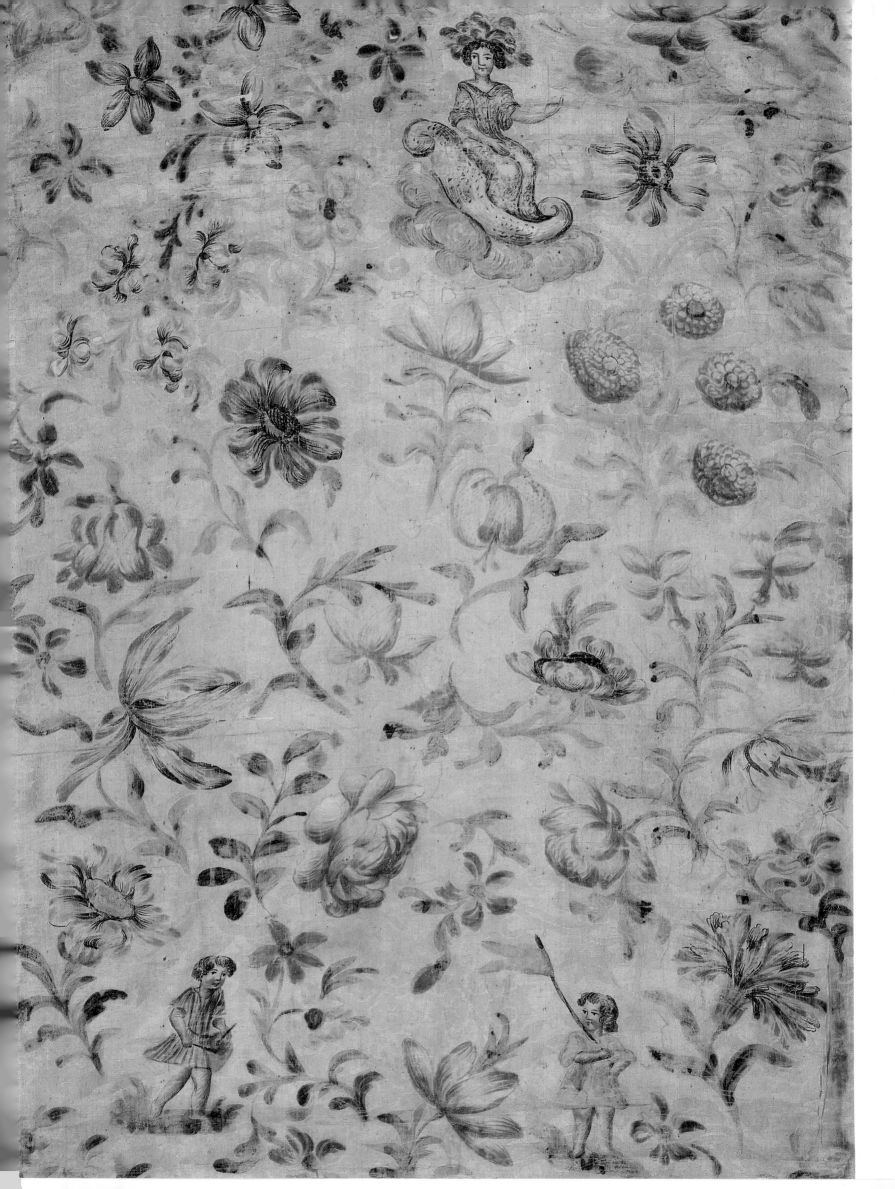

As with Tours, the early silks of Lyon followed the Italian Renaissance style, with large regal patterns influenced by the tastes and demands of the court and the Church, and used for dress and furnishings without noticeable differentiation, although towards the end of the sixteenth century designers started to scale down the proportions of patterns on silks that could be specified as being for clothing. Stripes, small checks, and spot motifs were woven in various techniques including velvets. The invention of new weaves allowed more variety in weight and thickness, and French silk-production concentrated on stimulating the concept of fashion with the constant creation of new costume-materials for society and the court.

When Henri IV came to power at the end of the sixteenth century, he encouraged sericulture in an attempt to make France independent of imported yarns. Thousands of mulberry trees were planted, and silk seed was distributed. Towards the end of the seventeenth century skilled Italian craftsmen were enticed to France, and one of these was the weaver Claude Dangon of Milan, who introduced the loom, already mentioned, known as the 'métier à la grande tire', which expanded the possibilities of drawloom weaving techniques. As Italian silk technology was the most advanced, it seems probable that this was a type of loom already in use in Italy.

The 1660s were a period of drastic reforms, as Colbert, Louis XIV's Minister of Finance, carried out his reorganization of industry. His programme of 1667 stipulated that manufacturers were to produce new patterns every year, and by the end of the seventeenth century new patterns were being produced twice yearly. The demand for talented and trained textile designers was unprecedented. These designers were often also the factory owners, for a knowledge of weaving techniques as well as skilled draughtsmanship, imagination, and a sense of fashion were all required.

Although silks are not usually dated, pattern drawings often are, and some of these drawings, now in the Victoria and Albert Museum, were brought by Huguenot refugees from France to Spitalfields in London (p. 207).

It has been suggested that the general view that the Revocation of the Edict of Nantes in 1685 was a disaster for the French silk industry has exaggerated its effect, and that the number of silk weavers was few compared with the overall number of Huguenot refugees.

The later seventeenth century saw a taste for all manner of floral motifs and fantastic vegetation in asymmetrical compositions. There was experimentation with metallic effects, and inventiveness in combining different lampas and brocading techniques, adding extra wefts and floats. Towards the end of the century designers introduced perspective into their patterns, creating an illusion of depth. These complex images resulted in the 'bizarre' silks, and the so-called lace-silks which developed simultaneously. In the bizarre silks, there is no particular direction of images, no 'top' or 'bottom', and the elements of fantasy are mixed with realistic

The young Marie-Antoinette, portrayed by Drouais wearing the lace-patterned silks and silk laces of the 1740s.

Above right Floral patterns of brocaded satin on a *chaise-longue* bearing the arms of the Marquise de Pompadour, *c.* 1750.

motifs in inventive and often witty juxtapositions (Pl. p. 177). Santina Levy has demonstrated how these bizarre silks became transformed into the meshes of the lace-patterned silk under the influence of the two-way East-West exchange of ideas at that time (*chinoiserie, les Indiens*). However, the laces of the period bore no resemblance to the hatched, meshed, serpentine designs that developed in the so-called lace-pattern silks (Pl. p. 202).

True lace with silk-like patterns and elaborate mesh filling belong to the late 1720s, the 1730s and the 1740s. The French and English silk weavers and the Flemish bobbin lacemakers served the same fashionable clientèle, and therefore aimed to produce complementary textiles, but their designs sprang from different traditions. The French needle-lace industry had suffered a set-back from the changing winds of early eighteenth-century fashion, when taste turned away from elaborate laces to light ruffles and gauzy fabrics and sought inspiration from French silks. For a period during the 1720s silk designs were reproduced in lace. The resulting elaborate lace fillings were in their turn borrowed back by the silk designers, and formalized in the late lace-patterned silks. Their ways soon parted again, but since the delicate diapers of the silks had by then become the hallmark of the mid-eighteenth-century laces, it is not surprising that, to later observers, it seemed as if the silks had emulated the laces, rather than the other way round.

Bizarre and lace-patterned silks were popular from the end of the seventeenth to the middle of the eighteenth century, apparently developing side-by-side, through abstract, exuberant, and increasingly naturalistic phases, until they were ousted by the fully naturalistic designs of the early 1730s. Although bizarre silks were manufactured in many different places, the genre undoubtedly originated in France.

The rococo of the 1730s was pioneered by Jean Revel, a painter turned silk designer, and his patterns showed flowers, landscapes, sometimes *à la chinoise*, or with the so-called *rocailles*, resembling wind-blown clouds. Brocade techniques had developed to a point where any type of representation was possible, and Revel invented a new technique, 'point rentré', which allowed gradual colour transitions. His successor, Philippe de Lasalle, became more famous. De Lasalle had studied with the flower-painter Bachelier, and then worked in the atelier of François Boucher, at that time at the height of his fame. De Lasalle became a decorator in Paris, and his path led him eventually to Lyon and commissions to designs silk for many of the grandest patrons, including the famous 'pheasant' furnishing silks for Catherine the Great (Pl. p. 186). Bird-cages, doves, garlands, ribbons, partridges with chicks, musical instruments, baskets of flowers and rose-entwined columns were part of de Lasalle's repertoire of romantic motifs, suited to the tastes of Louis XVI's court. The silks he designed for Marie-Antoinette's bedroom at Fontainebleau were never seen by the Queen herself, but in 1806 the Empress Josephine used them to decorate a room in the palace.

The striking colour and design of these silks ensured that the fashion was relatively short-lived, and by the 1740s a taste developed for floral patterns casually scattered with twigs and tendrils, making less remarkable but more wearable dress fabrics. A demand followed for simpler techniques which could be produced on simpler looms. Colours became more muted; flowers patterned a striped, checked or plain taffeta ground, and were sometimes juxtaposed with representations of lace or fur trimmings. Other new patterns included moiré, which some sources say was a technique invented in England (although Clouzot records that the technique was in

Waistcoat of 1787, woven in satin embroidered with sprays of flowers and the popular *chinoiserie* motif of monkeys.

use in Tours in 1638, applied to wool and cotton, but not to silk). For moiré the fabric is folded double and pressed in a calendre (cylinder, or roller) to obtain a 'watered' effect, hence it is sometimes called 'watered silk'.

Chiné, or chiné à la branche, was another popular effect, derived from ikat technique, a resist dyeing process performed before weaving. In chiné fabrics a cloudy effect was achieved by printing on the warp. The technique was used in various textures and combined with different techniques, for example alternating with bands of satin, and applied to velvet weaving. The collection of the Mobilier National has several examples of chiné velvet worked with large designs, such as those produced in Lyon for Napoleon's suites at the Tuileries and at Fontainebleau.

The silk industry naturally suffered severely from the effects of the French Revolution, but it responded to Napoleon's patronage and support. He decreed that all representatives of the French Republic, men and women alike, should wear fabrics from Lyon, and change these as often as possible. One of the most influential designers of Empire silks was Jean-François Bony, whose patterns are characterized by lozenges, and hexagonal, octagonal and circular cells which enclose and are joined by arrangements of many different motifs, including roses, peonies, fritillaries, oak leaves, laurel leaves, palms, olive branches, or ivy. Besides plant motifs, we find stars, Greek vases and amphorae, lyres, war-trophies, helmets, shields, Napoleonic bees and Imperial N's, eagles, swans – the classical allegorical designs found on the furniture of the period. Napoleon's taste was for rather military colours – crimson, deep green or strong blue, patterned with gold or golden yellow. Josephine's preference was for pastel shades, especially pale blue.

With the return of the Bourbons, the last vestiges of the Empire style appeared in the silk velvets and elaborate waistcoats of masculine court dress. While Lyon had received imperial support for its silk industry, the other silk-processing centres of France were not so fortunate, and offered little competition. Empire-line dresses in soft fabrics were worn with shawls, which had become an indispensable article of women's dress, and French looms, notably those of Nîmes, produced their versions of the Kashmir shawl, usually woven on silk warps, and sometimes entirely of silk. This achievement was facilitated by the invention of the Jacquard loom in Lyon in 1804.

The Jacquard loom relied on punched cards which read off the required design. The system opened up great possibilities for design and pattern work, and by the mid-1830s most Lyon looms were Jacquard.

The nineteenth century was to be the golden age of silk manufacture in France in terms of quantity, but the technical limitations had been beneficial from an aesthetic point of view, and virtuoso excess for a time succeeded quality. With mechanization we reach the story of silk and fashion in the modern world, to be continued in the final chapter.

Western Highlights

T

he attraction of silk is such
that at one time or another in its history, almost every country has attempted to develop silk weaving, and many countries have attempted sericulture, despite climatic inclemencies.

Beautiful silks have been woven in Denmark and Sweden, though like Russia, these countries are too northerly to be able to grow competitive quantities of silk. Political events in France encouraged silk weaving in Britain, and British and Spanish endeavours prompted attempts at sericulture and silk weaving in the New World. Switzerland, by virtue of its geographical location and a strong textile tradition, received weavers from surrounding countries and became an important centre, though with the emphasis on trimmings such as elaborate silk ribbons and galons. There have been a number of attempts to produce silk in Ireland, though in common with the Netherlands, Ireland is better known for mixed silk and linen. Each country developed individual embroidery styles and techniques which owe a great deal to the versatility and beauty of silk threads.

Although fresh mulberries were traded in season in London in 1170, and the monk and chronicler Gervais of Canterbury wrote that the knights who murdered Thomas à Becket at Canterbury in 1170 threw off their cloaks and gowns under a branching mulberry tree, we have no proof that these trees were used for sericulture. Nevertheless, the Church was always one of the main patrons of the silk trade and the silk industry. The English religious chronicler the Venerable Bede, writing in the seventh century, tells of an abbot who brought back two fine and beautifully worked silk cloaks from Rome, and states that King Alfred paid three hides of land on the banks of the River Ware for these. As early as the tenth century, Danish Vikings carried silks, some certainly yarn, to London and other centres, from the regions of the Dnieper and the Volga where they traded with Eastern merchants. As a rarity, silk was most economically and effectively used in embroidery, where its gleaming strands could be caught on a plainer surface, mixed with other precious threads of gold and silver, and patterned with many types of stitches to give a myriad textural effects. In this way, lesser fabrics were transformed into precious silken cloth.

The earliest surviving needlework in north-western Europe appears to be an Anglo-Saxon panel, *c.* AD 800, now in Masseik in Belgium. Worked in various stitches, including couching, with coloured silks and gold threaded on linen, it was originally embellished with seed pearls, though now only the tufts of thread that held them remain. The design is of arches, densely decorated with birds, animals and monograms, and the panels are believed to have been church furnishings rather than part of vestments. A group of small embroidered fragments from a ship burial at Øseberg in Norway, of similar date, was the decoration for the buried queen's robe.

Some of the finest early needlework is 'Opus Anglicanum' (Pl. p. 198), the general term for the ecclesiastical embroidery produced in England from *c.* 900 to 1500.

These English embroideries were widely exported, and famous throughout Europe; indeed, their name is derived from entries in European inventories of the time. The inventory of the Holy See, 1295, mentions Opus Anglicanum more frequently than any other embroidery, and in 1295 Pope Innocent IV demanded quantities of embroideries from the abbots of English Cistercian orders, writing that 'England is our garden of delight; truly it is a well inexhaustible, and from where there is great abundance, from thence much more may be extracted'.

In contrast to the richness of gold and silver and coloured silks was the German tradition of 'Opus Teutonicum', whitework, while another type of German embroidery, worked in silk, wool and metal threads on linen, was in a genre known as *weiberlisten*, 'the wiles of women', and drew stories from classical antiquity and the Bible, illustrating resourceful women thwarting powerful men. The designs, based on woodcuts, were worked by women of the patrician and burgher classes, and the characters portrayed wear contemporary dress.

From the thirteenth century both men and women worked in organized embroidery workshops, but needlework was considered an ideal occupation for nuns, and for women generally. The chronicler Thomas of Ely recorded that St Ethelreda, Abbess of Ely (d. 679), was renowned for her skill in working gold thread. Henry II (1216–1272) paid 'Joan, late the wife of John de Wuburn' for a 'cope of samite embroidered with the Jesse Tree', and he gave this to St Peter's Church in Westminster. Another notable embroiderer, whose name appears twenty-four times between 1239 and 1245 in the Liberate rolls of Henry III, was Mabel of Bury St Edmunds, and her last commission was an embroidered silk standard to hang near the altar in Westminster Abbey. In the early fourteenth century, London 'silkwomen' were working the material.

Traditionally craft skills were handed down from generation to generation, and surnames often contain clues to these, as in the case of the Settere family, whose name derives from a thirteenth-century Middle English term for embroidery, which in turn derived from silk-names such as Latin *serex*, Italian *seta*. By the thirteenth century, groups of workers formed guilds in order to safeguard their interests. The Worshipful Company of Weavers was founded in London in 1155, and granted a charter by Henry II. Few members of the company could have been concerned with weaving silk at this time, and what little silk there was available would have been used to produce ribbons, lace or passementerie. The English guilds and Livery Companies were important clients and patrons, commissioning embroidery for banners, hangings and ceremonial costumes. European knitting guilds also used silk, although most of their work was executed in wool and linen. Silk and gold thread gloves were part of church regalia, and some examples of sixteenth- and seventeenth-century knitted-silk waistcoats and jackets have survived. The undershirt worn by Charles I at his execution in 1649 is silk moss stitch, knitted in a

Detail from the Oxburgh hangings, embroidered by Mary, Queen of Scots, during her imprisonment (1568–7). Symbolically, it shows a hand holding a knife and cutting a vine. The caption translates as 'Virtue flourishes under wounding'. Her coat of arms, initials, and those of François I, are included in the design.

Detail from a 16th-century German silk-embroidered hanging: a vignette showing a lovers' tryst, perhaps?

damask pattern. When Queen Elizabeth I adopted silk stockings she insisted that her maids of honour should not do likewise, so that her own ankles clad in flattering silk had no rivals. A pair of Elizabeth's stockings (now in Hatfield House, Hertfordshire) has a plain top and delicate all-over lacy diamond design. There was a vogue for bright colours, and for stockings embroidered with clocks of coloured silk or gold thread.

Although the embroideries which Mary, Queen of Scots, left have been described as 'silent letters to posterity in handwriting of rainbow silks and metallic thread, telling of the misfortunes of a martyred Queen', some of her skilled needlework allows us to glimpse a spirited and witty personality: for instance an allegorical depiction of Queen Elizabeth as a ginger cat. Her housekeeping accounts show the purchase of old church vestments, brocades and velvets, for re-use. Period portraits are rich with details of embroideries and laces, and realistic flowers were copied from herbals, their life-like depictions set-off by disproportionate insects, birds, animals real or mythical, and rainbows which arch from silver-thread clouds that weep tiny glistening raindrops. Embroidered sweetmeat bags (Pl. p. 200), gloves, falconry sets, boxes and pictures display the many techniques of working silk. A particularly distinctive type was the padded 'stumpwork' of Elizabethan and Jacobean England. German and Hungarian baroque vestments were also highly embossed and encrusted with seed pearls.

Ireland had close trading connections with silk-producing countries, and usurers from the silk centre of Lucca were settled in Dublin. Excavations in the city have discovered silk trim on garments of the thirteenth century. Tenth-century Limerick boasted 'beautifully woven cloth of all colours and all kinds, their satins and silken cloth pleasing and variegated'. Story-tellers of the eleventh and twelfth centuries clothed the legendary heroes of ancient Ireland in silk tunics, though it is unlikely that silk would have been abundant in these earlier epochs. We have evidence that some Irish chieftains occasionally dressed in silk outfits in the sixteenth century, and silks, including a bolt of precious purple damask, have been retrieved from the holds of Spanish galleons sunk in the sixteenth century off the Irish coast, still recognizable after centuries immersed in salt water. Silk stockings have frequently formed part-payments for land sales, and a certain Paul Amyus signed away his lease to land in Bantry, Co. Cork, on payment of a pair of silk stockings, garters and roses.

Church patronage of embroiderers ensured a profusion of treasures, even in the more northerly countries where silk was scarce, and doubly precious. *Above* An exquisitely embroidered 13th-century South German ecclesiastical vestment, known as the Cope of the Four Evangelists, has the body of the garment entirely embroidered in a geometric pattern with silks, gold and silver thread. *Inset left* A virtuoso example of 14th-century English 'Opus Anglicanum': the Syon Cope, of silk and silver-gilt embroidery. The detail shows St George vanquishing the dragon, from the centre hem.

Left Embroidered *epimanika* – the cuff worn by the clerics of the Greek Orthodox Church. Pearls, gold and silver wire are worked with silk thread on a satin ground. The usual subject depicted is that of the Annunciation, with the Virgin embroidered on one cuff and the Angel on the other, among floral scrolls.

Opposite Reminiscent of an icon and found in Russia: a fragment of 17th-century silk brocade woven in Bursa in Turkey. The Ottomans were heirs to Byzantium, and continued the Byzantine tradition of providing silks for the Orthodox Church, exporting many to Russia.

An Elizabethan 'sweetmeat bag', embroidered with coloured silks and metal thread in a pattern of scrolling golden stems and three-dimensional flowerheads. Sweetmeat bags were frequently given to Queen Elizabeth I as New Year gifts, and exchanged as formal presents among the aristocracy – a case of a wrapping being more precious than the contents.

Demure but luxurious accessories: a pair of English gloves and a Bible, early 17th century. The gloves have tabbed silk gauntlets, tapestry-woven with metal thread, and decoration of ruched taffeta at the wrists. The Bible cover is tapestry-woven with silk and metal thread.

Left Formal 'undress', far too grand to sleep in: a 17th-century man's night cap, exquisitely embroidered with coloured silks, silver and silver-gilt thread.

Opposite above Lid of a rare surviving paper casket – silk-covered and silk-lined – showing a lady within an arch of flowers, accompanied by noble beasts – lion, unicorn, leopard and stag. The paper is covered with sleave (floss) silk and decorated with applied motifs of flossed paper, and the edges are bound with silver braid. This kind of fancy work was popular during the late 17th century.

Opposite An 18th-century mirror-frame decorated with English stumpwork, so-named because many of the figures of people and animals were derived from 'stamps', that is, engraved pictures. A combination of embroidery techniques was used, generally on an ivory satin or taffeta ground, with raised work and beadwork.

During the 18th century, fashions were reflected to and fro across the channel. *Above* In an early 18th-century English embroidery, multicoloured 'petit point' flowers highlight the cream silk 'rococo stitch' background.

Right A French-style lace-patterned silk, 1725–30, with fruit, flowers, pomegranates.

Opposite A delicate blue-and-silver brocaded Spitalfields silk by the English designer Anna Maria Garthwaite. It can be precisely dated to 1742 by the surviving pattern-drawing.

Quilt-cover from Epirus,
c. 1700. Ottoman influence
can be seen in the costumes of
the figures. Many regions of
Greece produced silk locally,
and each area developed its
own distinctive style of
embroidery. That of Epirus is
characterized by darning
stitch.

Below left Silk woven in
Sweden in the 18th century,
brocaded with silk chenille,
gold and silver thread on a
damask ground. Ravishing
silks were woven in the
Scandinavian countries at the
period.

Below right An early 19th-
century Russian brocade: a
popular type of dress silk.

Silk weaving in Ireland began in the seventeenth century, and after the Revocation of the Edict of Nantes in 1685 some Huguenot weavers made their way there. More came to Dublin in 1752, with the encouragement of the Society for the Relief of French Protestants, and in 1760 thirty families arrived at Innishannon, near Cork. As happened elsewhere, the Irish silk industry suffered fluctuations, including in 1763 riots against the introduction of labour-saving and therefore job-reducing machinery. A greater challenge came from imported silks, but official encouragement was given to the industry through the foundation of the Hibernian Silk Warehouse in 1765.

Poplin, originally made in Avignon – the papal city, hence the name – was first manufactured in Ireland in the late seventeenth century, and from its beginning, was appreciated for its sheen, strength and durability. Two branches of the trade developed, one weaving a poplin of wool weft and silk warp for dress goods and neckties, the other a poplin of wool, linen or cotton weft and silk warp for furnishing fabrics and coach trimmings.

In 1825 a company known as the British, Irish and Colonial Silk Company planted eighty acres of mulberry trees at Michelstown in Co. Cork, but the venture failed, and the promoters turned their attention to Malta and St Helena. History records a lecture on sericulture given in 1838 by a Dr Porter, entitled: 'A New Employment for the Female Peasantry of Ireland'. An experiment in sericulture was carried out at Innishannon but the venture was unsuccessful, and today all that remains are street names such as Mulberry Close.

In the twentieth century a group of Cistercian monks at Mount Saint Joseph Abbey, Roscrea, Co. Tipperary, became involved with an experiment in sericulture, and produced cocoons and wove twills, taffeta and satins, taught by Padraig Breathnach, last of Ireland's master weavers. The monks made their own vestments and sent gifts of their silks to the Pope, until in the mid-1960s their looms too were set aside.

It was not until James I became king in 1603 that serious attempts were made to introduce sericulture to England – although as James VI of Scotland, he is said to have had to borrow a pair of silk stockings from the Earl of Mar so that he could appear before the English ambassador appropriately attired ('For ye would not, sure, that your King should appear as a scrub before strangers?'). The King may well have sworn never to find himself short of silk hose again, but his interest in silk production was undoubtedly spurred by the arrival of Huguenot refugees from the Low Countries and France, in need of gainful employment. The largest influx of Huguenots occurred during the reign of Elizabeth, who, as a fervent Protestant, had welcomed and encouraged them to establish their trades in south-east England. Some settled in the port towns in southern England such as Sandwich, Rye and Winchelsea, and some moved to the north, for instance to Macclesfield, where later a

Knitted and embroidered silk
stocking, worn by Richard
Sackville, Earl of Dorset, for his
portrait painted *c.* 1616.

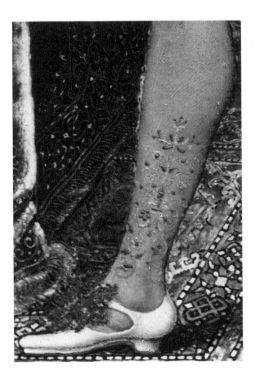

James I and his wife Anne of Denmark, *c.* 1605–10, portrayed wearing imported silks.

silk-weaving industry was established. Spitalfields has been mentioned in earlier chapters as the centre of the Huguenot tradition in Britain.

One of the most famous Huguenot families to become established in England, the Courtaulds, who fled France in the 1680s, were not originally a textile family, but in England they became rich silk weavers. A later descendant, Samuel Courtauld, developed the new synthetic silk called rayon in about 1910.

James's first attempts at silkworm-raising were at Greenwich. Here he employed John and Frances Bonnell to make 'Greenwich silk', and awarded them 'The survivorship of the Office of Keeping Silkworms at Greenwich and Whitehall'. A Monsieur Vetron from Picardy was put in charge of the importation, planting and management of mulberries, and this first official orchard was at Charlton House, Greenwich. James appointed a Governor of the Chamber whose duty required him to carry the insects 'withsoever His Majesty went'. The image of a determined and enthusiastic salesman with his trade samples comes to mind, royalty notwithstanding. It is difficult not to wonder whether the insects were literally carried around with the King, or whether, perhaps, the insects have become confused in the story's telling with a certain silk cushion embroidered with James's coat of arms surrounded with a design of entwined mulberry fruits, leaves and silkworm caterpillars. His wife, Queen Anne of Denmark, wore a dress of English silk taffeta to celebrate his birthday, on 19 June 1666.

The King commissioned William Stellenge to write a book on sericulture, and prepared for its publication and the promotion of sericulture by making available to the landed aristocracy a nursery stock of mulberry trees and seeds. Although Italy and France grew the white mulberry, the British selection of the black variety might have been made due to the black mulberry's greater tolerance of cold weather. The King wrote to all his lord lieutenants requesting them to plant mulberries, and offering to sell them seeds and trees. In 1618 two thousand mulberry trees were planted in Chelsea Park in London. Whether through lack of organization, insufficient silkworm eggs, or some other factor, is not clear, but the venture failed, despite James's obsessive enthusiasm, and as before, weavers had to rely on imported material.

A very fashionable type of glossy silk, favoured for ribbons, and known as 'lustring', was a speciality of Lyon and Nîmes, and in 1692 the Royal Lustring Company was set up in Spitalfields by an influential Lyonnais silk merchant, Etienne Seignoret. The following year all importation of lustring was banned in England. Seignoret was fined heavily for smuggling foreign lustrings in 1713, but despite this setback, the company flourished.

The English silks of Spitalfields became known as 'flowered silks', although the designs were more varied than the name suggests, and indeed encompassed all the distinctive patterns fashionable among the well-to-do of Europe (Pl. p. 202, below). For these complex patterns, a stronger silk was needed for the warp than for the weft, and the best was produced in Piedmont, though the East India Company supplied England with a strong yarn from China.

From its depots in Aleppo, Bursa and Istanbul, the Levant Company supplied quantities of silk from Persia and the Ottoman Empire. While previously British ships had sold most of their silk cargo in ports such as Leghorn and Amsterdam, now there was a ready home market. As the range of manufactured silks widened, demand grew for different types of silk, for example Persian silk (sherbassee), Turkish white silk (bellandine). Bengal and China silks generally were suitable only for the weft, and these were imported raw and thrown in English mills. Italian thrown silk, known in the trade as organzine, was found to be the best material for the warp of broad silk fabrics. Some silks were entirely woven from organzine.

Notable designers from this period were the Huguenots Christopher Baudouin, James Leman, John Vansommer and Peter Cheveney. Best known among the English were Joseph Dandridge, Anna Maria Garthwaite (Pl. p. 203), and Phoebe Wright, who was also renowned for her skill in embroidery.

Fashions were reflected to and fro across the Channel. The 'flowered silks' of Spitalfields, like the silks of Lyon and Tours, were woven with *chinoiserie*, rococo. and bizarre designs, combining nature, architectural elements and fantasy, and this early eighteenth-century taste was followed by lace motifs, and then in the 1730s, by

Spitalfields 'flowered silks', *c.* 1737. Sweeping leaves and large-scale floral design make up a man's coat with attached waistcoat front.

Krefeld velvet, a popular 19th-century furnishing fabric.

large-scale floral designs. Plain, small patterned, and striped materials were also woven, and by the last quarter of the century these, and small floral sprays, were very popular. The English silk industry gained an impetus with the introduction of a silk-throwing machine, its design plagiarized from an Italian model. The government paid one Thomas Lombe the impressive sum of £18,000 to relinquish his patent rights, and a large water-powered silk mill was set up at Derby.

English silks were exported, and in some markets, such as Vienna, French merchants complained of English competition. British taste was for imported French silks, and by 1668 silk was no longer the prerogative of the rich but was becoming widely worn by all classes of people. Political hostility between England and France led to the imposition of prohibitive duties on French goods, including silks, and these remained in force until 1738. French silk manufacturers were squeezed out of the English market, and illegally imported silks, laces, and of course French brandy, were the basis of many stories of smugglers, customs men, mysterious inns, and fires lit along the sea-shore to lure ships on to the rocks to spill their precious cargo.

The Netherlands, Spanish-held during the Middle Ages, maintained their woollen and linen industries for centuries, but silk was not a major product, although a certain type of half-silk called 'satin de Bruges' was well known, and many silk brocade and damask patterns were copied in linen, wool, and materials which combined silk with other yarns.

In Germany as in other parts of Europe, experiments were made in silkworm-raising. A gentleman boasted in 1653 that he had produced enough silk to make two pairs of silk stockings – in terms of cost and effort to output, surely some of the most expensive stockings ever produced. His hopes that the German Emperor would follow the example of the French King and ban Italian silk imports to favour home production, were alas in vain.

Italian silk dyers evidently worked in Nuremberg in the sixteenth century, and the German silk industry gained workers at the time of the Huguenot troubles. During the seventeenth century a Dutch family, the van der Leyens, traded in silks and linens in Krefeld, Germany, and set up a dye studio there in 1724. Krefeld produced ribbons, silk hosiery and small-patterned velvets popular for men's waistcoats, and its kerchiefs and scarves were famous worldwide.

Frederick the Great (1712–86) encouraged silk weaving, and built Frederickstad in Holstein as a 'silk port' for the raw materials. His embassy in Muscovy was intended to secure the purchase of Persian and Armenian silk, while in the Levant, Krefeld merchants acted as distributors of manufactured goods as well as purchasers of raw silk. The French occupation of the Rhineland under Napoleon (1794–1814) left the Krefeld industry struggling to compete with French textile centres, although Mulhouse and Elberfeld, east of the Rhine, managed to secure trading privileges

with France. Krefeld made a speciality of neckties, and the name cravat is said to derive from a regiment of Croats (Hrvate, Cravates) who served in the French army and wore a distinctive striped necktie. The industry in Berlin and its surrounding region flourished until the late nineteenth century. Although there is little silk-weaving in Germany today, the dyeing, printing and finishing of silk has remained an active industry.

In Switzerland, the weavers' guild gave refuge to workers fleeing the Inquisition of Pope Paul III in 1603, and attempts to establish sericulture were made in the Basle region. Weavers worked in their homes, but whereas the weavers of Lyon owned their looms, in Basle the looms were the property of the manufacturer. In order to take advantage of every hour of daylight the looms occupied the main window of the weavers' homes. Ribbon designs were often intricate and very luxurious.

The silk production of Zurich began in the fourteenth century and continues to the present day. When Richard Wagner was working in Zurich, his composition, it is said, was stimulated by the beauty of a particular yellow silk brocaded with scattered roses. The history of silk in Zurich is amply documented by the rules and regulations governing its production, and occasional sumptuary rulings limiting its wearing. During the eighteenth century many Huguenot weavers from Tours and Nîmes settled there, and the 'Zurich loom' was invented, allowing several ribbons to be woven in parallel. By the turn of the eighteenth century block-prints were increasingly replaced by copper-prints, and Mulhouse became an important centre for textile printing, profiting from its proximity to the printing centre at Basle, and to France and Germany, as well as from the enterprise of its early founders, who included the Koechlin family. The fashion for shawls and for Indian prints was combined in the production of silk shawls with patterns inspired by those of Kashmir and India. Today, one of the most important manufacturers for couture-quality silks is the Zurich firm of Abrahams, founded in the mid-nineteenth century.

The first Russian silk manufactory was established in Moscow in 1714. By 1727 there were sixteen, and in the second half of the eighteenth century many towns were producing silks. Shawls and kerchiefs were always an important item of Russian dress, and an important producer of silk kerchiefs woven with gold was Guri Levin, a merchant from Kolomna near Moscow. Kerchiefs with his trademark date back to the 1780s, and his mills were famous for their bridal veils. Such veils were all-enveloping, with gold-brocaded wide borders and repeating designs (flowers, rosettes, etc.) woven on ikat silk ground. They were very popular, and many were exported further east.

Rich peasant women wore superb festival *sarafans* of Russian-woven silks and brocades of silver and gold and many-coloured threads. The *sarafan* might be of cream satin brocade, with rose, blue and green floral embroidery and gold lace galloons and buttons. With this went an overblouse of white satin in a floral pattern

Swiss silk pictorial and commemorative ribbons.

and embroidered brocade lined with russet silk. The headdress – *kokoshniki* – was the most important item of dress, for by tradition a married woman had to hide her hair from strangers' eyes. *Kokoshniki* varied from region to region in a whole variety of picturesque and poetic shapes. They were made of silk in bright colours, red and raspberry coloured velvet, in cloth of gold ornamented with pearls, decorative glass, mirrors and foil.

Russian courtiers wore French and German fashions in the seventeenth century. An edict of 1719 permitted the import of silks and brocades from Western Europe, since the factory founded in 1717 by Fiodor Apraxim, Piotr Shatirov and Piotr Tolstoi for the production of all fabrics and brocades proved unable to fulfil demand. By the eighteenth century, many of the silks were already manufactured in Russia, and lists submitted to the Senate enumerate the types and variety; a list dated 1749 includes plain and figured velvets, plain and patterned silks, *grisettes*, plain and figured taffetas, flowered gros de Tours, and others. Much of the gold, silver, and silk lace and passementerie was produced in convents. The embroideries and woven silks produced in Russia can usually be indentified by a distinctive character, which is European yet oriental, or perhaps oriental yet slightly European.

In the Scandinavian countries as in Russia, attempts were made to establish sericulture, but climatic conditions were unfavourable. The first recorded attempt to set up silk manufacturing in Sweden was that of a Dutchman, Jakob van Utenhofen, in 1649, with the encouragement of Queen Christina. Attempts in Denmark included an encouraging ordinance stating that anyone who invested more than 500 dalers in a silk manufacturing enterprise would be entitled to dress 'above his station', or, more precisely, to wear 'velvets, taffetas, and other plain silks made in this country'. A number of impressive Danish woven silks survive, notably those in the collection of Rosenborg Castle.

The role of Vikings as traders in silks has already been mentioned. Many oriental silks have survived in Sweden's church treasuries, and Chinese and Byzantine silks from the Viking period were found in excavations at Øseberg and Birka in Norway. Silk was found in about fifty graves at Birka, a port with regular links with Byzantium and the orient via the Russian trade routes. A king of Norway, Sigurd the Crusader, is described in an Icelandic poem, sailing into Byzantium in 1110, the sails of his ships hung with 'pell' – rich oriental silks. A twelfth-century custom was to award Crusaders of the Knights of St John of Jerusalem a silk cloak (in the oriental tradition of the Robe of Honour) on their return from the Crusades, and such were probably the billowing silks that decked his sails.

The Greek islands belonged to Venice, Genoa or the Ottomans at various times, and before that the main influence had been Byzantine. Silk production in the islands appears to have increased in the sixteenth century, as it did in mainland Greece, Albania and the Balkans. Silk weaving and embroidery skills were a part of daily life.

Lavishly embroidered costumes and home furnishings were highly prized possessions until the nineteenth century, and each island and mainland area developed a distinctive embroidery type. That of Rhodes, which had fallen to the Ottomans in 1522, was worked in barely twisted, thick red and green silks on local linen or cotton; Skyros depicted an unmistakable cockerel, harpies and ships; Crete often included a double-tailed mermaid holding her tails; Naxos a distinctive geometric repeating leaf-pattern of darning stitch, usually in red silk but sometimes in green. One of the types peculiar to Epirus includes tulips, turbaned riders, and various animals and birds (Pl. p. 204). Rich mainland houses aspired to velvet and brocade bed-curtains and covers, and certain islands developed their own distinctive form of these, which might well be very ancient. Each curtain of the bed-tent tapered in shape, and was embroidered in the local style. When not in use, cushions were stacked one on top of another, often to a height of ten or more, hence their covers were often embroidered along the exposed sides only. Some of the patterns can be identified as versions of pomegranate designs, and Wace suggested that some of these embroideries were originally copies of the expensive brocades and velvets of Venice or Genoa.

Journeying westward, both Cabot and Columbus had hoped to find the land of the Great Khan; and in 1634 a French adventurer, Jean Nicolet, set forth to investigate rumours of a great inland sea from which a waterway led to Asia, its shores inhabited by a yellow-skinned people who, it was thought, could only be Chinese. When Nicolet reached Green Bay on Lake Michigan he presumed the cliffs ahead of him to be the coastline of China, and donned a robe of Chinese silk before landing, in order to be suitably dressed to greet the inhabitants.

More practically, in 1607 James I sent shipments of silkworms and mulberries to Jamestown, Virginia, the first English settlement in America. Huguenot weavers were among early settlers in the New World, and over the next twenty or so years, various attempts were made to establish sericulture further inland and down the coast. While some silkworm shipments were lost at sea, others reached their destination. By 1619 Jamestown colonists had devoted their energies to the project, and there were penalties for not planting mulberry trees. Initially the project was productive, despite many setbacks. Martha Washington reputedly wore a dress of Virginian silk when her husband George was inaugurated as President in 1789.

When Savannah in Georgia was settled, sericulture and silk production were given prime importance. The first Georgian silk was sent to England in 1735, and peak production was around the 1760s, when some 10,000 pounds-weight of silk were exported. However, the War of Independence (1776) curtailed production. The silk industry in Pennsylvania started in 1725 and was soon exporting to England, although the silk was generally of a lesser quality than the material imported from India, Persia, Italy, France and China.

Above American Indian cloth, embroidered and appliqué with silk ribbons and thread, *c.* 1820.

Right Cherokee buckskin coat embroidered with silk threads, 1865.

While the native American red mulberry was suitable fodder for silkworms, and white and black varieties had been imported and grown successfully, sericulture benefited in the 1830s from the discovery of a variety of Chinese mulberry that would grow rapidly, produce large leaves, and flourish in the United States. Speculation sent the price of seedlings rocketing, and pamphlets on sericulture promoted it as an ideal home activity and family industry. Other crops were abandoned, and many people were ruined when silk production languished. A blight of mulberry trees dealt the final blow. Nevertheless, some fine silk textiles were woven in Utah by Mormons during this time, and in Pennsylvania, from about 1830 to 1851, the Harmonist Society raised silkworms and wove silk in their own mills.

The Shakers in Kentucky persevered longest with silk, and produced scarves and kerchiefs on treadle looms for their own community into the twentieth century. Settlers saved every scrap of cloth to use over and over again, and some of their treasured patchwork quilts were made with silks, like a Quaker quilt in 'Tumbling Blocks' pattern, of 1852 (title page, top).

Although James I is credited with introducing sericulture to the eastern states, the Spanish had done so in Mexico at least a hundred years earlier. The skills and expertise of Andalusia had profited 'New Spain', and in the 1540s more than fifty towns were raising silkworms. Optimistic predictions that New Spain would become the greatest silk producer in the world were not fulfilled after the Manilla trade developed, and mulberry silk-raising was extinct by the end of the eighteenth century. A small domestic oak-silk industry continued to supply thread for accenting woven designs and embroidery. Early Mexican embroideries are usually hispano-mauresque in design, but it is thought that the later embroideries, rich with multi-coloured blossoms, were copied from the Chinese silk embroideries that reached New Mexico in the eighteenth century. Mexican dress is brilliantly coloured, and relies extensively on embroidered and woven decoration.

Silk brought colour, elegance, and a touch of softness and beauty into lives that were frequently harsh, difficult, insecure, and devoid of many of the comforts that today we take for granted. To dress in silk, have furnishings of silk, represented a certain standard of living. Western highlights are those fabrics worked by skilled fingers to exacting standards, and whether woven, embroidered or knitted, they were never mass-produced, always individual. Western highlights are also the discoveries and inventions made possible by the widespread availability of silk, and such technological progress led on to industrialization, and to mass production.

 Silk in the Modern World

he heart-moving statement embroidered on an eighteenth-century sampler, 'Polly Cook did it and she hated every stitch she did in it', conjures up a child who would obviously have preferred activity to the stillness, concentration and patience required by needlework. Textile skills continued to be essential in an age before mechanization replaced home spinning, weaving, knitting and embroidery, but this was to change in the nineteenth century. The Jacquard loom of 1804 was an automated version of the drawloom that speeded up production of patterned fabrics, reduced labour costs, and brought silks within the reach of many more people than ever before. It marks the beginning of a new era – silk in the modern world.

With mechanization, the history of textiles changed dramatically, but lower costs resulted in lower quality, with detrimental effects on standards of design and taste. Silk manufacturers were faced with the problem of how to fulfil public demand for quantities of cheaper silks while maintaining the standards that had brought them fame. In France the status of the artist-designers in textile companies was an important and established tradition, and in the long run it was probably the designers' efforts that saved the silk industry of Lyon from destruction. Elsewhere, various schools of art and design were set up, and interest in works of excellence of previous centuries found expression in a series of artistic revivalist movements. By the 1840s the Gothic Revival was well under way in Britain and America, and towards the middle of the century the church architects A.W.G. Pugin, G.E. Street and G.F. Bodley were encouraging interest in the techniques of gold and silk liturgical embroideries in the tradition of Opus Anglicanum (Pl. p. 198). At the Great Exhibition of 1851, Gothic Revival prints and embroideries were displayed by the Birmingham firm of Newton, Jones & Willis, and the British entry for the exhibition was a 'Medieval Court' devised by Pugin. Ecclesiastical furnishings based on medieval and Renaissance damasks and velvets were made by firms such as Watts & Co. in London.

Home furnishings were lavishly hung and draped; even pianos, tables and firescreens were swathed and be-tassled. The extravagant use of fabric in women's dress in the 1840s encouraged experiments in decorating cloth, and the nineteenth century saw great progress in printing designs on silk, and in dyeing. For the first time, cloth was dyed as woven lengths rather than as yarn, and chemists in England and France applied their skills to formulating synthetic dyes for new and exciting hues. These, known as anilines, produced some startling shades unknown in nature, although the early dyes were fugitive, fading to drabness. A particular shade of fuschia remains associated with the Lyon textile chemist Verguin. One of the earliest of the anilines was W.H Perkin's mauve, later known as 'mauveine'. When Queen Victoria appeared at the Great Exhibition wearing a mauve silk dress, the new colour became a fashion rage.

Bright aniline colours made a dramatic impact on patterned fabrics, but technology also produced innovations in decorative weaving. A delicious example is the romantic dress-silk woven in Lyon for the young Victoria, a combination of techniques which suggests layers of lace, velvet and satin, but is in fact a single fabric. The Queen's wedding dress in 1832 was white Spitalfields silk satin, and in 1837 her coronation train was woven by Richard Atkinson of Dublin in white and gold, with the union symbol of shamrock, rose and thistle. Despite such bright beginnings, the Victorian era is better remembered for the period of Victoria's widowhood, and the fashion she set for wearing black. Following the Queen's example of lengthy mourning, all families with sufficient means and social pretensions wore black for at least a year after the demise of a close relative, a frequent occurrence in a time of large families and early deaths. During the eighteenth century black silk crêpe had been imported to England, but by the nineteenth century, several silk-weaving firms in England were producing and exporting 'crêpe anglaise' to enthusiastic customers in France. One of these firms was that of Samuel Courtauld, who developed a particular type of light, compact, power-operated loom especially suited for crêpe-weaving, a discovery which resulted in 'considerable pecuniary advantage'. By the end of the century Courtaulds was one of the largest firms in the British silk industry.

Silk woven in Lyon for the young Victoria, in a combination of techniques to give the impression of layers of different silks.

Movements to counter the excesses of industrialization were gaining momentum by the 1880s. William Morris is credited with reviving interest in Arts and Crafts. He established the firm to be known as Morris & Co. in 1961, and proclaimed hand techniques and handcrafts far superior to any machine processes. The textile industry's enthusiasm for the new aniline dyes had made traditional methods of dyeing almost obsolete, and Morris and Thomas Wardle, a silk-dyer from Leek in Staffordshire, devoted years until 1881 to researching the old skills. The embroidery section of Morris's Merton Works near London was directed by Mary Morris, and her husband urged embroiderers to think of their work as gardening with silk and gold, inspiring a movement for Art Embroidery.

The textile firm of Warner & Sons, founded in Spitalfields in 1870 and mainly producing furnishing silks and velvets, had become involved in reviving figured silk waistcoats. In 1895 it took over a bankrupt silk-weaving firm in Braintree, Essex, and after moving out of London went from strength to strength, weaving silks and velvets for the coronations of 1902, 1911, 1937, and 1953. For the Franco-British exhibition of 1908 it revived alto-e-basso and other decorative velvet techniques, and reproduced Italian examples of the fifteenth and sixteenth centuries.

After Cobden's treaty of 1860 removed the duty levied on imported silks, the United Kingdom's imports doubled, Paris dictated fashion, and French silks undercut comparable fabrics in England and Ireland. Specialist manufacturers survived, for example those in Macclesfield producing men's accessories (who still today produce ties and silk hankerchiefs), and a small group of manufacturers who continued to produce heavy, highly priced furnishing silks for a relatively small but consistent market.

National styles grew out of the Arts and Crafts movement, and in one of these, Art Nouveau, the curving lines of nature were developed and stylized in a distinctive manner. The flow and shimmer of silk and the subtle shades it could be dyed made it the perfect choice for Art Nouveau textiles (Pl. p. 221). Today the name Lalique conjures up glass and fabulous jewels such as those made for Sarah Bernhardt, but Lalique also designed silks, and some of these, long sashes or scarves known by descriptive titles such as Peacock Scarf, Cornfield, Moths, and Field of Daisies, were woven in silk and gold thread by Maison Atuyer, Bianchini-Ferier & Cie, of Lyon, and were exhibited in the Salon de la Société des Artistes Française in 1907.

The most dramatic and far-reaching fashion change of the century was the rise of the organized couture house. One of the first was that of the designer Charles Frederick Worth, who opened his 'House' in Paris in 1858 and enjoyed enormous success under the patronage of the Empress Eugénie and her court. Taste in dress at the mid-century favoured shot silk, satin and velvet, fashioned into the full skirts of the crinoline: the artist Winterhalter portrayed Queen Victoria and the Empress Eugénie in full-skirted, off-the-shoulder gowns. Worth next pulled skirts up and back into a train, its exaggerated form emphasized by tightly laced corsets. His use of rich fabrics throughout the second half of the century inspired the silk manufacturers of Lyon, and he continued to enjoy the patronage of European courts. Outside court circles, in reaction to such constricting fashions, the Aesthetic and Rational Dress Movement of the 1870s advocated full-sleeved, soft, flowing robes influenced by Pre-Raphaelite art.

Another development of Arts and Crafts was closely associated with the geometrical lines of the Scottish architect Charles Rennie Mackintosh, whose 'Glasgow style' was characterized by the organic forms of Art Nouveau set on a geometric grid, well illustrated in the needlework of Glasgow School of Art. Mackintosh's work was influential in Austria, where the Wiener Werkstatte Studio was founded in 1903, and throughout its existence until 1939 its textile department produced thousands of designs, both for interior furnishing and fashion. The painter Gustav Klimt designed caftan or kimono-type garments for the workshop. Magnificent textiles and textural effects dominate his paintings, in which the individuals portrayed are almost incidental to the textiles, patterned with gold and jewel-like colours, and reminiscent of Byzantine icons in their intense, rich splendour.

As preceding centuries had seen vogues for the exotic in *chinoiserie* and *turquerie*, late nineteenth- and early twentieth-century fashion was fascinated by the orient. After centuries of cultural isolation, Japan signed a commercial treaty with Britain and America in 1858, and in London the Exhibition of 1862 introduced the public to

arts and crafts as varied as those of Japan and Morris & Co. An oriental warehouse opened in Regent Street was to be the training ground for the young Arthur Lasenby Liberty, who set up shop on his own in 1885, at first selling only Eastern silks. The demand for these was so great that he commissioned English designers to produce a range of soft, pliant silks and rayons inspired by eastern designs, known as 'Art Silks' (Pl. p. 221). Thomas Wardle, working with Morris, devised what came to be called 'Liberty colours', delicate pastels in total contrast to the strident aniline dyes and heavy fabrics that had become the rage of Victorian fashion. A number of Morris, Art Nouveau and Aesthetic designs are still in production, and have become international classics. One of these is a pattern of peacock feathers, designed by Arthur Silver who formed the Silver Studio in 1880. The firm of Warner & Sons also made fabric designs for Liberty, some based on eighteenth-century Spitalfields silks.

Just as Queen Victoria had supported the British silk industry in patriotically selecting Spitalfields silk for her wedding dress, the Duchess of Teck was a keen supporter of the Silk Association and President of the Ladies' Committee, and in 1891 she commissioned British silks for the wedding of her daughter the Princess May (later Queen Mary). The Silver Studio books illustrate a group of fifteen designs entitled 'The May Silks'. The silk selected for the bridal gown was white and silver, patterned with union roses, shamrocks and thistles, May blossoms, and True Lovers' knot. Other designs from the series were woven for her trousseau, and there is an established tradition for British royal brides to wear British silk wedding gowns.

The various artistic and revivalist movements in Europe had their counterparts in the United States. The influential New York Decorative Art Society was formed in 1877. A founder member, and America's best-known textile designer of the period,

Portrait by Gustav Klimt of a patron, Fredericke Maria Beer, dressed in a silk tea-gown printed with a Wiener Werkstatte pattern, 'Marina', 1911 designed by Dagobert Peche.

Allegorical design by Leon Victor Solon, block-printed on a silk square by the firm of Thomas Wardle & Co. in 1893.

Printed furnishing silk by the American designer Candace Wheeler, 1885.

was Candace Wheeler, and in 1879 she joined Louis C. Tiffany and others in a collaborative venture under the name of Associated Artists. In the same year she was awarded the Society's first prize for a painted and silk-embroidered *portière*. In 1883 when Tiffany started a separate decorating company, Wheeler continued with Associated Artists, whose all-women team of designers produced textile patterns for many American manufacturers.

By the turn of the century Paterson in New Jersey had become the silk centre of America. Silks were imported from Japan and dyed in the soft waters of the Passaic river. The Paterson textile firm Schumacher & Co. was producing furnishing fabrics in the nineteenth century, and is still one of America's leading manufacturers, with extensive historical archives. Apart from a wide range of furnishing fabrics, silks were produced for a variety of purposes, including Jacquard-woven silk ribbons with commemorative subjects. This type of illustrative ribbon was fashionable for a period in Europe and America. Another Paterson firm, Hamil & Booth, produced small-patterned dress fabrics and plain weaves.

As the pace of transatlantic travel accelerated, so did the traffic in Old World antiques and art. American museums and private collectors amassed fabulous treasures, and around the turn of the century these were the inspiration for American weavers to produce some fine furnishing silks copied from examples in museum archives: Byzantine, Sassanian, Sicilian, and many more.

Paris from the turn of the century was alive with artists from all over Europe and America, attracted by the new modern art movements. Art and fashion became more closely related, and the colours and moods of painted canvases were echoed in silks from Lyon's looms. French style had been popular in Tsarist Russia throughout the nineteenth century. Now Paris in turn was taken by storm when in 1909 Serge Diaghilev presented the Ballet Russe. Big embroidered Central Asian suzani hangings, ikat silks and the intense, exciting colours of the Russian Steppes inspired designers to be as daring.

One of those strongly influenced by Bakst's Russian ballet designs was Paul Poiret, who affected oriental dress of brocade jackets tied with wide belts, and gave a famous Thousand and One Nights party which resulted in an avalanche of orders for his lampshade skirts, harem trousers and oriental embroideries. The prevailing tastes of the Belle Epoque, as the period leading up the World War I was known, the pastel tones of sugared almonds, shades of sweet pea and evening stock, cloyingly frilled and feathered, were anathema to Poiret, and in total contrast, his decorative art workshop, the Atelier Martine, produced designs with brilliant primary colours in bold juxtaposition. To achieve a completely fresh effect he employed young girls with no design training. A characteristic design of Poiret's silks are naive roses with vague cloudlike shapes. Much of his work was an intimation of the Art Deco movement which made its first tentative appearance before World War I.

Orientalism lingered on in Art Deco: curves and angles were juxtaposed in dramatic designs, metallic threads gave reflective emphasis to patterns that were frequently whimsical, such as Raoul Dufy's 'Coquillages', a brocade of silk and silver threads patterned with spouting whales, cockle shells, waves, and surprised little horses with floating manes, designed for, and woven by, Bianchini-Ferier in Lyon. Poiret exhibited an evening dress made from this brocade at the 1925 Exposition des Arts Décoratifs. American designers too were producing the geometric designs with stepped and jagged edges of Art Deco, and some of the less conservative companies such as Cheny Brothers and the Stehli Silk Corporation commissioned designs to illustrate contemporary features of the American way of life. Their titles bring these vividly to the mind's eye: 'Mothballs and Sugar' by Edward Steichen; 'Aspirin' by R. Green; 'Manhattan Thrills', based on a roller coaster.

The concern which united Art Deco designers and craftsmen was not the end product alone, but the whole process, from drawing board to finished work, and in Venice Mariano Fortuny (1871–1949) arrived at the same conclusion: the artist must be the master of every step of the process that achieved his creation. Fortuny created some of the most remarkable fabrics and dresses of his century. The drape, fall, texture and colours of his silks transformed the wearer's body into fluid sculpture, a daring concept in an era of whalebone stays. He devised new printing techniques in subtle shades and metallic hues, to give an impression of rich, metal-brocaded velvet. A large silk rectangle, the Knossos scarf, printed with geometric motifs inspired by Cycladic art, was made in countless variations, and from these Fortuny developed his production of dresses. The Delphos robe first appeared in around 1907, and its finely pleated silk pongee became his hallmark. More than any other designer, Fortuny promoted the revival of gold and silver textiles – evoking once more the wonder of Byzantine, Persian and Islamic silks, or the great silks of Europe during the Renaissance (Pl. p. 226).

Perhaps the last of the dream worlds was the endless party of the Twenties and Thirties known as 'les Années folles', the 'Crazy Years', and here Fortuny's dresses and textiles took their proper place. Proust was among those contemporaries who wrote admiringly about Fortuny's silks, and in *A la Recherche du Temps Perdu*, dressed Albertine in Fortuny's sunset-shaded silks. Inevitably Fortuny had his copyists, and of these Gallenga and Babani were the most significant. In the Italian Pavilion of the 1925 Exposition des Arts Décoratifs in Paris, Fortuny displayed his silks, but the Grand Prix was awarded to Gallenga, whose metallic stencilled velvets were imitations of Fortuny's techniques and inventions.

Another important name among the artists who used the medium of silk and textile techniques as expression was Sonia Delaunay. Russian by birth, she married the Cubist painter Robert Delaunay, and together they developed their theories on colour relative to form, space and movement, which they called

Raoul Dufy's design for a silk and silver brocade: 'Coquillages', 1925.

Simultaneous Colour. From appliqué she explored printed and painted fabrics, for which silk was the perfect medium. A Lyon silk manufacturer commissioned a collection of fifty fabric designs, and when these were produced in 1923 they were received with acclaim. Her designs are geometric (Ill. p. 213), sometimes with subtle shading, sometimes dramatic in colour contrast. In the Thirties she opened an embroidery studio to produce her geometric designs, and in the Sixties Zika Ascher reproduced her designs in his collection of limited edition artist-designed silk squares.

Colette, after a visit to Maison Ducharne in Lyon, wrote of 'celui qui tisse le soleil, la lune, et les rayons bleus de la pluie . . .' (he who weaves the sun, the moon, and the blue streaks of rain). The Twenties and Thirties were a period of great inventiveness in silk weaving. Mechanized weaving was applied to numerous techniques and textures: silk mousselines, crêpes, voiles and toiles de soie, fluid chiffons that floated and flowed, cut velvet chiffon. A fabric which perhaps summed up the inventiveness and patience of the weavers was *velours sabres*. Extremely laborious and exacting to produce, this was a satin with a double warp, one of which was structural and the other, floating, was handcut with a tiny instrument called a *sabre*. By cutting every second thread within designated motifs, a fine pile resulted, and this was raised with a hog's hair brush, to give a velvet effect against a satin field.

Such was the reputation of Lyon that for a time the Casino de Paris finished its show with a special review called 'Soieries'. A curtain of gold tissue lifted, and the beautiful girls shimmered on stage, each swathed in a type of silk whose different character they represented – regal gold brocade and duchesse satin, rich mysterious velvet, floating ethereal chiffon, jewel-hued printed silks. The costumes were designed by Zinoviev.

Beaded crêpe and chiffon flapper dresses, light silks that skimmed the wearer's body, and crêpe de chine, bias cut to flutter and flow, were the epitome of chic. Madeleine Vionnet perfected the bias cut, and Mme Grès's complex draped and pleated chiffon, pinned and created on living models, must have caused sighs of envy on Mount Olympus.

Silk stockings might have seemed like a gift from the gods to the owners of shortened hemlines and visible legs, but in the Twenties, when this fashion outrage broke on an unsuspecting world, pulpits across Europe and America rang with threats of fire and brimstone to the wearers: the Archbishop of Naples declared that the recent earthquake in Amalfi was God's expression of anger against skirts that skimmed the knee. Despite the fact that sumptuary laws have been spectacularly ineffective throughout history, various American states attempted to legislate on hem-length, and a book entitled 'The Word of God on Women's Dress' was published in 1922. The invention of nylon in the 1930s brought the demise of silk stockings.

Even in the era of Art Deco and the '*Années folles*' of the Twenties and Thirties, floral motifs never entirely lost their popularity. *Above* Detail from a silver lamé dress by Babani, the skirt and deep cuffs decorated with flower-like roundels and geometric motifs, mainly in crimson and pink, set off by black silk crêpe. *Right* An American crewel tablecloth worked on silk grosgrain by Mariska Karasz, 1931. The witty design incorporates a backgammon board against a pattern of flowers.

Opposite Les Jets d'Eau, satin with damask effect, designed for the 1925 exhibition in Paris that gave its name to Art Deco.

Left Fresh as springtime in 1908: Paul Poiret's green chiffon tunic, trimmed with mink and embroidered with green beads, silk and gold thread, worn over a yellow satin dress.

Below Balenciaga's taffeta balloon-dress rustled down the catwalks in 1953.

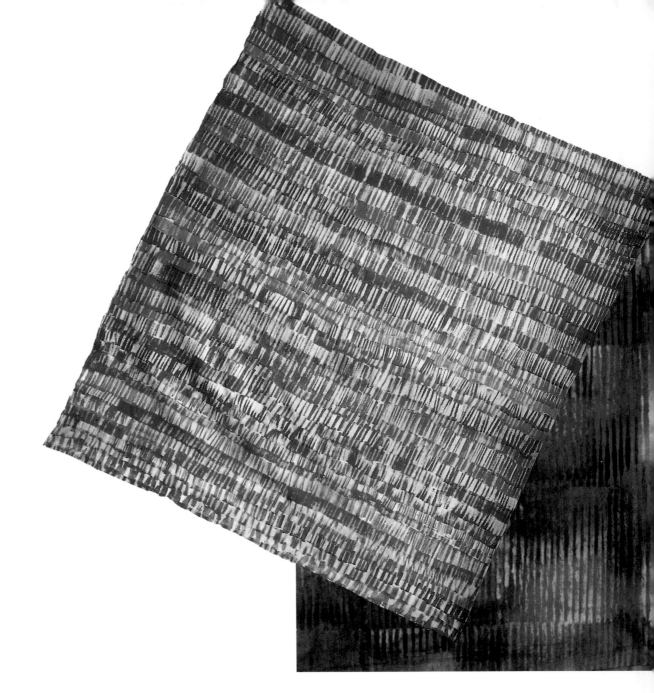

Left and below Mariano Fortuny (1871–1949) created gold-stencilled velvets that give a theatrical impression of the brocaded velvets of earlier centuries. *Left* A dress with a 'Persian' floral motif; the silk *faille* label which Fortuny gave to all his velvet garments can be glimpsed inside the neck. *Below left* One of the Renaissance-inspired velvets, with palmettes and sweeping meanders.

Left Fortuny's silk Delphos dresses, twisted to preserve their fine pleating. They could be adjusted in wear by a system of interior ribbons, and silk-rouleau fastenings caught with tiny Venetian glass beads.

Designs printed on velvet by Noralene (Nora and Helen Ferruzzi, painters who acquired Fortuny's paints and other equipment at the sale of his studio). Their inspiration is Venice: its stones, skies, and water.

Right Silk shawl by the firm of Ratti, inspired by a painted ceiling at Dunhuang, along the ancient Silk Road. Antonio Ratti at Como is one of Italy's foremost silk manufacturers, with a valuable archive and collection of silks.

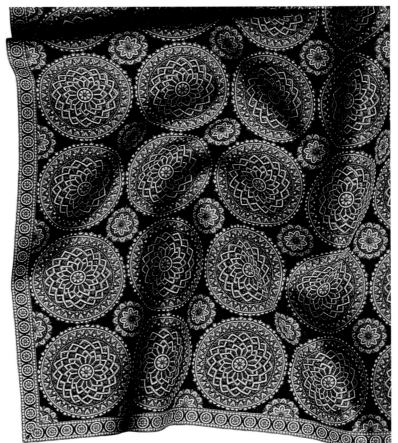

In fashion and design there is always a search for inspiration, reinterpretation, and in recent years the collector's instinct has encompassed textiles. As haute couture climbs steadily in price, and mass production cannot but lack the intimate touches and fine detail that make the difference to the discerning, classic couture from past collections has been caught in the upward swing of collecting precious fabrics. Balenciaga, an architect and sculptor where Fortuny was a painter and magician, returned to heavy duchesse satins, organzas and taffetas for his elegant forms (Pl. p. 225), and was responsible for the invention of a new fine silk weave, gazar. Yves St Laurent's collections were never so exciting as when he was reinventing cossacks, Arabian princesses, oriental beauties, for the salons of the West. Meanwhile, in the auction rooms purist collectors bid feverishly for scraps of Byzantine brocade, hispano-mauresque silks, Ottoman velvets, Mogul khanats. A market has developed for carefully conserved and mounted silk fragments, in appreciation of the qualities and techniques of earlier times. These precious silks are once again worth their weight in gold.

During World War II, silk, like other luxuries, was scarce at any price. Maison Ducharne, whose silks had delighted Colette, hid their supply of raw material, and during the German occupation of Lyon, secretly wove their silk into a tapestry of a modern allegorical scene, the hero a cavalry officer of Saumur. Maison Ducharne's post-war designs were inspired by such images as a cane-backed chair, the hilt of a samurai sword, a wrought-iron balcony, domino masks, aeroplanes and trains, and black and white were used as contrasts to the dramatic colourings of rich and varied silks.

Despite the inventiveness and excitement of silk in the early twentieth century, the industry had sustained severe blows. Production was devastated by the silkworm disease pebrine, disrupted by the impact of two world wars, and challenged by the rise in popularity of synthetic fibres. By the 1950s the great silk manufacturers of Lyon were producing a variety of fabrics, ranging from the best silks for the couture houses, through other natural fibres and silk-mixes to the various synthetics. That France's silk-weaving skills are still very much alive is demonstrated by the historical silks reproduced from original patterns commissioned for the restoration of Versailles, Fontainebleau, and other important palaces.

There are at present only five Western European countries left with substantial silk industries: France, Germany, Italy, Switzerland and the United Kingdom. Of these, only Italy is also a silk-producer on any scale, although since the Chinese 'Silk War' of 1988, attempts have been made to rekindle interest in French sericulture, and the Cevennes region has maintained a certain amount of silk production. The firm of Hermès, best known for their distinctive silk squares, are among those with current silk-producing programmes. The name Hermès is synonymous with silk and saddlery. Founded in 1837 as a harness-making firm, in 1928 it diversified its activities and started to produce leather garments. The silk scarf was already an essential accessory, and the hallmark of Hermès is still saddlery or equestrian motifs. Hermès annually present collections to themes, the silks are produced in Lyon, and their extensive archives contain over two thousand designs, with a shade catalogue of over two thousand colours.

A number of Italian universities have programmes of sericulture, some sponsored by manufacturers and silk associations, and these include experiments in simplified intensive feeding processes. In the Seventies Italy invented silk tweed, and her knitted silks vied in luxury with cashmere. New technology, computers, and wide shuttleless looms have enabled some of the larger Italian weavers to compete on more equal terms with silks from developing countries and the Far East.

Japan in the nineteenth century made enormous strides in silk production, importing machinery and technology from France and studying European textile designs. For a period until World War II Japan was the major supplier of raw silk to the West. After the war, Japan restored her silk production, with vastly improved reeling, inspection and classification of her raw silk. She remained the world's biggest producer of raw silk, and practically the only major exporter of raw silk, until the Seventies, when her broader industrial expansion led to a corresponding decline in sericulture, and China made a concentrated effort to recapture her historic position as the world's biggest raw silk producer and exporter.

Statistics showing a continuing decline in Japanese sericulture hide the very great interest that the Japanese have in silk. The rising cost of labour and agricultural land renders labour-intensive sericulture less attractive, but the quest continues to increase the yield of cocoons and to replace the mulberry leaf with artificial foodstuffs. If sericulture can be automated, it will certainly be the Japanese who discover how this may be achieved. Silk is being used increasingly for purposes other than clothing and furnishings, such as cosmetics and surgery (allergies to silk are unknown), and these do not require the prodigious quantity of raw silk needed to make a kimono. Kimonos are no longer *de rigeur*, even for weddings, but despite the adoption of western clothing in Japan, traditional garments are still very important.

At present the main silk producers after China are Brazil, India, the ancient Silk Road producing-regions of Uzbekistan, the Caspian and the Black Sea, and Korea and Thailand. Though sericulture in Korea dates back some two thousand years, its present-day development sprang from the Japanese presence in pre-war days, which reactivated the dying silk industry. Japan is one of Korea's main clients for raw silk. Thailand too has an ancient tradition of silk, but her emergence as one of the great silk producers in modern times is due largely to the enthusiasm and dedication of an American, Jim Thompson, whose name is inextricably associated with Thai silk for many foreign tourists, and perhaps even for a few Thai. The distinctive texture of

Elsi Giauque's silk sculpture
Colonne Blanche, 1978.

Thai silk, what Thompson described as 'humps and bumps', is due to the use of two different silk yarns – the fine, smooth, thrown thread of Bombyx mori as warps, and the untwisted, irregular, bulky native raw silk as weft. Today, some Thai silk is made entirely from native yarn, some entirely from imported silk, but often a combination of yarn is used. The characteristic slubs are sometimes created intentionally in the weaving process.

A compulsive collector with eclectic tastes, Thompson started to buy sarong lengths, attracted not only by the texture but also by the often startling colour combinations – a plaid of acid green and magenta for example, or deep blue and shocking pink. Thompson tracked down the remaining weaving families, and formed a company to produce and promote silks. His suitcase crammed with samples, he flew to New York and spilled these on the desk of Edna Woolman Chase, then editor of Vogue. As far as Vogue was concerned, Thai silk had arrived, and it was soon to feature, cut and stitched as couture garments, on its international pages.

Not until washed silk in the Eighties, its attractive peach-bloom surface obtained by tumbling in drums with sand, was silk so universally affordable as Thai silk. The costumes for the film 'The King and I' could be made from no other fabric, and other important early orders ranged from the principal costumes for 'Ben Hur' (for which special weaves were created), to the refurbishment of the Canaletto Rooms in Windsor Castle. Perhaps the most celebrated and influential customer was the beautiful Queen Sirikit of Thailand, whose Pierre Balmain wardrobe for the visit she and the King made to America in the early Sixties included many special Thompson silks. Balmain continued to use Thai silk extensively in his couture collections, and other designers did likewise.

It is part of silk's power that it retains its aura of luxury, its sense of being special, whether worn as a shirt with levis or as regal brocade for ceremonial occasions. In recent years Japanese artists, designers and technicians have devised many innovative textures and weaves, notably in synthetic or synthetic-natural fibre mixes. Japanese designers have also made great impact on fashion, inventing shapes and textures, a completely fresh approach which, nevertheless, in truly Japanese character, grows from its tradition-steeped roots, the desire for excellence in every detail. The genius of Issey Miyake, to name just one, demands a new term that includes, but goes far beyond, the confines of 'fashion'. Though he works in all types and mixtures of textile fibres, his inventiveness with silk, too, challenges traditional concepts of its application and use. Japanese artists have also worked with silks for sculptural structures, notably Machiko Agano, who showed at the 11th Biennale his *Untitled*, of white silk organza, wood and cords, a series of suspended, gently balanced floating veils.

Today among the many artists and ateliers working with silks, the San Francisco-based firm of Obiko deserves mention. Silk designers work with new and traditional

techniques – for example Japanese *shibori*, and Fortuny-inspired metallic printing – on innovative and classic *pret-à-porter* garments.

Among the most beautiful illustrations of the use of silk in contemporary weaving is the work of the Swiss artist Elsi Giauque. A contemporary of the Bauhaus weavers, Giauque was born in 1900. Her textile sculptures, for example her suspended columns of free-floating silk threads, caught at precise points, like *Colonne Blanche*, 1978, are in a sense architectural. The American artist Sheila Hicks, on the other hand, took her inspiration from the techniques of Mexico and South America, and constructed giant sculptures of silk and mixed fibres in complicated systems. The term 'twining' has been coined to describe these twisted forms.

All over the world today artists work with silk in both traditional and innovative techniques, painting, sculpting, combining it with other media, marvelling at its adaptability. Galleries like Julie's in New York exhibit 'Art to Wear' – garments which can be displayed effectively as paintings or sculpture as well as worn. Though the concept seems so modern, it is in fact ancient. We read classical Greek and Arabic texts describing glorious robes hung to decorate the walls of ceremonial tents, and elegant stands were devised in order to display the beauty of kimonos.

The display of excellence is traditional in the story of silk. Its history is an eternal silken thread, linking the centuries, encircling the globe, turning and returning.

A Compendium of Information

Terms and Techniques

Abr or *ebru:* Turkish, literally 'cloud'; term for fabric woven with the warp or weft resist-dyed before weaving. The yarn is tied or otherwise protected from colour before immersion in the dyestuff. Also known by the Indonesian term 'ikat' and French 'chiné'.

Aerophane: Fine thin silk crêpe, popular in the early nineteenth century for decorative appliqués, as raised motifs, or applied and re-embroidered, and for pleated and gathered dress-trimmings.

African silk: Chiefly the wild silk of the Anaphe species, found in Uganda and other parts of Africa, where the silkworms feed on fig leaves and construct large nests containing clusters of cocoons. The fibre of cocoons and nest are processed by being spun together to form a thread. In Nigeria, anaphe silk is mixed with cotton. Also the wild silk of Gonometa rufubrunnea, recently discovered in Botswana and neighbouring countries; this silkworm gives a silk of fineness and tensile strength intermediate between Bombyx mori and tussah. See also *Wild Silks*.

Alto-e-basso: See *Velvet*

American silk: Wild silks from species introduced from Asia, such as the Ailanthus, and also a number which are native to the continent. In the mountains outside Oaxaca wild silk is harvested and woven into a thin crêpe which is dyed bright magenta and used for a wrap-around belt; it is suggested the custom may pre-date the Spanish conquest.

Antheraea mylitta: See *Wild silks*

Antheraea perynl: See *Wild silks*

Antioch, cloth of: Silk named for the city in Syria, famous as a market and textile centre. During the time of the Crusades 'cloth of Antioch' referred generally to rich silks from the East, and sometimes more specifically to a type of figured brocade patterned with birds, whose heads, beaks, feet and roundels on the wings were picked out in gold thread, or with animals such as gazelle, similarly highlighted with areas of gold. The brocades may have been woven in several areas around the Mediterranean.

Atlas: Satin weave used in the Near and Middle East, and in India. Attacus atlas is the Atlas silkmoth (see *Wild silks*).

Aya cloth: Japanese name for one of the earliest types of figured silk, first introduced into Japan via Korea not later than the third or fourth century A D. Judging from the few fragmentary textiles that have been preserved from the Tang period (A D 618–906) 'aya' cloths were constructed with a 'twill' ground.

Baldachin, baldaquin: Canopy of rich silk and gold material. The name derives via Old English *baldekin* from Italian *baldacchino*, originally denoting a rich patterned silk from Baghdad.

Bandhani: Indian silk, tie-dyed to give a spotted pattern.

Batiste: Fine, thin, plain-woven cloth of silk, cotton, etc. Named after its inventor, Baptiste Chambrai, a thirteenth-century French weaver.

Batting: Silk fibre used for quilting and insulation, twenty per cent warmer than the best down.

Baves: Silk threads as they are drawn off the cocoon complete with their gum or sericin coating. See also *Reeling, Sericin, Spinning*.

Beaded roundel: An ancient repeat-motif enclosing traditional designs such as single, or confronted, or addorsed, animals or mythical beasts, or hunting scenes, often with a Tree of Life. The motif was adopted and developed by the Sassanians, and widely copied.

Bed hangings: Curtains which trimmed the four poster bed, and usually included two large and two small curtains, a tester or canopy with inner and outer valances, coverings for the head and footboards and matching counterpane. In the Greek Islands around the seventeenth century, a unique style developed, where typical local embroideries formed a tent-like structure suspended from a wooden ceiling rose. Bed furnishings included matching embroidered cushions and valances.

Bengaline: Fabric with silk warp and cotton or wool weft, and prominently ribbed silk surface.

Bizarre silks: Silks woven with non-directional exotic designs, fashionable in Europe from the late seventeenth century to *c.* 1720. While the silks reflect the influence of Oriental designs, they appear to have originated in Lyon, and were imitated in other centres.

Blackwork: Monochrome embroidery, usually in black silk, sometimes enriched with metal threads, fashionable in sixteenth-century Europe. It has been associated with Catherine of Aragon, although it was an international style, known from the Middle Ages and stylistically related to Arabic and Moorish designs. Also known as Spanish or Holbein work.

Blonde: Natural colour of undyed silk. The term for early nineteenth-century laces of undyed silk.

Bombasine, bombazine, bumbazine: A black twill weave, of silk or other fibres, much used for mourning clothes and especially popular during the nineteenth century.

Bombyx: Term (literally, 'cocoon') for indigenous silk known to the Roman world, said to have been first spun in the island of Cos by Pamphile, daughter of Plates. Cos had been famous in antiquity for 'coa vestis', a gauzy sheer fabric.

Bombyx mori: The domesticated silk moth which is

the source of most of the world's silk production.

Bouclé: Fabric-texture produced when a secondary weft, usually of metal thread, is pulled up to form loops on the face of the textile. Nowadays a general term for looped yarns and weaves.

Boulting cloth: An open-mesh raw silk, used for silk-screen printing and as a foundation for embroidery. The warp is a fine, hard twist organzine, and the plain gauze square mesh is held in place by silk's natural gum (sericin).

Bourrette: Yarn of silk or other fibre with rough uneven texture, and fabric woven of such yarn.

Brigandine: Pattern of a small-scale repeating spot or circle enclosing a pointed star, woven in velvet or brocade, inspired by a form of armour composed of overlapping metal or leather scales.

Brin: A single filament of silk drawn off from a cocoon, after degumming (removal of sericin).

Brocade: Compound weave in which additional colours are added, originally by means of hand-held bobbins (brocading shuttles), while a 'draw-boy' manipulated the warps for the pattern. As in embroidery, the additional threads are decorative, rather than constructive. The ground can be any weave: satin was popular in the West, twill is used in Japan and in many Persian and Byzantine brocades. Philippe de Lasalle began the use of chenille (tufted yarn) wefts to give areas with the effect of velvet. Brocade is now woven on a mechanized or computerized Jacquard loom.

Brocading weft: An additional weft introduced into a ground weave, with movement limited to the width of the area where it is required, i.e. which does not travel from selvedge to selvedge.

Brocatelle: Weave related to the damask weave, usually with a satin or twill figure on a plain satin ground. The pattern appears raised, since the weave contains a double warp (more warp threads than will lie together in one plane). Like damask, brocatelle seldom uses more than two colours.

Calender, calandre: A machine with rollers (cylinders) which press the fabric to give a moiré or 'watered' effect by flattening the surface in irregular creases.

Cannele: Weave with ribbed surface formed by warp floats (warps carried over two or more wefts).

Canut: Sharp-bladed instrument used to cut loops to form velvet pile; also the colloquial term for the silk weavers of La Croix Rousse district of Lyon.

Caterpillar Club: International club whose membership is limited to persons whose life has been saved by a parachute. Caterpillars can lower themselves to the ground by the silk thread they spin; and during the world wars parachutes were made from silk.

Chain stitch: The chief of many linked, loop stitches. Ancient and universal, the stitch has been used for outlines and infilling, and is done either with a needle or hook.

Chantilly: Fine black and also blonde silk bobbin lace, first popular in the eighteenth century. Now made at Le Puy and other centres around Paris.

Charmeuse: A type of soft-textured satin especially popular for lingerie.

Chenille: A velvet or tufted yarn, originally silk, with a furry appearance like that of some caterpillars (French, *chenille,* caterpillar).

Chiffon: Transparent silk woven like fine muslin, with a semi-dull lustre and gauze-like grainy texture. Chiffon, organdie, voile, and grenadine are all light, mat fabrics made from fine twisted yarns, spaced out to make the fabric transparent, and are part of the taffeta group of fabrics. Chiffon patterned with areas of silk pile was invented and fashionable in the 1920s. Also called crêpe georgette.

Chikan: 'Whitework' embroidery made by Italian Moslems and confined to Dacca and Calcutta in Bengal, and Lucknow. Bengali work was mainly for export to Europe, but in Lucknow it was for local patrons. Floral patterns were embroidered on fine muslin. Some of the most beautiful chikan used threads of the wild yellow silk of Antherea mylitta of Assam and Bengal.

Chiné, chiné à la branche: Textile with polychrome patterns resist-dyed on the warp before weaving. See *Ikat.*

Chinoiserie: European imitation of Chinese decoration, often recognizable by caricatured features.

Cloud-band: Chinese motif widely adopted during and after the Mongol expansion. It resembles an undulating ribbon, often decorated with tiny scrolls along the edges.

Cintamani: Pattern-motif widely disseminated during the period of Mongol dominance, consisting of triple dots arranged as a pyramid, over a pair of wavy lines, originally an auspicious Buddhist symbol, denoting wisdom (fully opened Third Eye) above serenely smiling lips. The motif was freely adapted, particularly by the Ottomans.

Cisele: See *Velvet*

Cloth of gold: A heavy silk enriched with gold thread.

Coa vestis: See *Bombyx.*

Colifichet: Floss-silk embroidery on paper.

Compound weave: A construction with more than one set of warp threads and/or weft threads. One set usually appears on the face, the other on the reverse. A general term for a complex weave. Compound weaves, for example damask, are used to create contrasting textures and the more elaborate patterns and colour effects, and are generally produced on a loom with an attached Jacquard or a Jacquard-like computer.

Cope: Ecclesiastical cloak worn by dignitaries, a large semi-circular garment.

Couching: Technique in which a thread is laid over fabric and attached to it by oversewing, especially used to apply metal threads.

Counted-thread stitches: Embroidery based on a build-up of simple stitches over a regular number of threads in canvas or fabric.

Crêpe, crape: Fabric made of yarn which has been highly twisted before weaving, giving suppleness, a rough mat surface and crisped texture (Latin, *crispus*, curled). Crêpe twisted yarns are twisted either to the right or left, and threads of each twist are used alternatively in the fabric, in both filling or warp. The crêpe effect is achieved in fabric by the contrary pull of the two tightly twisted threads when they are released from their set condition by the degumming process (removal of seracin). All crêpe twisted yarns are degummed *after* weaving. Varieties of woven crêpes include crêpe de Chine, crêpe marocain, crêpe georgette (also known as chiffon).

Crêpe de Chine: Fabric woven from raw silk in various weights, a popular dress fabric, also used for silk sheets. It is opaque, with a semi-dull lustre and smooth, slightly crinkly texture, with soft drape.

Crêpe georgette: Chiffon fabric named after a Paris designer Mme Georgette de la Plante. See *Chiffon.*

Crêpe marocain: Heavy Chinese silk with very marked grain.

Cross stitch: Simple and ancient double stitch in the form of an X, used in almost every part of the world.

Damask: An early Chinese patterned weave, predating brocade. It takes its name from Damascus, the important city in Syria on the East–West trade routes. Among the early silks, all of which originated outside Europe almost down to the ninth century AD, damasks figure prominently. However it is not the case that Damascus became the sole centre weaving damask cloths. For example, Procopius in the sixth century refers to Tyrus, Berytus, and Antioch as principal places of silk manufacture, with no mention of Damascus. Damask is characterized by the use of different weave-structures to achieve a pattern in a single colour cloth, and has a flat, reversible design made by combining warp-faced and weft-faced satin or twill weaves. Where two colours appear, the warp is generally one colour, the weft the other. Any fibre can be used in a damask cloth, and other weaves may be incorporated. From 1350 onwards 'drap de damas de Luccque', or Lucchese damask, was a standard item in inventories and bills. By the fifteenth century Venice had become a well-established silk centre, and elements of design such as palmettes, fruit, flowers and so forth were adopted and modified by Venice and Florence as well as other Italian silk centres. These provided the impetus for both Spanish and French damask-weaving styles in the sixteenth century. The seventeenth-century fashion for hanging walls with lengths of silk spurred the damask weavers, and large-figured patterns incorporated variations of pomegranates, palmettes, lotus, artichokes, crowns, and large sinuous meanders became features. Frequently chairs and seats were upholstered in the same fabric as the walls, giving a room uniformity. The crisis caused in all silk-weaving by the French Revolution was alleviated by the introduction of the Jacquard loom and mechanization of the silk industry.

Darning stitch: Economical embroidery technique in that the thread is shown on the pattern side only.

Decreusage: French term for the process of removing the gum (sericin) from silk by immersion in an alkaline solution.

Denier: Unit of weight equal to about eight-and-a-half troy grains, the measure by which silk yarn was weighed and its fineness estimated in 1839.

Diasprum: See *Lampas*

Diocletian Edict: The Emperor Gaius Diocletian (AD 284–305) issued a list of many regulations pertaining to silk weaving, tailoring and the wearing of silk clothes, indicating that silk was a well-known and important fabric in the Roman Empire in the third century.

Disease of silkworm: See *Pebrine*

Double weave: Construction that produces two textiles, one above the other, by means of at least two sets of warp and two sets of weft.

Douppion: Double cocoon containing male and female pupae, producing a tangled thread. The resulting yarn and woven cloth have a slubbed, irregular texture.

Drawloom: Handloom with a system of cords for lifting the warps for the passage of the weft, used to produce complicated repeat patterns. The Chinese term for this translates as 'pulling the flowers', French is 'tirer les lacs'. The cords were manipulated by a 'drawboy', an assistant perched at the top of the loom.

Droguet: Small-patterned silk textile popular in the eighteenth century.

Duchesse satin: A heavy, luxurious dress fabric.

Dyeing: Silk was dyed as yarn, rather than as fabric, until *c.* 1815–30. Piece-dyeing of fabric was introduced in Lyon around 1849. See also: *Resist-dyeing, Tie-dyeing*

Ecru: Silk thrown (i.e. twisted) or woven while still in its natural gum-coated state.

Eri: Silk from Philosomia ricini and Philosamia cythnia, Indian wild silk moths feeding on castor leaves, nowadays cultivated indoors. The silk requires spinning; it cannot be reeled.

Fagara: Silk produced from the Atlas moth, Attacus atlas.

Faille: Thick, soft taffeta, usually yarn-dyed, sometimes given a moiré finish.

Fancy or *composite weaves:* Fabrics which combine two or more weaving techniques.

Fardet, torsello: Long, narrow, canvas-covered bales of raw or woven silk, in a convenient size and shape for transportation by pack animal. Emblem of the Lucchese silk merchants and of the Court of the merchants.

Ferronerie: Curved, linear woven patterns reminiscent of decorative wrought-iron work, an effective decoration in voided velvet. See also *Velvet.*

Fibroin: Amino acid which hardens as the silkworm ejects it into the air, to form the fibre element of raw silk.

Figured fabrics: Fabrics (velvets, etc.) with woven rather than embroidered patterns.

Filament: Term for an extremely long fibre. Silk is the only natural (as distinct from manmade) filament.

Filature: Factory where raw silk is reeled from cocoons.

Fingernail weaving: Method used in China and Japan for fine silk tapestry, where the weaver's nails were sometimes finely serrated to beat down the weft. The Japanese term, *tsuzure-ori,* nowadays generally refers to any fine hand-woven silk tapestry.

Float: A yarn carried over two or more yarns of the opposite set between interlacings. A warp float passes over two or more weft, a weft float over two or more warp.

Florentine stitch: Wavy, zig-zag embroidery in shaded colours, used as an all-over pattern for wall hangings, bed curtains and upholstery. Originated in Hungary in the late Middle Ages, and later practised in Italy and most of Europe. Also known as Hungarian, Bargello or Flame stitch.

Floss: Silk from the outside of the cocoon, used as soft untwisted strands; in embroidery often laid and couched.

Flowered silks: The silks produced in Spitalfields, London, in a variety of patterns in the eighteenth century.

Foulard: Tie- or scarf-weight twill-woven silk.

French knot: Knot-like stitch used in embroidery, similar to Chinese Pekin knots.

Frisé: Crinkled thread composed of a lamella (fine strip of metal) wound on a spiral core.

Galons, galloons: Trimming-braid for uniforms, upholstery etc. of silk, metal or other threads.

Gauze, gaze: Sheer fine silk, able to hold a shape, as in trimmings for hats.

Gazar: Sheer silk invented and extensively used by the French couturier Balenciaga.

Genoese velvet, velours de gêne: Polychrome floral voided velvets, also called 'garden velvets'; made in other centres as well as Genoa.

Georgette: See *Chiffon.*

Gilded membrane, paper or *parchment:* Flat gilded strips, which came into use for weaving and embroidery in China during the Yuan (Mongol) dynasty.

Gold thread: Silk thread wrapped in finely beaten-out gold foil. Pure gold was used in the early Middle Ages, but later silver-gilt replaced it. An alternative to gold thread was fine gold leaf laid on thin animal membrane or paper, see above. Also known as *lamella.*

Green cocoon: Fresh cocoon.

Grogram: Coarse fabric of silk, or mohair and wool, or these mixed, after stiffening with gum. John Evelyn saw grograms being produced near Tours in the seventeenth century.

Gros de Tours: Heavy, strong taffeta with a pronounced ribbed surface.

Grosgrain: A plain ribbed silk.

Ground: Field or background of the pattern.

Gul-u-bulbul: 'Rose and nightingale', the phrase generally used to describe bird-and-flower motifs in Persian art.

Gum: Sericin, the gummy substance holding filaments of raw silk together.

Gynaeceum: Literally, 'women's quarters' in a Roman or Byzantine household, eventually the name for textile-producing workshops, no longer specifically for women workers.

Gypsy moth: Oak-feeding moth. In 1869 the American Leopold Trouvelot tried to interbreed Bombyx silkworms with gypsy moths. Accidentally released at Medford, Mass., they multiplied into millions and now constitute a defoliation hazard in the north-east USA.

Habutae: Plain-woven light silk from the Far East, popular as a lining material.

Harness: Frame that holds the heddles of a loom; also called a shaft.

Heddle, headle, heald: String, metal or bone eyelet through which individual warps are threaded, in an order determined by the pattern.

'Hit the silk': War-time usage dating from 1942, meaning to parachute from an airplane, that is, make a timely exit. See also *Caterpillar Club.*

Holosericum, holoserica: Latin term for garment made entirely of silk, as opposed to one decorated with silk elements or thread. The Roman child emperor

Elagabalus (AD 218–22) was reputedly the first Roman to wear holosericum. He kept a silken rope of purple and scarlet to hang himself, should this appear to be necessary, and was fond of dressing up as a female prostitute, perhaps in his silks, and going to the port of Ostia.

Honan: Hand-woven Chinese wild silk fabric.

Huguenots: French Huguenots, subject to religious persecution in the sixteenth and seventeenth centuries, who fled the country in large numbers. Among them were expert throwsters and weavers who contributed significantly to the development of the silk industry in Germany, Britain, Ireland, Italy and Switzerland.

Ikat: Indonesian name for fabric woven with the warp or weft (or in 'double-ikat', as for the Indian saris known as *patolas*, both warp and weft) resist-dyed before weaving. The yarn is tied or otherwise selectively protected before immersion in the dyestuff. Also known by the Turkish terms 'abr' or 'ebru' and French 'chiné'.

Irish poplin: See *Poplin.*

Jacquard loom: Type of loom named after Joseph-Marie Jacquard (b. 1752, Lyon), who was apprenticed to his father at the age of twelve and set to work pulling the loom-strings (*tirer les lacs*) which controlled drawloom pattern-weaving. In 1804, by modifying Vaucanson's invention of 1745 and Falcon's in 1734, Jacquard devised a perforated pattern-card to carry the weft in place of the 'drawboys'. He received the Legion d'Honneur in 1819, and his statue stands in the Place de la Croix in Lyon. The process is now computerized.

Jardinière: Garden velvet. See: *Genoese velvet.*

Kesi, kesa: Japanese priest's robe, consisting of a rectangle and seven or nine specifically placed patches.

Kesi, k'ossu: Chinese silk tapestry.

Kimono: Japanese national dress, from *ki* meaning 'silk', *mono* meaning 'wearing'.

Kincob: Persian and Indian term for metal brocade, from Chinese 'chin', gold. Herat was especially famous for gold brocade, and Persian weavers brought to India by the Moguls taught the technique to Indian weavers. Kincob became a speciality of Benares.

Kinran: Japanese term for gold brocade.

Knitted silk: Hand-knitted silk gloves and hose were formerly part of regal and Church regalia. In the fifteenth and sixteenth centuries, knitted silk garments were sold throughout continental Europe as flat segments to be stitched together to fit the purchaser. Many fine and beautiful examples can be seen in various museums. Knitting machinery was invented by William Lee from Calverton, Nottinghamshire, in 1589. Refused a patent by Elizabeth I, he moved to France. In machine knitting, there are two types of warp-knitted silks: tricot and milanese. Tricot is characterized by fine vertical wales on the face and crosswise ribs on the back. In Milanese the threads are interknitted at every course in which the threads run diagonally. A fine rib on the face and a faint diagonal or diamond effect on the back are characteristic. These fabrics are run-resistant, and are used for women's gloves and lingerie and, after printing, for women's lightweight crease-resisting dresses.

K'ossu: See *Kesi.*

Laidwork: Embroidery of long threads, often floss silk, laid on fabric and fixed at points by couching threads.

Lamé: Tissue with most of the pattern made up of gold and silver threads.

Lamella: Flat strip of precious or base metal, or gilt or silvered parchment, metal or paper used for yarn. It may be used flat or wound around a core.

Lampas: Figured textile in which a pattern composed of supplementary warp and weft is added to a foundation weave, such as a pattern of twill weave on a satin foundation. Additional warps or wefts are also used in the patterned areas to create extra colours, and when not required are woven into the back of the cloth. Also called 'diasprum'.

Lutestring, lustring: Glossy silk used in dresses, or as a ribbon, a speciality of Lyon and Nimes in France. Import to England was banned in 1692, after the formation of the Royal Lustring Co.

Magnanerie: French term for silkworm-rearing room or house.

Maltese lace: Heavy silk bobbin-lace, usually cream (blonde). Also found in black silk. Characterized by short wheatears, often in the form of a Maltese Cross.

Mashru or *masru:* Silk-and-cotton or silk-and-linen fabric, usually striped with a silk-satin surface.

Moiré: See *Calender.*

Momme: Unit of weight, denoting quality, of woven silk.

Monovoltine: Term for silkworm species with one generation each year.

Mordant: Chemical agent used to fix dyestuff to a fibre.

Moriculture: Mulberry cultivation, as opposed to sericulture which includes the breeding of silkworms.

Mousseline: Very light silk.

Mukhmal, makhmal: Arabic term denoting pile fabric, velvet (Indian, 'makmali').

Mukta: Silk spun from the cocoons of moths which have made their natural escape, yielding coarse thread favoured by various Indian sects who abhor the taking of life. Used as a foundation thread in heavy gold and silver brocades (kincob), such as those from Benares.

Mulham: Cloth with silk warp and cotton weft, a speciality of Moslem Spain.

Multivoltine: Term for silkworm species with numerous generations each year.

Noil: Short-stapled waste obtained in spinning silk.

Opus Anglicanum: General term for ecclesiastical embroideries produced in England from approximately AD 900 to 1500.

Opus Teutonicum: Medieval German 'whitework' embroidery, in contrast to the bejewelled and colourful embroidery of other countries, especially England.

Organza: Sheer fabric, yarn-dyed before the gum is removed. It is almost transparent, with a dull lustre and a mesh-like, flat, firm, stiff texture.

Organzine: Silk yarn made of two strands of raw silk, each twisted and then thrown together with a reverse twist. Useful as a warp yarn. See *Throwing.*

Orphrey: Band, usually embroidered, superimposed in cross or Y formation, or as border, on chasuble, cope etc.

Paris velvet: Inexpensive pile fabric combining waste silk with cotton.

Passementerie: Elaborate braids and trimmings.

Patola: Double ikat, fabric with weft and warp resist-dyed before weaving, a speciality of ·Gujerat, used to make the most expensive type of wedding sari.

Pebrine: An epidemic disease in silkworms, which in the nineteenth century devastated sericulture all over Europe and the Near East, identified and researched by Louis Pasteur.

Pekin knot: Knot-like stitch used in embroidery, similar to French knot, but more loop-like in appearance.

Petersham: Stiff, ribbed-silk ribbon used for hat bands and waistbands.

Petit point: Tent stitch, term usually applied to finer work.

Pile weave: Construction with extra sets of warp or weft, making a three-dimensional surface, as in velvet, corduroy, etc.

Pique: Embroidery in which the design is outlined with cord and infilled with stitches, resembling a figured fabric.

Plush stitch: Loop stitch, taking its name from plush fabric, which has a nap longer than that of velvet. Loops may be left or trimmed to various degrees to give a sculptural effect.

Ply: Yarn of two or more single strands twisted together.

Point rentre: Method of shading introduced by textile designer Jean Revel in the early eighteenth century. The shades of colour are dovetailed in weaving to give an illusion of three-dimenstional forms.

Polonnaise: Type of silk-and-metal-thread rug or kelim, made in various weaving centres in Persia, such as Kashan.

Polyvoltine: See *Multivoltine.*

Pongee: Taffeta-type of soft, heavy silk.

Poplin: Fabric formerly woven with silk warp and wool worsted weft, with corded surface. Originally made in Avignon, a papal seat, hence its name, from French *popeline* and Italian *papalina.* Poplin became a typical Irish fabric and now refers to a strong cotton with an attractive sheen, although legally the term 'Irish Poplin' can only be applied to a mix of pure silk and pure wool.

Porpola, purpura: The colour of precious murex-dyed cloth. By the eleventh century the term had come to mean merely precious silk fabric.

Raw silk: Silk retaining its natural gum or sericin. Though lustreless, it is in its strongest and most durable state. Dye does not penetrate the gum evenly, and the silk is usually de-gummed by immersion in an alkaline solution.

Reeling: The process of unwinding cocoons to make raw silk. The pupa is killed in the cocoon by heat or steam. Threads from two or more cocoons (depending on the final thickness or size of thread desired) are formed into one continuous, uniform and regular strand that constitutes commercial raw silk. The process, which is extremely delicate, has been mechanized and automated; the establishment in which it is done is called a filature. The cocoons are first sorted to remove the douppions (double cocoons), pierced cocoons and any other unreelable cocoons (these cocoons are spun). Those fit to be reeled are boiled in water for 10–12 minutes to soften the natural gum or sericin which holds the filaments together. The ends of the filaments are caught with revolving brushes and wound on reels. The reels are unwound into skeins of the desired circumference, length and weight. See also: *Spinning, Throwing.*

Resist-dyeing: Process in which wax or clay is applied to cloth or yarn, or it is bundled or tied, to prevent the dye reaching certain areas and so create a pattern. In ikat, the warps or wefts are resist-dyed before weaving. In double ikat, both warps and wefts are resist-dyed before weaving.

Samite: Heavy lustrous weave which has been compared to satin. It was used for clothing, tents, furnishings, shrouds and funeral palls, and was reputedly decay-resisting. Sometimes samite was patterned. It is often mentioned in medieval texts and romances, and that red samite hose are mentioned in a bill of settlement between merchants of Calatayud and the cathedral at Toledo in

1278, is an indication of the wide variety of clothing-uses to which the fabric was put.

Sarcenet: Fine light silk, said to have been first made by the Saracens, popular for veils.

Satin: Opaque fabric, with a bright lustre on the face side, with a slick, smooth touch and soft or firm texture as desired. It may be piece-dyed or yarn dyed. There is a wide range of satins: duchesse satin, double-faced radzimir satins, satin crêpes with a weft made from twisted yarns, charmeuses (satin crêpes with a very soft feel).

Satin de Bruges: Mixed silk-and-linen or silk-and-wool fabric woven in the Netherlands.

Satin stitch: Straight, parallel embroidery stitch, a mass of which gives a flat, shiny appearance.

Schappe silk: A spun silk which has had 90 per cent of its gum or sericin removed.

Seed, grain: Silkworm eggs.

Selvedge: The lengthwise, finished edge of a woven fabric.

Sendal: Strong taffeta, much used for banners, as in the Spanish banner of St Isidore. Gomez-Moreno, however, has listed as 'sendal' the sheer material forming part of the headwear of Eleanor of England and Maria de Almenar, found in their tombs at Las Huelgas, a type of fine linen woven with stripes of white or coloured silk. Florence May suggested that 'sendal' was a general term, applied alike to light and heavyweight fabrics, as the word 'silk' is used today.

Sericin: Gummy protein that holds together fibroin filaments in a cocoon, and later in raw silk. It forms 25–30 per cent of the substance of raw silk. It prevents even dyeing, and is removed by immersion of the raw silk in an alkaline solution.

Sericulture: Cultivation of mulberries and silkworms to make cocoons.

Shantung: Chinese wild silk fabric, opaque with a semi-dull lustre, woven with tussah or douppion wefts, which result in a soft slubbed texture.

Shibori: Japanese term for tie-dye.

Shot silk: Fabric woven with different coloured warps and wefts, to given an iridescent sheen.

Shuttle: Holder for weft thread as it is interlaced with the warps.

Siklatun, ciclatoun: Silk as a dress fabric. Ciclatoun 'with gold' is often cited. The Cid and his daughters dressed in garments of ciclatoun.

Silk, silk moth, silkworm: Silk is the natural protein filament extruded by various categories of mollusc, spider, and moth. Only Lepidoptera, the silk moth family, produce enough fibre for commercial textile purposes. It is scientifically grouped into seven main moth families spread across the New and Old Worlds. The two moth families which produce more silk than any other group are the Saturniidae and the Bombycidae to which the Bombyx silk moth belongs. There are many varieties of Bombycidae yielding continuous filaments. The primary source in terms of quality and quantity is the cultivated species Bombyx mori (literally, 'mulberry cocoon'). Unlike some of its spectacularly beautiful cousins (in particular the Saturniidae), Bombyx mori is pale greyish white, is blind, has no digestive organs, has lost the ability to fly, and is unable to survive outside a human-managed sericultural environment. The many varieties of Bombyx mori yielding continuous filaments are the subject of research by institutes in the sericultural countries, all with the objective of producing ever more perfect and competitively priced silk. The eggs, known as seed or grains, are cold-stored to control the hatching period. (They hatch at *c.* 22°C/71–72°F). However, breeding cycles are affected by hours of sunlight, even though the caterpillars live in an artificial environment. In Europe and the Middle East, Bombyx mori silkworms produce one generation annually; in Japan two or three harvests per year are possible, while in parts of India and China breeding cycles are almost continuous. Six species of Bombyx, differing from Bombyx mori but also mulberry-feeding, have been semi-domesticated in India. All are polyvoltine and form variable but reelable cocoons. There are many mulberry-feeding species of silk moth that remain wild. See also: *Wild silk.*

Silk, properties of: Strength: a 1 mm silk yarn will support a weight of 45 kilos; fineness: a cocoon weighing 3 gr. gives 1,000 m. of yarn; high absorbency; rot-resistance; non-conductivity, making it an excellent electric insulator; a non-allergen.

Silk-screen printing: The silk-screen printing process is the modern commercial form of stencil printing. Since the screen may be made from wire gauze, cotton fabrics and other materials as well as from silk boulting cloth, the process is generally called 'screen printing' by commercial printers. Artists use specialized techniques, and call their method serigraphy to distinguish it from the commercial variety. The design is painted on, or affixed to, a sheet of silk boulting cloth or other screen material that is stretched tightly over a wooden or metal frame. The design is transmitted in terms of open and blocked areas of the screen. Each colour requires a separate screen. Silk-screen stencils can be prepared by a variety of methods, and photography is increasingly employed.

Slubs: Irregular lumps in threads, as in Thai silk.

Slucz: Silk-weaving centre in Poland, famous for its sashes.

Soie grège: Raw, untwisted silk in its natural gum, sericin.

Spinning, spun yarn: Spun silk is yarn composed of shorter or broken filaments that are unsuitable for reeling, and require twisting together in the manner of cotton, wool etc. Broken cocoons of wild and breeding silk moths, and the beginnings and ends of Bombyx mori cocoons, will usually be spun. Spun silk yarns are used for shirtings, blouse and dress material, silk 'tweed' and sewing and embroidery threads. The combings left after the processing of the spun silk fibres are called 'noils', and are blended with other fibres or spun into coarse yarns. One cloth woven from these yarns was used for artillery powder bags: because silk is a protein fibre, it burns to a hard bead-like ash that will not clog the mechanism of guns.

Spitalfields: See *Huguenots.*

Split stitch: Fine stitch worked in untwisted silk thread where each stitch pierces the thread to give tiny, fine, chain-stitch appearance, used for delicate detailing, as of facial features in Opus Anglicanum.

Stamped velvet: Plain cut velvet impressed with a pattern by means of a heated, incised cylinder.

Staple: The length of a pure natural fibre when teased out. For silk this can be up to *c.* 250 mm.

Stencil: Ancient method of fabric decoration, commonly used in China and Japan by AD 500. A highly developed method was used in Japan from the late seventeenth century to recent times. The intricate designs were cut in separate pieces of parchment which were then glued or tied in place by numerous crossing-strands of silk or human hair. Stencilling was widely used in the USA after 1800 for interior decoration, and stencilling patterns on silk velvet was considered a suitable accomplishment for young ladies.

Stifle: To kill the pupa in a cocoon by heat.

Stumpwork: Mid-seventeenth-century embroidery, usually figurative and worked from figures derived from engravings or 'stamps'. Often applied to pictures, caskets or mirror frames, it involves much raised work, appliqué, needlepoint and beadwork.

Surah: In the US, the term is synonymous with 'tie silk'. Printed surah is known as 'foulard' in the men's trade.

Tabby: Streaked or 'watered' silk (see *Calender*). The term is said to derive from Attabi, a textile-producing district in Baghdad, and may have originally described a striped or ikat cloth. One observer likened it to zebra skin.

Tabby weave: Term for plain over-and-under basic weave.

Taffeta: One of the terms for fine, plain, silk cloth woven by intertwining a warp and a weft yarn in the simplest way. Taffeta is usually shiny, though not highly reflective as satin weaves; yarn-dyed, very fine-grained, with a dry and rustling feel.

Tambouring: Chain stitch worked with a small hook over a tambour (or drum frame). A fast and effective method of embroidering large surfaces.

Tapestry: Weave characterized by mosaic-like patterning with discontinuous wefts. The blocks of colour may be dovetailed or separate; if separate, the splits between blocks may be sewn up after weaving to make a reversible cloth.

Tartar cloths: By the fourteenth century, a term for figured silks patterned in gold with birds, animals and mythical beasts.

Thread: The filament used for sewing, manufactured as part of the throwing operation, but considered a distinct and separate branch because some additional equipment must be used in manufacture, and great care taken in every operation, especially spooling, to make a smooth, knotless thread.

Throwing, thrown yarn: The one process between reeling of the long filaments of Bombyx mori and weaving. Between two and ten cocoons are reeled simultaneously. The silk thread is twisted gently in varying degrees either to the left or right (from the Anglo-Saxon *thrawan*, to twist). Each twist is called a 'turn', and the greater the number of turns per inch/cm, the greater the contraction of the thread. Many fabrics are woven with yarns containing little or no twist. The most frequently used types of thrown yarns are tram, organzine and crêpe. Some couched embroideries are made with untwisted (floss) silk.

Tie silk: Firm opaque silk, usually twill weave. See also *Surah.*

Tiraz: Woven bands, products of Moslem textile workshops, and also the workshops.

Tie-dyeing, tie-and-dye: The process in which an area of yarn or cloth is secured from colouration by firmly wrapping, tying or stitching it before immersion in a dye. See also: *Resist-dye.*

Tram: Yarn of two or more threads twisted together with only a few turns per inch/cm, used for the filling or crosswise thread.

Tussah: See *Wild silk.*

Twill: Fabric in which the weave gives an effect of diagonal ribs and grooves. The main fabrics using this type of weave are the serges, surahs, diagonals, herring-bone and diamond weaves.

Twisting: Process of turning together two or more filaments or unit-groups of filaments, to form a twisted yarn. See: *Throwing.*

Velvet: Ancient weave in which pile is produced by raising the warps by the introduction of rods or wires during weaving. The loops may subsequently be cut. Velvet consists of three elements: a structural warp, a structural weft, and a non-structural or supplementary warp. Velvets may be described as 'solid' when the ground is entirely covered with pile, or 'voided', when areas of the ground are left free of pile. The voided areas may be plain satin, or brocaded with metal. In 'alto-e-basso' (pile-on-pile velvet) the pile is woven in two or more heights, to achieve a pattern. The loops formed may be cut or uncut. In 'ciselé velvet' the pattern is formed by cut and uncut pile, the cut pile being higher than the uncut. These types may be further embellished by the addition of metallic threads, in different sizes and heights of loops. 'Ferronerie' denotes a pattern reminiscent of wrought-iron-work, hence its name. 'Velours de Gêne' (named for Genoa although not specific to the city) are multi-coloured velvets patterned with flowers, popular for upholstery, also known as 'jardinière' or 'garden velvets'. The ancient method of using wires to create the pile was time-consuming, and in the 1830s in Lyon an unknown weaver devised a double-woven cloth in which the pile-thread was anchored in both top and bottom layers. As the cloth came off the loom it was sliced apart, producing two pieces of finished plain velvet. The technique was refined and adapted to power looms by a Spaniard, Jacinto y Cortes, and this is the process used for commercially produced velvet today.

Warp-faced: Term for a fabric with many more warp than weft, so that the weft are covered by warp.

Warps: Lengthwise yarns in woven fabrics.

Weft: Interlacing yarns in woven fabric. Also referred to as 'picks', 'filling' and 'woof'.

Wild silks: Term for both truly wild and less-cultivated species. The latter include Indian tussah (from Sanskrit *tasar*, a shuttle), eri and muga. The family of giant silkworms (Saturniidae) includes several species that produce commercially marketable silk, although the quality is not so fine as that spun by Bombyx mori. The moths are large, with distinctive 'eye' markings on their wings. The mezankoorie moth of Assam yields a valuable cocoon, as does Attacus atlas, one of the largest silk moths, measuring up to 10 in (25 cm) across the wingspan, found throughout India, Ceylon, Burma, China and Java. Samia cynthia, which feeds on a variety of plants including Ailanthus (tree of heaven) and castor-oil plant, spins a loose, flossy cocoon, either orange-red or white. Antheraea mylitta feeds on the leaves of the jujube tree in India and spins a large, compact silver-grey cocoon. Antheraea assama is domesticated to some extent in its native Assam. Antheraea pernyi, an oak-leaf feeder native to Mongolia and northern China, produces the brownish tussah silk imported extensively into Europe. This moth was one of several native species introduced to Europe and the USA at the end of the nineteenth century to replenish stocks decimated by pebrine disease, and has since naturalized in various regions of Spain, including the Balearic Isles. Another oak-leaf feeder, the Japanese Antheraea yamamai, which produces a large, bright green cocoon with strong white silk, failed to flourish when the eggs were brought to Europe in the early 1860s. The polyvoltine Eri (Ailanthus, Arrindi) silk moth is a native of Bengal, Assam and Nepal. It makes loose, flossy cocoons, orange-red or sometimes white, up to seven times a year. A hardy species, it was introduced to Italy in 1856 and to Spain a few years later for domestication. It now lives in the wild at sea level in the region of Barcelona, where it breeds as one generation on prunus, ilex, ligustrum, sorbus and viburnum. In many parts of Europe and the USA it has naturalized itself in city parks. Its Ailanthus name recalls one of the caterpillars' food plants, the 'tree of heaven', a widespread species of urban environments in western Europe. Antheraea peryni, the Chinese oak silk moth, a native of northern China, was introduced to Europe and the USA for silk rearing at the end of the nineteenth century, and to Spain, *c.* 1875, and like the Eri silk moth is now naturalized in certain regions.

Yarn: Silk which has been reeled and then thrown, or else spun. See *Reeling, Spinning, Throwing.*

Why collect? There is the thrill of the chase, the possibility of surprise, perhaps the desire to extend an inherited collection, or interest in the art and artefacts of a particular country or period of history. Silk collections are sometimes based around specific techniques or even designs. The choice of direction is very personal; types of collection are as varied as collectors themselves.

How select?

Visiting museums and exhibitions, poring over study collections, books, specialist magazines and journals, can all help to develop the indispensable 'eye' and good visual memory of a collector. (It is said that a collector needs an 'eye', and a 'nose', the latter a sort of sixth sense.) Even the sense of touch is important. While museums and galleries, understandably, cannot allow exhibits to be handled, they can provide valuable information about specialist clubs and lectures, symposia, arranged visits to collections, including some that might not be open to the public generally, and a collector should combine these sources with viewing and attending auctions, where physical examination of the items is essential. It is important to be able to make comparisons, to understand the physical condition of silk materials, to recognize alterations, and know how these factors relate to quality and rarity.

Where to buy?

Dealers, auction rooms, markets, bazaars, and other people's collections are all important sources, but silks may be found in less obvious places. A sculpture dealer might have something worn but wonderful which arrived as packing-material for a bronze, or perhaps a beautiful silk has been used as the lining of a box, or at the back of a Tibetan tangka. Such discoveries are part of the thrill of collecting.

Costume is apt to be worn out, or altered, or cut up to be recycled as furnishings, but precious silks have sometimes survived as scraps, perhaps re-used as decorative appliqué, or patching another fabric. Occasionally interesting fragments can be discovered in this way, and rescued.

Silks have survived as wrappings for holy relics. The source for many important collections of silk was the closure in the nineteenth century of religious houses on the Continent. Their vestments of precious silks were cut into pieces and sold to separate institutions, which explains why precisely the same design can be seen in museums in Britain, on the Continent and in America. After the Boxer Rising in Peking, the palace was looted, and imperial silks came on to the market. The Topkapi Palace held a series of auctions during the early 1920s. The likelihood of silks in such quantity ever coming on to

the market again seemed remote, but after the Chinese invasion of Tibet, the devastation of the monasteries brought extraordinary silks and other treasures to the West.

Until comparatively recently, textiles were not regarded as important archaeological finds, and were treated fairly dismissively, even thrown away during digs. Often they crumbled or burned when exposed to light and air. Tiny scraps of brownish material were not appealing to eyes seeking gold or spectacular works of art. Real archaeology, as opposed to treasure hunting, is an invention of the twentieth century. Techniques are still being developed to safeguard fragile materials, and some fabulous silks have been saved to enrich museum collections around the world.

Be your own curator

It is a good idea to catalogue every item at the time of acquisition, making a note of the place and price of purchase, and any clue as to identification and provenance. If silk is purchased in auction, mark the catalogue and keep the receipt. Any detail of provenance or history adds significantly to interest and value. An inventory with photographs is also important. Any restoration or cleaning should be noted, with 'before' and 'after' photographs if possible.

The nature of collections is to expand, therefore space for storage and display is a vital consideration. Flat textiles are easier to store than complete garments. The conditions of storage are all-important.

Improving a collection

As a collection grows, inevitably the collector will want to sell items. Perhaps a better example of the same type becomes available. This is where a good rapport with a reputable and knowledgeable dealer is valuable. Good dealers are keen to work with their clients and to help them to improve and develop their collections. They should always be prepared to buy back an item they have sold to a client, or take it in part exchange for another item, or offer to sell it on the client's behalf. Knowing other collectors with similar interests will sometimes lead to a direct exchange.

Fakes and forgeries

Textile art is not a field where forgeries generally flourish. One reason is that prices have not been so high as to encourage the considerable time and effort required to make an effective fake. However caution is advisable in certain areas. During the boom in Ottoman art in the late 1970s and 1980s, for example, embroideries were sometimes 'restored' to a point where there was more restoration than original material. The dealers were encouraged to do this by collectors who sought items in perfect condition, and were unable to judge the balance of new and old.

The numerous revivalist movements have prompted the reproduction of ancient silks, obviously with no intention to deceive. So in nineteenth-century Persia, silks from the sixteenth, seventeenth and eighteenth centuries were rewoven. Here the copies can easily be distinguished by the way the newer dyes have faded and aged. In Europe and America, many eighteenth-century designs were reproduced in the nineteenth and early twentieth century, especially the furnishing textiles and silks used for vestments. In the late nineteenth century, the Gothic revival prompted reproductions of medieval silks, and at Krefeld in Germany, silks were woven which recreated ninth-century fragments excavated from the tombs of early saints. Unscrupulous dealers (and collectors too) have been known to remove the selvedges and deliberately 'age' the fabric. In some instances old materials have been used to counterfeit even more ancient textiles. In such a case, only careful and scientific examination of techniques and dyes, and pattern-comparison, can reveal the truth.

Care and Conservation

How have silks survived?

Sometimes silks survive despite adverse circumstances, but usually they do so because they have been valued, and cared for in various ways.

Separately, each fibre survives according to its built-in characteristics and earlier treatment, but when different fibres are combined in a weave, their reaction to humidity alters. Pure silk survives better than a textile woven of silk combined with a different fibre.

Causes of damage

All natural fibres will decay, and start to do so from the moment they are picked or cut. Even if the natural process of decay cannot be reversed or halted, it can be slowed down by conservation and sensitive handling.

Natural damage

The deterioration-rate of silks is accelerated by light, dust, dirt, grease, excess moisture and excessive dryness. Of first importance is protection from light. Light fades colours, and also attacks fibres so that they become brittle and break. Dust and dirt contain small particles of grit which in time will cut the fabric, so it is important to keep dirt well away.

Water can mark silks and cause dyes to run. Together with heat it provides the conditions for mould to grow. Dryness will make the fibres brittle, so that they break: correct moisture content is necessary for suppleness.

Destructive treatments

At the turn of the century silks were subjected to disastrous finishing treatments. Among ingredients used to 'weight' or 'dress' the fabrics were metal salts, often used to excess, so causing the severe deterioration seen in these materials. The dressing was used particularly on silk taffetas made into linings and petticoats, to give their lovely rustle to the dresses of the 1890s and 1900s, but it can also be found on the satins and silks produced for wedding and evening dresses. In the worst instances of damage, the silk is reduced to powder.

In seventeenth- and eighteenth-century tapestries, where silk was used extensively bleached for highlighting certain areas, and for the sky, the silk content is often beyond conservation. There is no remedy for shattered silk.

Harsh treatment of fabric continues after it has left the loom and factory. In shops, the rolls of cloth are subjected to touch, dust and light. At the tailors or dressmakers a whole range of mechanical and hand-processes add their own strains: the fabric is cut, pinned, gathered, pleated, steamed.

Silks used for furnishings and for dress encounter a variety of hazards such as perspiration, smoke-filled rooms, food and drink stains. Cleaning agents may be harsh, but worse still is neglecting to wash or clean dirty fabric. Grease and food stains can be difficult to remove once they have become fixed, and will attract dust, and can also encourage insect and other animal life. Such creatures, in the process of eating the food, will make holes in the fabric.

Frequent washing, even by a trained conservator, is to some degree harmful. Dry cleaning is a harsher treatment than washing, often involving some mechanical action, and although it is sometimes the only practical step, it is advisable to keep it to the minimum.

Temperature

The ideal storage and display temperature is between 12° and 18°C, but this can rarely be maintained outside museum storerooms. In private houses, rooms with textile displays should never be warmer than 20°C, for the cumulative damage could be considerable.

Humidity

A stable humidity of 50 to 55 per cent is optimum for display and storage. Humidity, like temperature, is affected by the number of people in a room at any one time. People generate heat and have humid breath. As fibres absorb moisture they expand, as they release it they contract, and constant readjustments of this kind can be destructive, especially of silk woven with other types of fibre.

Storage

Silks should be stored in a dark place, at a moderate and constant temperature, and carefully wrapped in acid-free tissue paper. Layers of fabric should be protected from each other, and garments should have crumpled tissue paper inserted inside sleeves and folds to inhibit cracking. Wrappings should be replaced when yellowed.

Objects should be stored lying flat, or larger pieces may be rolled on well-washed calico- or acid-free-tissue-covered rollers. Hanging is best avoided, and should it be necessary, the weight must be supported on padded hangers. Prevention of damage is the best form of conservation.

Family heirlooms are often stored in old chests, particularly chests of cedarwood with its reputation for keeping away insects. The most precious silks were put away in wrappers, often made of old sheets or table linen, or even petticoats, for protection from dust and contact with bare wood. Cathedral treasuries are supplied with custom-built storage, shaped to fit copes and chasubles. Their conservation has preserved untold wealth, and the corresponding care given to their archives has sometimes preserved essential information on the source, date and purpose of the objects.

Display

It is a sad truth of a collector's life that all display is destructive, and this applies whether the object is shown under open conditions or in a showcase. Silks should be kept in darkness, but filters of colourless or near-colourless ultra-violet-absorbing acrylic sheets, available as Perspex VE or Plexiglas 201 or Oroglas UF 3, may be used in place of glass for showcases and picture frames. Acrylic sheets are lighter in weight than glass, and do not change temperature so rapidly. There should always be a 'cushion' of air between a textile and its framing material, so that the surfaces do not touch. Conventional spotlights should be avoided, for they not only destroy the organic materials they light, but have a detrimental effect on the temperature and humidity of a room. Low-voltage tungsten halogen lamps used for spotlighting have high luminosity without heat, and are therefore safer, though they should be fitted with ultra-violet filters. The safest form of lighting is fibre-optics which generate no heat at all. Never fix a display with adhesive tape, and never use glue on any textiles.

In a domestic context it was customary to have blinds and lined curtains to keep out the light when rooms were unoccupied, and loose covers, which would only be removed on very special occasions, to protect fine furnishings from wear and tear. Oriental carpets were protected from everyday use by druggets. When embroidery skills occupied many hours, the owners would look after their work with care, and value it.

It is the conditions in which they are kept, not age alone, which govern the life of textiles. Ideal conditions have been found in the dry, dark tombs of Peru and Egypt, in the stillness of Tibetan monasteries high in the Himalayas, in deep caves, in the ice and permafrost of Asian tombs, or sometimes with the embalmed or mummified bodies buried in churches and graveyards. Some silks have been retrieved from refuse heaps where a stratum of sand may have provided the necessary conditions. The earliest surviving silks we know, found in China, were protected from direct contact with soil by woven basketry, and in Europe, Roman lead coffins have protected silks. These survivals are inspirations to those who have the care of silks today.

Museums and Collections

In addition to specialized museums, those with general collections usually include textiles, and among them silk will be found. Silks have also been conserved by Cathedral Treasuries, and in some cases are still in situ; museums in major cities can provide information, and will also have details of associations who in turn can indicate further collections. In the U.S.A, many large companies have formed textile collections, and these are exhibited from time to time.

AUSTRIA

Vienna	Kunsthistorisches Museum ● Österreichisches Museum für Angewandte Kunst

BELGIUM

Brussels	Musées Royaux d'Art et d'Histoire

CANADA

Montreal	The Montreal Museum of Fine Arts
Ontario	Royal Ontario Museum
Ottowa	National Museum of Man
Saint John	New Brunswick Museum
Toronto	Royal Ontario Museum
Winnipeg	Ukrainian Cultural and Educational Centre

CHINA

Chengde	Summer Palace Museum
Fujian	Fujian Provincial Museum
Hubei	Jingzhou Museum
Hunan	Hunan Provincial Museum
Peking	Imperial Palace Museum
Suzhou	Museum
Xinjiang	Archaeological Museum Museum of the Autonomous Uighur Region

DENMARK

Copenhagen	Davids Samling ● Rosenborg Castle

EGYPT

Cairo	Museum of Islamic Art

FRANCE

Lyon	Musée Historique des Tissus
Mulhouse	Musée de l'Impression sur Etoffes
Nancy	Musée Historique Lorrain
Paris	Mobilier National ● Musée National des Arts Africains et Océaniens ● Musée des Arts Décoratifs ● Musée du Monde Arabe ● Musée Carnavalet ● Musée de l'Hôtel de Cluny ● Musée Guimet ● Musée de l'Homme

Sens	Trésor de la Cathédrale de Sens
Strasbourg	Musée des Arts Décoratifs
Tourcoing	Centre de Documentation des Fils et Tissus
Tours	Musée des Beaux Arts ● Musée du Chateau du Plessis: a new museum to celebrate the history of silkweaving and sericulture. Among others, the Cathedrals of Auxerre and Metz conserve examples of precious Byzantine silk masterpieces.

GERMANY

Berlin	Staatliche Museen, Stiftung Preussischer Kulturbesitz ● Museum für Islamische Kunst
Krefeld	Deutsches Textilmuseum Krefeld
Munich	Staatliches Museen für Völkerkunde
Stuttgart	Linden-Museum Stuttgart

GREECE

Athens	Benaki Museum ● Folklore Museum
Nafplion	Peloponnesian Folklore Foundation
Soufli	Silk Museum

HOLLAND

Amsterdam	Rijksmuseum
Utrecht	Rijksmuseum

HONG KONG   T.T. Tsui Museum

INDIA

Ahmedabad	Calico Museum of Textiles

ITALY

Como	Fondacion Ratti
Florence	Museo Nazionale del Bargello Church of Sta. Trinità
Genoa	Museo d'Arte Orientale Edouardo Chiossone
Milan	Castello Sforzesco, Museo d'Arte Applicata
Prato	Palazzo Pretorio
Rome	Vatican Palace Museum
Turin	Museo Nazionale della Montagna Duca degli Abruzzi
Venice	Centro Studi di Storia del Tessuto e del Costume, Palazzo Mocenigo ● Museo Correr e Quadreria Correr

JAPAN
Honshu Ishikawa Prefectural Museum of Art
Kyoto   Costume Museum ● Kyoto Municipal Museum of Traditional Industry ● Kyoto Yuzen Dyeing Hall ● Kyoto National Museum
Nara   Nara Prefectural Museum of Art ● Office of the Shoso-in Treasure-house ● Toshodaiji Treasure-house ● Museum Yamato Bunkakan
Osaka   Osaka Castle Museum
Tokyo   Kanebo Collection ● Tokyo National Museum ● Tsubouchi Memorial Theatre Museum ● Silk Museum

PORTUGAL
Lisbon Museu Calouste Gulbenkian

RUSSIA
Leningrad Hermitage Museum ● Ethnographical Museum

SPAIN
Burgos   Real Monasterio de las Huelgas
Granada   Museo Islamica
Madrid   Instituto de Valencia de Don Juan
Terrassa Museu de la Seda
Toledo   Sta Catedral Primada

SWEDEN
Malmö   Stadsmuseet
Stockholm Östasiastika Museet

SWITZER-
LAND
Basel   Museum für Völkerkunde
Riggisberg Abegg-Stiftung
Zurich   Museum Rietberg

TAIWAN
Taiwan Museum of Art

TURKEY
Istanbul Sadberk Hanim Museum ● Topkapi Saray Müzesi ● Turk ve Islam Museum

UK AND
IRELAND
Bath   American Museum in Britain ● Museum of Costume and Fashion Research Centre

Bedford   Cecil Higgins Art Gallery and Museum of the Decorative Arts
Belfast   Richard Atkinson & Co. ● Ulster Museum
Braintree Working Silk Museum
Bristol   City of Bristol Museum and Art Gallery
Cambridge Fitzwilliam Museum
Dublin   National Museum of Ireland
Durham   Gulbenkian Museum of Oriental Art
Edinburgh Royal Scottish Museum
Glasgow   Art Gallery and Museum, Kelvingrove ● Burrell Collection
Liverpool Merseyside County Museum
London   Bethnal Green Museum of Childhood ● British Museum ● Horniman Museum and Library ● Museum of London ● William Morris Gallery ● Museum of Mankind ● Victoria & Albert Museum
Macclesfield Silk Education Services
Manchester   Whitworth Art Gallery, University of Manchester ● Gallery of English Costume, Platt Hall
Newcastle-Upon-Tyne Laing Art Gallery and Museum
Nottingham   City Art Gallery and Museum, Nottingham Castle
Oxford   Ashmolean Museum
Whitchurch Whitchurch Silk Mill

USA
Baltimore Baltimore Museum of Art ● Walters Art Gallery
Bloomfield Hills Cranbrook Academy of Art, Museum
Boston   Museum of Fine Arts ● Isabel Stewart Gardner Museum
Cambridge, Mass. Fogg Art Museum ● Peabody Museum of Archaeology & Ethnology, Harvard University
Chicago   Art Institute of Chicago ● Field Museum of Natural History
Cleveland The Cleveland Museum of Art
Denver   Denver Art Museum
Detroit   Detroit Institute of Arts
Granville, Ohio Museum of Burmese Art and Culture

Indianapolis	Indianapolis Museum of Art		Old Chatham,	Shaker Museum
Kansas	Nelson-Atkins Museum of Art ● University of Kansas Museum of Art		Paterson, N.J.	The Paterson Museum
			Philadelphia	Philadelphia Museum of Art ● University Museum, University of Pennsylvania
Los Angeles	Los Angeles County Museum of Art		Providence, R.I.	Museum of Art, Rhode Island School of Design
Minneapolis	Minneapolis Institute of Art		San Francisco	M.H. De Young Memorial Museum
Newark, N.J.	Newark Museum			
New Haven	Yale University Art Gallery		Seattle	Seattle Art Museum ● Costume and Textile Study Centre Museum, University of Washington
New York	American Museum of Natural History ● The Brooklyn Museum ● Cooper-Hewitt Museum, Smithsonian Institution National Museum of Design ● The Fashion Institute of Technology ● The Hispanic Society of America ● The Metropolitan Museum of Art ● Museum of American Folk Art ● The Museum of Contemporary Crafts ● Museum of Modern Art		Washington D.C.	Dumbarton Oaks Research Library and Collections ● Smithsonian Institution ● Textile Museum
			Williamsburg	Colonial Williamsburg Foundation
			Winterthur	Henry Francis du Pont Winterthur Museum

Publications

General

Algoud, H., *La Soie* (Paris 1912). Valuable for silk history, especially for France, and specifically for Lyon.

Barber, E., *Prehistoric Textiles* (Princeton 1991). Not specifically on silk, but with fascinating information on the development of textile skills in the Near East.

Barham, H., *Essay upon the Silkworm* (London 1719). Includes an ingenious theory of Noah and the silkworm in China.

Boulger, G.S., *The History of Silk* (*Asiatic Review*, Vol. 16, 1920).

Cox, R., *Les Soieries d'Art* (Paris 1914). Often quoted.

Dale, J.S., *Art to Wear* (New York 1986). The work of contemporary American artist-designers, beautifully illustrated.

Dunlevy, M., *Dress in Ireland* (London 1989). Includes silk.

Emery, I., *The Primary Structure of Fabrics* (Washington D.C., 1966). The most comprehensive explanation of techniques.

Errera, I., *Catalogue d'Etoffes Ancienne et Modernes* (Musées Royaux, Brussels 1927). No colour, but allows present-day collectors to see the riches available in the early part of this century.

Falke, O.v., *Decorative Silks* (New York 1922). Classic reference work, frequently quoted.

Feltwell, Dr J., *The Story of Silk* (UK 1990). Strong on sericulture.

Frank, I.M., and Brownstone, D.M., *The Silk Road* (Oxford 1986). Filled with anecdotes and information.

Gaddum, H.T., *Silk* (Macclesfield, 1948–). Available from the Silk Education Service and the Macclesfield Silk Museum. Concise and useful.

Geijer, A., *A History of Textile Art* (London 1979). Valuable and informative book by a highly respected textile historian.

Gervers, V. (ed.), *Studies in Textile History, in Memory of Harold B. Burnham* (Toronto 1977). A collection of articles by textile historians, worth seeking out.

Hermitage Museum, Leningrad (now St Petersburg) *The Art of Costume in Russia 18th–20th century* (1979). Well illustrated with paintings and silks, showing the influence of French fashion on the silks of the Russian aristocracy.

Hunter, G.L., *Decorative Textiles* (New York 1918). For furnishing silks, especially in the USA.

Hyde, N., and Wolinsky, C. 'Silk', *National Geographic*, January, 1984.

Lubell, C. (ed.), *Textile Collections of the World*, Vols 1, 2, 3. Guide to the textile holdings of museums in France, the United Kingdom and Ireland, Canada and the USA.

Paine, S., *Embroidered Textiles* (London 1990). Designs from many sources.

Patterned Threads – ikat traditions and inspirations (Exhibition catalogue, Minneapolis Museum of Art, 1987). Ikat well illustrated, clearly explained.

The Pile Thread (Exhibition catalogue, Minneapolis

Museum of Art, 1991). Velvet and carpet techniques clearly illustrated and explained.

Rheinberg, L., *The Romance of Silk* (Textile Institute, 1992). Accurate and up-to-date account of the international silk market, valuable also for its technical information.

Samte Velvets Velours (Exhibition catalogue, Krefeld Museum, 1979).

Staniland, K., *Embroiderers – Medieval Craftsmen* (London 1991).

Synge, L., *Antique Needlework* (London 1982).

2000 Years of Silk Weaving (Exhibition catalogue, New York, 1944). No colour, but a valuable work of reference for dealers and collectors.

Wilson, K., *A History of Textiles* (USA 1974). Useful text and bibliography.

Egyptian, Byzantine and medieval silks

Abegg-Stiftung Museum, Riggisberg, *Alte Gewebe und Ihre Geschichte* (1987).

Bellinger, L., 'Textile Analysis: Early Techniques in Egypt and the Near East' (Textile Museum Workshop Notes No. 2, 1950).

Bellinger, L., 'Repeats in Silk Weaving in the Near East' (Textile Museum Workshop Notes, No. 24, 1961).

Bellinger, L., 'Textiles from Gordion' (*Needle and Bobbin Club Bulletin*, 1962).

Carroll, D.L., *Looms and Textiles of the Copts* (California 1986). Not on silk, but relevant to silk's history.

Granger-Taylor, H., and Wild, J.P., 'Some Ancient Silk from the Crimea in the British Museum' (*Antiquaries Journal*, 1981).

Kendrick, A.F., *Catalogue of Textiles from Burying Grounds of Egypt*, Vol. III (London 1922). Includes silk.

Lopez, R.S., *The Silk Industry in the Byzantine Empire* Cambridge, Mass., 1945). The classic source, frequently quoted.

Lucas, A., *Ancient Egyptian Materials and Industries* (London 1989). Mentions silk excavated in Ptolemaic burial.

Marzouk, M.A., *History of the Textile Industry in Alexandria* (Alexandria 1955).

Pfister, R. 'Le role de l'Iran dans les Textiles d'Antinoë' (*Ars Islamica*, 1948).

—, *Textiles de Palmyre*, I–III (Paris 1934, 1937, 1940).

Rutschowskaya, M.-H., *Coptic Fabrics* (Paris 1990).

Volbach, W.F., *Early Decorative Textiles* (trans., New York 1969).

Silks of China, Japan and South-east Asia

Burnham, H., *Chinese Velvets* (Toronto 1959).

Cammann, S., 'Notes on the Origins of Chinese k'ossu Tapestry' (*Artibus Asiae*, Ascona, 1958).

Clunas, C. (ed.), *Chinese Export Art and Design* (London 1987).

Drege, J.-P., *La Route de la Soie* (Paris 1986).

Ecke, G., *Chinese Domestic Velvets* (Tokyo 1963).

Egan, P. (ed.), *Out of China's Earth* (London 1981). Archaeological discoveries, including silks.

Gittinger, M., *Master Dyers to the World* (Textile Museum, Washington D.C., 1982).

Gittinger, M., and Lefferts, H.L.Jr., *Textiles and the Tai Experience* (Textile Museum, Washington D.C., 1992). Published in conjunction with an exhibition.

Hanyo, G., *Soieries de Chine* (Paris 1987). Especially useful for archaeological material, and well illustrated.

Hitchcock, M., *Indonesian Textile Techniques* (1985).

—, *Indonesian Textiles* (London 1991).

In the Presence of the Dragon Throne (Exhibition catalogue, Royal Ontario Museum, Toronto, 1977).

Ito, J., *Tsujigahana, the Flower of Japanese Textile Art* (Tokyo 1985).

Kennedy, A., *Japanese Costume* (Paris 1990).

Laumann, M.M., *The Secret of Excellence in Ancient Chinese Silks* (China 1984).

Le Coq, *Buried Treasures of Chinese Turkestan* (Oxford 1987).

The Manchu Dragon (Exhibition catalogue, The Metropolitan Museum of Art, New York, 1981). Silk Dragon robes illustrated.

Maxwell, R., *Textiles of Southeast Asia* (Oxford 1990).

Meister, M.W., 'The Pearl Roundel in Chinese Design' (*Ars Orientalis*, Vol. VIII, 1970).

Milanesi, M., *La Via Della Seta* (Italy 1985).

Minnich, H.B., *Japanese Costume* (New York and Tokyo 1963).

Needham, J., *Science and Civilization in China* series, Vol. 5, Part IX: 'Reeling and Spinning'. Best available source of background information on early sericulture and silk technology.

Rawson, J., *Chinese ornament, the Lotus and the Dragon* (London 1984).

Riboud, K. and Vial, G., 'Les Soieries Han. 1 Aspects Nouveaux dans l'Etude des Soieries de l'Asie Centrale. 2 Analyse Technique sur un Specimen de Noin Oula' (*Revue des Arts Asiatiques*, Vol. xvii, Paris 1968).

Riboud, K. (ed.) *In Quest of Themes and Skills – Asian Textiles* (Ahmedabad 1989). Includes articles on Indian textiles.

Schafer, E.H., *The Golden Peaches of Samarkand* (Berkeley 1985).

—, *The Vermilion Bird* (Berkeley 1985). Fascinating background to the Tang, including anecdotes about silk and silk-weaving.

Silk Roads, China Ships (Exhibition catalogue, Royal Ontario Museum, Toronto, 1984). For the China trade with the West.

Stein, A., *Serindia* (Oxford 1921).

—, *Innermost Central Asia* (Oxford 1928).

Sylwan, V., 'Silk from the Yin Dynasty' (*Bulletin of Far Eastern Antiquities*, 1937).

Tsien, T.H., *Written on Bamboo and Silk* (Chicago 1962). Further uses for silk.

Walters, D., *Chinese Mythology* (London 1992).

Warren, W., *Jim Thompson, the Legendary American of Thailand* (Singapore 1976). On the revival of silk in Thailand.

Whitfield, R. and Farrer, A., *Caves of the Thousand Buddhas* (London 1990). Published in conjunction with a British Museum exhibition of silks found at Dunhuang.

Xin, Y., and Naixiang. *Art of the Dragon* (London 1989). Includes paintings on silk, and silk textiles.

European silks

Art of Textiles (Exhibition catalogue, Spinks, London, 1989).

Boileau, E., *Le Livre d'Etienne Boileau, 1258* (Paris 1837). Information about textile skills, early guilds and trade in medieval Paris.

Bosseboeuf, Abbé L., *Histoire de la Fabrique de Soieries de Tours, des Origines au XIXᵉ Siècle* (Tours 1800).

Bussagli, M., *La Seta in Italia* (Milan 1986). Lavish and informative publication.

Clouzot, H., *Le Metier de la Soie en France 1466–1815* (Paris, before 1925).

Diderot and d'Alembert, *L'Encyclopédie de la Soie* (Paris). For looms and techniques.

Five Centuries of Italian Textiles (Exhibition catalogue, Prato, 1981).

Les Folles Années de la Soie (Exhibition catalogue, Musée Historique des Tissus, Lyon, 1975).

Fortuny (Exhibition catalogue, Musée Historique des Tissus, Lyon, 1979).

May, F.L., *Hispanic Lace and Lace Making* (New York 1939).

—, *Silk Textiles of Spain* (New York 1939). Chiefly concerning Moorish Spain. Florence May died while still working on the companion volume, intended to bring the history up to date. However, the Hispanic Society intend to publish the work posthumously.

Morris, B., *Liberty Design* (UK 1989).

Mozziconacci, A., *Le Ver a Soie du Murier* (Paris 1921). On sericulture.

Origo, I., *The Merchant of Prato* (London 1963). The story of a medieval silk merchant, an historical account from surviving documents.

Osma, G. de Fortuny, *Mariano Fortuny: His Life and Work* (London 1980). Comprehensive account of a genius's life and work with silk.

Parry, L., *Textiles of the Arts and Crafts Movement* (London 1988).

Pifferi, E., *La Seta* (Italy 1984).

Reynier, E., *La Soie en Vivarais* (Marseille 1981).

Rothstein, N., *Silk Designs of the Eighteenth Century. From the Collection of the Victoria and Albert Museum* (London 1990). For the so-called 'flowered silks' of Spitalfields.

St Leger, A., *Silver Sails and Silk – Huguenots in Cork 1685–1850* (Cork 1991).

Schoeser, M., and Rufey, C., *English and American Textiles* (London 1989).

La Seda a Espáñya (Exhibition catalogue, Museu de la Seda, Terrassa, Catalonia, 1991).

Soieries de Lyon (Exhibition catalogue, Musée Historique des Tissus, Lyon, Commandes Imperiales, 1983).

Soieries de Lyon (Exhibition catalogue, Musée Historique des Tissus, Lyon, Commandes Royales au XVIIIᵉs, 1989).

Tessuti Serici Italiani 1450–1530 (Exhibition catalogue, Castello Sforzesco, Milan, 1983).

Thornton, P., *Baroque and Rococo Silks* (London 1965).

Indian silks

Alkazi, R., *Ancient Indian Costume* (New Delhi 1983).

Bunting. E.-J., *Sindhi Tombs and Textiles, the Persistence of Pattern* (USA 1980).

Calico Museum, *Treasures of Indian Textiles* (Ahmedabad 1980). *Historic Textiles at the Calico Museum* series, Vols 1–4.

Dhamija, J., and Jain, J. (eds.), *Handwoven Fabrics of India* (Ahmedabad 1989).

Irwin, J., and Hall, M., *Indian Embroideries* (Ahmedabad 1973).

Irwin, J., and Schwartz, P.R., *Studies in Indo-European Textile History* (Ahmedabad 1966). Small book packed with fascinating information.

Master Weavers; Festival of India (Exhibition catalogue, Royal College of Art, London, 1982).

Murphy, V., and Crill, R., *Tie-dyed Textiles of India* (London 1991).

Paine, S., *Chikan Embroidery* (1989).

Les Textiles de l'Inde, et les Modèles Crée par Issey Miyake (Exhibition catalogue, Musée des Arts Décoratifs, Paris, 1985).

Sassanian (pre-Islamic Persian) and Islamic silks (including Moorish Spain, Ottoman Turkey)

Al-Andalus (Exhibition catalogue, The Metropolitan Museum of Art, New York, 1992).

Arabesques et Jardins du Paradis (Exhibition catalogue, Musée des Arts Décoratifs, Paris, 1989).

Atil, E. (ed.), *Turkish Art* (USA 1980).

Davis, R., *Aleppo and Devonshire Square* (London 1967). The origins and history of the Levant Company.

Ferrier, R.W., (ed.), *The Arts of Persia* (Yale U.P., 1989).

Gervers, V., *The Influence of Ottoman Turkish Textiles and Costume in Eastern Europe* (Toronto 1982).

Gursu, N., *The Art of Turkish Weaving* (Istanbul 1988).

Islemeler (Exhibition catalogue, David Black, London, 1978). Ottoman domestic embroideries.

Johnstone, P. *A Guide to Greek Island Embroidery* (London 1972).

Kalter, J., *The Arts and Crafts of Turkestan* (London 1984).

Kuhnel, E., *Abbasid Silks of the 9th Century* (*Ars Orientalis*, Vol. 2, 1957).

—, *Islamische Stoffe aus agyptischen Grabern* (Berlin, 1927).

Mackie, L.W., *The Splendor of Turkish Weaving* (Washington D.C., 1974).

Migeon, G., *Les Arts Plastiques et Industriels – Manuel d'Art Musulman* (Paris 1907).

Neumann, R., and Murza, G., *Persische Seiden* (Leipzig 1988).

Oz, T., *Turkish Textiles and Velvets* (Ankara 1950).

Petsopoulos, Y. (ed.), *Tulips, Arabesques and Turbans* (London 1982). Textile chapter by Walter Denny.

Ramazanoglu, G., *Turkish Embroidery* (Istanbul 1987).

Renaissance of Islam – Art of the Mamluks (Exhibition catalogue, Smithsonian Institution, Washington D.C., 1981).

The Royal Hunter (Exhibition catalogue, The Metropolitan Museum of Art, New York, 1978). Sassanian art.

Scarce, J., *Women's Costume of the Near and Middle East* (London 1987).

Serjeant, R.B., *Islamic Textiles, material for a history up to the Mongol conquest* (Beirut 1972). Valuable text, not illustrated, with translations from Arabic texts concerning textiles.

Spuhler, F., *Islamic Carpets and Textiles in the Keir Collection* (London).

Suleyman the Magnificent (London, British Museum; Paris, Musée des Arts Décoratifs; Washington, Smithsonian Institution, etc.). A travelling exhibition, 1989/91, which included magnificent Ottoman textiles.

Trilling, J., *Aegean Crossroads* (Washington D.C., 1983).

Upham-Pope, A., and Ackerman, P. (eds.), *Survey of Persian Art* (New York 1938-9).

Wiet, G., *Soieries Persanes* (Cairo 1948).

Acknowledgments

Many people have helped in various ways, and I am deeply grateful for their friendship, generosity and support:

My mother, Irene Gillam, who never stopped believing, and my daughter, Chloe Franses, who did sterling work tracking and identifying transparencies.

My agent, Anne Engel.

In Ireland, 'the silk monk', Father Dermot at Mount Saint Joseph Abbey; Tim Severin (whose 'China Voyage' sails are protected with silk stitches); and the good fairies who first transported me across the water to that isle and its magic.

Derek Content, who introduced me to the world of word-processors despite my protestations, and gave years of encouragement.

Richard Trescott, who frequently revived flagging spirits with libations of the bubbles that cheer.

The International Silk Association's Ron Currie (in Lyon) and Leslie Rheinberg (in the UK).

Many people were generous with suggestions, their time, and transparencies of silks, and I would like specifically to thank Dr Nurhan Atasoy (Istanbul University), Dilys Blum (Philadelphia Museum of Art), Judy Brittain, Professor John Carswell (Sothebys), Massimo Corona, Michael Dillon, Professor Sammy Eilenberg, Johnny Eskenazi, Kaffe Fassett, Lynn Felcher (FIT, New York), Esther Fitzgerald, Francesca Galloway, Sevgi Gonul (Sadberk Hanim Museum), Jack Haldane (Abingdon Books), David Halevim, Lady Pamela Harlech, Monique Jay (Lyon, Musée Historique des Tissus), Gyan Lall, Vishnu Lall, Clive Loveless, Mayotte Magnus, Alan Marcuson (*Hali*), Roland and Sabrina Michaud, Philippe Missillier, Penny Oakley, Ioanna Papantoniou (Peloponnesian Folklore Foundation), Kerry Taylor (Sothebys), Roddy Taylor, Nabil Saidi, Sandra Sakata (Obiko SF), Jacqueline Simcox (Spinks), Edmund de Unger (the Keir Collection), Joseph Uzan, Anne Wardwell (Cleveland Museum of Art).

Last, and most important, the countless generations of anonymous silkworms.

P.S.

Locations of works and photo sources

The following abbreviations are used: *a* above, *b* below, *c* centre, *l* left, *r* right.

Ahmedabad: Calico Museum of Textiles 64; *Aix-la-Chapelle*: Cathedral Treasury 107; *Amsterdam*: Rijksmuseum-Stichting 193; *Assisi*: Museo Tesoro, Basilica S. Francesco (photo Abegg-Foundation, Riggisberg) 81; *Athens*: Benaki Museum, Inv. No. 3899 122*l*; *Auxerre*: Saint-Eusèbe (photo Lauros-Giraudon) 84; *Bamberg*: Bamberg Cathedral Treasury (photo Ingeborg Limmer) 91; *Barcelona*: Museu d'Art de la Catalunya 166*a*; *Bath*: The American Museum in Britain, Claverton Manor 2*a*; *Basle*: Gewerbemuseum, Museum für Gestaltung 209*a*&*b*; *Beirut*: Photo courtesy the Museum of the American University of Beirut 85; *Berlin*: Staatliche Museen Preussischer Kulturbesitz 118; *Boston*: Courtesy, Museum of Fine Arts. Ellen Page Hall Fund 108*l*; *Bristol*: City of Bristol Museum and Art Gallery, Oriental Section 73*r*; *Cairo*: Museum of Islamic Art 101*l*; *Cleveland, Ohio*: The Cleveland Museum of Art, Purchase from the J.H. Wade Fund 96, 101*r*; *Como*: Ratti 227*b*; *Cracow*: Wawel State Collection of Art 121; *Dublin*: National Gallery of Ireland 166*b*; *Edinburgh*: Royal Museum of Scotland. © Trustees of the National Museums of Scotland 122*r*; *Florence*: Galleria degli Arazzi (photo Alinari) 2*b*, Galleria degli Uffizi (photo Scala) 13, Museo Nazionale, Collezione Franchetti (photo Alinari) 150, Palazzo Medici-Ricardi (photo Scala) 156; *Genoa*: Museo d'Arte Orientale Edoardo Chiossone 43*ar*&*cr*; *Hatfield, Hertfordshire*: Courtesy of the Marquess of Salisbury, Hatfield House 194; *Hong Kong*: photo courtesy The Commercial Press (Hong Kong) Limited 25, 28*b*; *Istanbul*: Topkapi Saray Museum 115, 116, 126*l*&*br*, 127*bl*; *Krefeld*: Deutsches Textilmuseum 208, Gewerbesammlung der Textilingenieurschule 162; *Leningrad*: Hermitage Museum 24, (photo D.W. Belons) 53*a*; *Ligerz*: photo Marlen Perez, courtesy Käthe Wenger *London*: Royal Collection. St James's Palace. © Her Majesty the Queen 184, Bernheimer Fine Art Ltd 32, 56*ac*&*bc*, 200*a*, British Library 42, 43*bl*, 50, 127*br*, 171, 172, British Museum 49, 141*r*, Georgina von Etzdorf 228*al*, Esther Fitzgerald 71*ar*, India Office Library 73*l*, By Courtesy of the Keir Collection 14, 15, 112*al*, 154*br*, Liberty Archives, Westminster City Archives 221 (insert), Clive Loveless, 56*ar*&*br*, 70*al*, 128*al*&*bc*, 204*a*, Mallett & Son (Antiques) Ltd 80, 201*b*, 202*a*, Mayotte Magnus 30*a*&*b*, 31*a*, Ajit Mookerjee Collection (photo Thames and Hudson) 62, Phillips Fine Art Auctioneers 222*a*, Rossi & Rossi 27*r*, Philippa Scott 12*ar*, 56*al*&*bl*, 58, 59*a*, 98*a*, 128*ar*&*br*, 138*al*, 199, 226*a*&*br*, (photo Mayotte Magnus, London) 9, Sotheby 133, 55*r*, 72*b*, 104*a*, 105*l*&*r*, 111*cb*, 127*a*, 140*ar*&*br*, 141*br*&*al*&*bl*, 142, 143, Spink & Son Ltd 7, 11, 16, 26*l*&*r*, 27*l*&*c*, 28*a*, 43*al*&*br*, 55*l*, 65, 67*l*, 68*ar*, 69, 70*b*&*ar*, 71*b*&*ac*, 106, 128*c*, 157*l*&*r*, 158, 159*b*, 160*b*, 177, 178, 179*ar*&*bl*, 185, 186, 188, 197, 198*b*, 200*b*&*r*, 201*a*, 202*b*, 226*bl*, By Courtesy of the Board of Trustees of the Victoria & Albert Museum 31*b*, 39*b*, 52*l*, 53*b*, 61, 68*bl*, 74, 78, 83, 97, 119, 137, 147, 190*l*&*r*, 191, 196, 198*c*, 203, 204*br*, 205, 207, 213, Reproduced by permission of the Trustees, The Wallace Collection 170; *Los Angeles*: Copyright © 1989 Museum Associates, Los Angeles County Museum of Art. All Rights Reserved 135*a*; *Lugano*: Thyssen-Bornemisza Collection 73*c*, 149; *Lullingstone*: R.C. Gooden: 21; *Lyon*: Musée Historique des Tissus (photo René Basset) 10, 53*bl*, 68*al*, 82, 98*b*, 108*r*, 126*ar*, 138*bl*, 139*r*, 155*b*, 159*a*, 160*a*, 173, 187*l*&*r*, 198*a*, 215, 219; *Madrid*: Academy of History 102; *Manchester*: Whitworth Art Gallery, University of Manchester 217*r*; *Metz*: Cathedral Treasury 92; *Milan*: Eskenazi 20, 154*l*; *Milwaukee*: Milwaukee Public Museum 212*r*; *Nara*: Horyuji Temple 53*bc*, Museum Yamata Bunkakan 47, Shoso-in Treasure House 34; *Newark*: Collection of The Newark Museum (Purchase 1979 The Members' Fund) 2*cr*, (Purchase 1969 Harry E. Sautter Endowment Fund) 130; *New York*: Christie's 144, Cooper-Hewitt Museum, National Museum of Design, Smithsonian Institution Art Resource (© CHM Gift of J.P. Morgan, from the Miguel y Badia Collection 1902-1-82) 93, (1902-1-221) 94, (Bequest of Marian Hague, 1971-50-149) 39*a*, © Julie: Artisans' Gallery, New York (photo Otto Stupakoff). From *Art to Wear* by Julie Schafler Dale, Abbeville Press 228*b*, The Metropolitan Museum of Art (Rogers Fund, 1926, 26.231.2) 135*b*, (Gift of Mrs Boudinot Keith, 1928, 28.70.1-25) 218, The Solomon R. Guggenheim Museum 217*l*; *New York and Delhi*: V. & G. Lall 67*r*; *Ontario*: Photo courtesy of the Textile Department, Royal Ontario Museum, Gift of Mrs John David Eaton 138*r*&*139l*; *Osaka*: Fujita Art Museum 35; *Oxford*: Reproduced by courtesy of the Curators of the Bodleian Library (MS Ouseley Add.173, no.13) 66; *Oxfordshire*: Richard Purdon 54; *Paris*: Balenciaga Collection (photo Jacques Boulay) 225, Bibliothèque de l'Arsenal 175, Bibliothèque Nationale 77, 103, 104*b*, 174, Collection Union Française des Arts du Costume (photo Jacques Boulay) 224, Hermès 18, Christian Lacroix 19, Musée des Arts Décoratifs 167, (photo L. Sully-Jaulmes) 44*a*&*b*, 221, 223, Musée de Thermes et de l'Hotel de Cluny (photo Hirmer) 86, (photo J. Hyde) 112*br*, Musée du Louvre 79, (© Photo R.M.N.) 5, (photo Archives Photographiques) 100*l*, (photo Giraudon) 169, Cabinet des Dessins, Musée du Louvre (© Photo R.M.N.) 163, Musée Guimet (© Photo R.M.N.) 22; *Philadelphia*: Free Library of Philadelphia (photo Photo Illustrations Inc.) 72*a*; *Private Collection* 2*l*, 12*al*&*bl*, 59*b*, 111*cr*, 123*al*&*ar*&*br*, 128*ac*&*bl*, 176, 206*l*&*r*, 222*b*; *Riggisberg*: Abegg-Foundation 111*a*&*c*&*l*&*br*, 153; *Rome*: Vatican Museums 52*r*; *Sens*: Sens Cathedral 134; *Stockholm*: Kungl. Husgerådskammaren. The Royal Collections (photo Karl-Erik Granath) 140*l*, Kungl. Livrustkammaren 136, Nordiska Museet, Anders Berch Collection (photo Mats Landin) 204*bl*; *Stuttgart*: Staatliche Schlösser und Gärten (photo Abegg-Foundation, Riggisberg) 17; *Taipei*: National Palace Museum 29; *Tokyo*: Nezu Institute of Fine Arts 41, National Museum 46*b*; *Uppsala*: Cathedral Treasury 151; *Vaucluse*: Cathedral Treasury of Art 100*r*; *Venice*: Noralene 227*a*; *Vienna*: Kunsthistorisches Museum 4, 154*a*–155*a*, Museum für Völkerkunde 212*l*, Österreichisches Museum für Angewandte Kunst 87, 125, 146; *Woburn*: From the Woburn Abbey Collection, reproduced by kind permission of the Marquess of Tavistock and Trustees of the Bedford Estates 206*r*.

Index

Page numbers in *italics* refer to captions

Introductory Illustrations